CONTENTS

Section II: Addressing the Needs of College Seniors

Section III: Facilitating the Transition Out of College

The SENIOR Year

CULMINATING EXPERIENCES AND TRANSITIONS

Mary Stuart Hunter, Jennifer R. Keup,
Jillian Kinzie, and Heather Maietta
Editors

NATIONAL RESOURCE CENTER

FIRST-YEAR EXPERIENCE® AND STUDENTS IN TRANSITION

UNIVERSITY OF SOUTH CAROLINA

Cite as:

Hunter, M. S., Keup, J. R., Kinzie, J., & Maietta, H. (Eds.). (2012). *The senior year: Culminating experiences and transitions*. Columbia, SC: University of South Carolina, National Resource Center for The First-Year Experience and Students in Transition.

Published by
National Resource Center for The First-Year Experience® and Students in Transition
University of South Carolina
1728 College Street , Columbia, SC 29208
www.sc.edu/fye

Production Staff for the National Resource Center
Project Manager: Toni Vakos, Editor
Design and Production: Josh Tyler, Graphic Artist

Library of Congress Cataloging-in-Publication Data

The senior year : culminating experiences and transitions / Mary Stuart Hunter ... [et al.].
     p. cm.
   Includes index.
   ISBN 978-1-889271-85-9
   1. College seniors—United States. 2. College students—United States.   I. Hunter,
Mary Stuart.
LA229.S435 2012
378.1'980973—dc23

                                                                        2012028152

List of Tables & Figures

Tables

Figures

FOREWORD

John N. Gardner

It is high time good thinkers, scholars, and practitioners in undergraduate education improvement work turn their attention to the concluding college experience. This work is long overdue and has remained so since the 1998 publication of *The Senior Year Experience*, co-edited and co-authored by myself and Gretchen Van der Veer. Much has happened since then to impact seniors and, hopefully, what we do to prepare them for the real world.

Like many higher educators, much of my work has been and continues to be influenced by my own undergraduate experiences. The world was a very different place when I graduated from college in 1965:

- Women did not begin to have the opportunities they do now to prepare for and enter almost any profession they might seek.

- There was no federal student loan debt incurred by students as Title IV of the Higher Education Act had not yet been enacted.

- The massification of public higher education was just beginning with the passage of the 1965 Higher Education Act.

- It would have been unthinkable for me to go back home and live with mom and dad after commencement.

During my senior year, the college I attended did not offer any capstone course or require a senior thesis or project. Nor did I participate in a senior-year transition experience offered by student affairs professionals or engage in career planning with a career counselor (both professionals and opportunities were nonexistent for the most part and at my small college in particular). The capstone I provided myself, however, was a stint in student government leadership, which had a profound influence on me in terms of what I learned about how colleges really function and resist change (but that is another story). All of these experiences (and lack of) created my empathy for today's seniors, even though their times are very different from my own.

Four years after establishing the University of South Carolina's (USC) National Center for the Study of The Freshman Year Experience (NRC and today's National Resource Center for The First-Year Experience and Students in Transition) in 1986, my codirector and editor of this volume, Mary Stuart Hunter, and I had an epiphany: College seniors were the next student transition we needed to pay attention to. Seeing the University through the eyes of my college-aged son and witnessing what he needed but was not receiving, coupled with the interest shown toward other transitions, especially the one out of college, from educators attending our First-Year Experience conferences influenced this epiphany. There are many parallels between the entering and departing experiences: (a) both are critically important; (b) both are times of stress and transition, for the student and the family; (c) in both cases, students could be helped in special transition seminars; and (d) both transitions could be improved through intentional partnerships among faculty, academic, and student affairs administrators. So beginning in 1990, we offered annual Senior-Year Experience conferences, which evolved into the Students in Transition conference now sponsored by the NRC every fall.

During this same period, USC piloted the first effort to replicate University 101 for seniors—University 401, Senior Experience Seminar. This senior seminar, which I developed is probably the most rewarding course I ever taught. The seminar was granted permanent approval by the USC Faculty Senate on April Fools' Day, 1998, the same year Jossey-Bass published *The Senior Year Experience.*

Since the publication of that book,

- Female seniors are now graduating at higher rates than men.

- Seniors have accumulated more college-related debt than the cumulative credit-card debt in the United States.

- Graduates are deferring home ownership, marriage, and parenting for longer periods.

- More graduates than ever are living with family after graduation, many of these students never having left their family homes to attend college.

- Recent college graduate unemployment rates are higher than at any time since these data have been tracked.

- The U.S. Census Bureau reports that in a number of major metropolitan areas, females who are single, childless, college graduates, between 22 and 30, are now earning higher salaries than comparable men.

- The prospect of students continuing their education after commencement has become much more expensive as cash-strapped institutions are forced to raise tuition rates.

- Demands for greater accountability and transparency on the part of colleges and universities have greatly increased.

- Regional accreditors exert more influence over colleges and universities to demonstrate learning outcomes and added value for graduating seniors.

- Many graduating students find themselves underemployed and in holding patterns for the lives they went to college to secure.

- For those graduates fortunate enough to find positions in the world of work, that job environment has changed profoundly to one of global connectivity and rapid, and frequently unpredictable, rates of change.

This list is only a partial enumeration of the changes over the past 14 years and provides this new volume's focus on the importance of the senior year and what we can do to improve its impact on our students. The contributors offer the reader an overview of the history of the senior year, current trends, and rationales for the need for more attention to this period as well as a context for the larger role of the senior-year experience on campus.

After my many years of working on the first-year transition, I wondered if I would ever see a comparable level of interest in the senior-year transition. For a complete college education, which delivers on its potential, we need to be as thoughtful, supportive, and intentional about what we offer our seniors as we are for our first-year students. It is my hope this volume will make that case and show the way—and that the readers' inspired actions will help narrow the gap in interest and commitment between first and senior-year transitions. Thank you for being open to where this book can take you. Your seniors will thank you, too.

John N. Gardner
Senior Fellow, Distinguished Professor Emeritus
University of South Carolina

INTRODUCTION

Mary Stuart Hunter, Jennifer R. Keup, Jillian Kinzie, and Heather Maietta

Anthropologists have long understood the importance of transitions related to individuals' life stages and the ways in which cultures embrace these natural rites of passage. The senior year is indeed an important transition period in the lives of college students. Yet, the senior year as a transition point in the undergraduate experience has received relatively little attention in the academy. Of the three major phases associated with rites of passage, including separation, transition, and incorporation (van Gennep, 1960), the senior year represents a significant and sustained separation experience. Transition cannot occur without separation as a first step. If higher educators are to support senior students as they navigate this final transition in the undergraduate experience, opportunities must exist to create meaningful and educational experiences in the separation phase of this rite of passage. This book is designed to call attention to that final transition, the senior year, and challenge educators and institutions to make the most of the culminating experiences of students.

The Meaning of the Senior Year

Undergraduate education in the United States has a distinct beginning and end. The poignancy of going off to college and the pageantry of commencement are celebrated traditions. The first and final years of college have unique transition symbols, such as submitting a first college essay or presenting a senior project, and make distinct contributions to student achievement and success. The rites of passage associated with the senior year, including traditions of senior week and graduation, are perhaps the most sacred of college experiences. Although the first year of college has enjoyed considerable definition and attention, particularly given its importance to transitioning into college and contributions to student persistence, the senior year is equally distinct in terms of moving out of college and its significance to student achievement and postcollege outcomes. The senior year represents the final and culminating phase of the undergraduate experience leading to entry into graduate school or the workplace and is an occasion to bring coherence to a program of study and to look toward a future beyond the baccalaureate degree.

The final year of college encompasses significant personal and educational transition. For many students, the senior year signifies the last year of university life—the final year to enjoy life as a student, before becoming a real person who goes to a job every day and no longer lives according to the academic calendar. The transition aspect of the senior year can be unsettling and bring about some of the same kinds of anxieties as the first college year, such as moving into another new and more independent life phase, forging a new identity (this time not associated with being a student), leaving friends and known comforts and routines, and new financial pressures (now repaying those loans vs. trying to fund college).

The institution's point of view on the senior year is also one of transition and culmination. The transition focus aims to help students increase their capacity to take charge of their own existence, prepare for their future, and move on to postcollege life. Institutions may organize programs and courses, such as from-backpack-to-briefcase workshops, career development seminars, and senior recognition ceremonies, and offer interventions to support students through their transition and ensure their success. In addition, as the culmination of the undergraduate program, the senior year is the site of distinct academic initiatives, including capstone courses, senior theses or projects, comprehensive examinations, internships or practica, senior presentations and recitals, and other educational experiences designed to cap off the degree. These academic experiences coupled with career and student affairs programming are intended to foster synthesis; bring coherence across years of work in the major; and offer students the opportunity to demonstrate breadth and depth of knowledge, growth, and competence. Lastly, culminating experiences, like senior projects and comprehensive exams, are also viewed as an important rite of passage and often one of the hallowed traditions of undergraduate education.

Although the culmination and transition aspects of the senior year have long been acknowledged at colleges and universities, the important qualities and purpose of the senior year garnered scholarly attention only in the late 1980s when a growing circle of educators and prospective employers raised concerns about the preparation of seniors for life after college. Leadership by John Gardner and the National Conference on the Senior-Year Experience (Gardner, 1999) broadened the discussion to include consideration of the developmental and transition needs of seniors and emphasized college and university's moral obligation for helping students transition out of college. Educators began studying facets of the senior year, detailing key student needs and identifying what campuses could do to improve the final college transition experience (Gardner, Van der Veer, & Associates, 1998; Henscheid, 2000).

Since the explication of the senior-year experience, references to the senior year have evolved from simply meaning the in- and out-of-class experiences of students in their final year of college to a comprehensively designed effort that

- addresses the needs of seniors;
- assists them through their transition with holistic support and an appreciation of the role of ritual and rites of passage;
- brings closure, integration, and reflection to the undergraduate journey; and
- helps students graduate with the skills they need to be successful in life beyond college (Gardner, 1999; Gardner et al., 1998).

These goals can be achieved by (a) creating curricular coherence and bridging the curriculum to the world of work; (b) fostering seniors' personal development in terms of making career connections and clarifying an adult identity; (c) establishing relationships with students with an eye toward encouraging alumni commitment, as well as connections to employers and graduate schools; and (d) identifying institutional accountability and outcomes assessment activities to examine educational quality.

In essence, the senior-year experience is "a variety of initiatives in the academic and co-curricular domain that, when implemented in a coordinated effort, can promote and enhance learning, satisfaction, and a successful transition during the final quarter of the baccalaureate educational experience"

(Gardner, 1999, p. 7). According to Chickering and Schlossberg (1998), it is important to be intentional about experiences in the senior year because it represents the institution's final opportunity to do something positive for students to help them leave college with a sense of being in charge of their future and as effective agents for their personal and professional development.

Trends and Developments

The senior-year experience movement initially outlined issues related to the transition out of college and why it was important for institutions to adopt a strategic and intentional approach to this time (Gardner et al., 1998). It was envisioned as a bookend to the well-defined, successful first-year experience (Barefoot, 2000) and as the vehicle for raising awareness of and addressing the important issues and goals related to the senior year listed above.

Over the last two decades, the senior year of college has continued to receive steady attention from higher education scholars and educators (e.g., Collier, 2000; Gardner, 1999; Gardner et al., 1998; Henscheid, 2008a; Taub, Servaty-Seib, & Cousins, 2006). The themes advanced in recent literature include more detailed senior student development issues and needs; the importance of establishing a comprehensive campus approach to addressing these needs; the value of senior curricular experiences, including capstones and field experiences; and holistic career transition programs to help students further refine skills needed for success in a competitive workplace and global economy.

The theme of developing a more comprehensive approach to addressing senior student needs has been facilitated through greater partnerships between student and academic affairs units. This alliance is a necessary component of creating a more integrated, seamless curricular and cocurricular experience in the senior year. Student and academic affairs offices have partnered around the creation of senior leadership programs, rites of passage experiences, career and life transition courses and workshops, and in assessing student learning outcomes. Student and academic affairs collaboration is important to implementing a comprehensive first-year experience; this same partnership contributes to an integrated, cohesive senior-year experience.

Discussion about the quality of the senior year and concern about student outcomes has intensified recently given the sagging economy, rising student debt load, and indicators that college graduates may lack the skills needed for a 21st century economy (AAC&U, 2007; Hart Research Associates, 2009, 2010; Schneider, 2012). Concerns about whether students actually leave college with the rich portfolio of learning that employers seek and society needs, including broad knowledge, strong intellectual and practical skills, grounded commitments to personal and social responsibility, and demonstrated capacity to deal with complex challenges, has placed greater demands on the senior year as a central point for reflecting on student learning outcomes and preparation for employment. The senior year has become a key time to assess what students know and can do as a measure of institutional quality and also what students can communicate to prospective employers.

Much of the literature on the senior year has documented the serious transition issues new graduates face. As students get closer to graduating and moving on to the next stage in their lives, they are faced with significant challenges, including a competitive job market or the rigors of a graduate program. Navigating a first job, establishing financial independence, separating from college support systems, deciding about graduate and professional school are but a few of the transitions that graduating seniors encounter (Pistilli, Taub, & Bennett, 2003). The career development and transition programming on campus has become more refined and specific to helping students make the most of their senior year and address postcollege needs in a more holistic way.

Gaff, Ratcliff, and Associates (1997) identified the senior-year experience as one of the more important changes taking place in the curriculum at numerous colleges and universities. Many senior capstones and projects were launched in the late 1980s in response to concerns about eroding quality in undergraduate education and possible fragmentation in the curriculum. According to Durel (1993), the capstone course is defined as a "crowning course or experience coming at the end of a sequence of courses with the specific objective of integrating a body of relatively fragmented knowledge into a unified whole" (p. 223). Dickinson (1993) suggested that the capstone course could also function as bridge to the world beyond college. Increasingly, institutions are designing senior-year experiences that require students to pull together their learning and demonstrate their abilities through demanding senior seminars, research projects, portfolios, artistic productions, and internships.

As the assessment movement has taken hold in higher education, the senior year has become the focal point for assessing student learning outcomes, particularly in the major. Outcomes like critical thinking or writing could be examined using standardized tests or by reviewing senior capstone projects or portfolios employing a critical thinking rubric, such as the Valid Assessment of Learning in Undergraduate Education (VALUE) tool provided by the

Association of American Colleges and Universities (AAC&U). Similarly, the systematic analysis of comprehensive exam results over time can help a department identify key concepts that students are failing to grasp or theories that may be getting insufficient coverage across courses. Similarly, performance on these exams could help inform course redesign, suggest alternative course sequencing, or indicate other necessary changes in curricular requirements. Seniors have an important perspective for assessment activities as they are in a good position to render a judgment about the quality of their experience, and they provide the institution with a more complex picture than students at earlier points in their degree.

Another trend associated with the senior year is the need to make clear to students their role in giving back to their institution as alumni. Campus development offices and alumni associations see the senior year as a time to build loyalty among students and to help them understand the responsibility they have to invest in the education of future students. Alumni associations are reaching into the senior year to begin the transition to alumni status early and to help students understand the responsibilities and privileges of being an alumnus.

Overall, these trends have resulted in colleges and universities devoting greater attention to five broad categories of programming in the senior year. These include (a) senior seminars and capstone courses, (b) programs and workshops to prepare students for postcollege life and careers, (c) opportunities for students to make intellectual connections across course work, (d) events that celebrate the achievement of becoming a senior, and (e) activities that work toward cohesion among seniors class and alumni (Henscheid, 2008b).

Preparation for Life Beyond the Undergraduate Experience

Students leaving their undergraduate years enter a new phase of life. Traditional options include graduate school; military service; volunteer efforts; domestic life; and for the majority of graduates, the work force. Many college leavers will engage in multiple options simultaneously (e.g., work and attend graduate school while starting a family). Adjusting to new situations can be challenging as navigating new waters is difficult without preparation and guidance. The decade of one's 20s, what Jay (2012) termed the defining decade, is a critically important time:

Again and again, 20-somethings hear that they have infinite time for the dreaded adult things but so little time for the purportedly good stuff. This makes living in the present easy. It's connecting the present with the future that takes work. (p. 191)

It is the preparation for this connection to postcollege life that seniors need and that educators can influence.

The economy of the future requires an educated, well-trained workforce, so preparation for the college-to-career transition is increasingly important. Yet, many new graduates are not ready to manage complex issues, think critically and creatively, solve problems, speak and write clearly, accept responsibility and accountability, take the perspective of others, or meet employer expectations (Keeling & Hersh, 2012). According to the Bureau of Labor Statistics (2011), while the economy is recovering, educated young professionals are still having a difficult time finding and securing employment. Competition depends not only on the credential of a degree but also on a number of additional skills or qualities (i.e., competencies) that employers seek in new hires.

How can institutions help their students close the gap between what they are learning in the classroom and employer expectations? One solution is to encourage students to participate in cocurricular programming and experiential learning opportunities (e.g., internships, co-ops, practica, study abroad, directed research) to enhance the academic experience, increase skills, and provide important out-of-class connections to the world at large. Recent research (NACE, 2012) showed that employers prefer to hire candidates with relevant work experience acquired through an internship or co-op.

Preparation for the postcollege transition must accompany students' ability to not only take advantage of integrated learning experiences but also to connect and process these experiences to academics so they are truly prepared to meet our current and future workforce demands. Seniors who participate in cocurricular activities gather new knowledge about their chosen area of study, industry, and themselves—all important aspects of learning. However, as Taylor (2011) points out, "Facilitating such deliberate reflection beyond the individual classroom experience appears to be largely absent in our institutional practices" (p. 16). Preparing today's seniors for the world of work suggests that higher education examine how institutions can actively create and foster learning within and beyond the classroom.

Further, institutions should factor in employer preferences and needs during outcomes assessment associated with the senior year. A recent publication by Arum and Roska (2011) found that students did not improve significantly in their critical reasoning and writing skills while in college. Additionally, poor performance in these areas tended to be associated with programs such as business education, where team projects rather than individual assignments have a tendency to be the norm. Findings such as these may be an indication that what the academic community sees as important and what the business community finds valuable in a college education are at odds. It is unlikely that what students study in college will be the same as what they end up doing in their career, since the average number of jobs an individual with a bachelor's degree will hold in their lifetime is 12 (Bureau of Labor Statistics, 2010) and the number of career changes a person goes through in his or her lifetime is approximately five. Such change requires the ability of young people to hone and identify their transferrable skills—attributes that are not learned from a textbook—and explore the variety of ways to apply them to the workforce. Therefore, institutional assessment in the senior year must be broad enough to include measures of the competencies needed in the workplace as well as the transferability of skills and knowledge learned in the undergraduate program.

By 2020, 2.6 million new jobs will require an advanced degree, with a projected increase of about 22% for jobs requiring a master's degree (CGT & ETS, 2012). As such, graduate education also plays a critical role in the success of our workforce and economy, attracting and producing influential leaders, researchers, and problem solvers. Graduate school admissions are at an all-time high. This is not surprising given that 26.3% of the class of 2011 reported plans to attend graduate school, up from 20.6% in 2007 (NACE, 2012). The decision to attend graduate school often occurs early in the senior year. Although students are ultimately responsible for their careers, universities, industry, and policy makers must also play a role in helping identify career pathways for students, which often includes graduate school. The role of institutions in preparing seniors for decision making with regard to graduate school is to establish programs aimed at understanding the connection between undergraduate education, graduate education, and potential career paths so that students can determine routes of progression and whether graduate school is the right choice for the college-to-career transition.

New and young professionals entering the workforce struggle to find career opportunities because there is an expectation that graduates be equipped with a higher level skill set and knowledge base than in the past. Further, economic conditions prohibit employers from providing an abundance of on the job training opportunities and out-of-the-gate professional development. In other words, new graduates are expected to come prepared. Providing students with resources and information about themselves and their postcollege options (e.g., continue their education, travel, volunteer, accept a full-time job) supports them in their transition and ensures that the workforce has the young professionals it needs and that society has the creative individuals required to tackle the problems and challenges of the 21st century.

Rationale for Attending to the Senior Year

Gardner (1999) identified a handful of reasons that seniors need and deserve greater attention. First, seniors have high expectations for capping off their undergraduate experience and unique needs as students in transition. The senior year offers the institution its last chance to ensure students a rewarding education and sufficient preparation for postcollege life. Seniors will soon be alumni and potential donors and supporters of the institution. As such, institutions must cultivate an ongoing relationship with them. Another practical rationale for attending to the senior year is that seniors are the students on campus most likely to graduate and to be judged as a reflection of institutional quality (Gardner et al., 1998). Finally, there is the moral imperative to ensure an enriched senior year—students simply deserve a more defined and effective culminating experience (Gardner, 1999).

The rationale for attending to the senior year has both a student and institutional perspective. From the students' point of view, the senior year carries considerable expectation. Seniors have made it this far, and have invested significantly in their experience. They want their education to amount to more than just a diploma. Students expect the senior year to be substantive, involve reflection, and bring coherence to their education. It should also help students transition to postcollege life.

Although Cuseo (1998) concluded the senior-year experience is really a student-centered movement, in that it aims to support students in transition to life beyond college, the institution is also a beneficiary. Most institutions acknowledge the importance of having collaborative relationships with prospective employers and business leaders. Senior-year experience programming can foster such relationships through partnerships between the college or university and corporations on career preparation workshops and job fairs. Similarly, the institution benefits from seniors who have a positive experience and become loyal alumni. More specifically, the institution gains when students are prepared for and experience postgraduation success, which in turn makes them better alumni and college ambassadors. In addition, curricular experiences, such as capstones, senior-year presentations, and interdisciplinary seminars in the senior year can offer invigorating faculty development opportunities. Further, assessment data from seniors can provide institutions a wealth of information about program quality and educational outcomes— information that can be used to improve curricular coherence or to retool the undergraduate program.

There is also a societal rationale for attending to the senior year. Pressing national issues over that last decade, including a constrained economy, the demand for more Americans to earn college degrees, and concerns about graduates lacking skills desired by employers, amplify the justification for attending to the senior year. The pressure on colleges and universities to increase graduation rates and to reduce time to degree makes it incumbent upon institutions to ensure that the path to the senior year is clear and that seniors get the support they need to make it to the graduation stage. A tough economy and rising student loan debt makes it even more important for students to have good job-search skills and know how to manage their finances. Finally, the U.S. economy needs students who possess the skills and talents that employers desire and that our global labor market demands. Institutions must ensure that seniors are prepared to navigate the increased challenges of current economic conditions and rising employer demands.

The Chapters Ahead

This book is organized in such a way as to help readers understand the senior student first, consider how institutions can address student needs in the collegiate context, and then attend to actual strategies that can be employed to assist seniors in their transition out of college.

In section I, Jennifer Keup provides a helpful portrait of the needs and demographic charactericstics of today's seniors. Tracy Skipper builds on this portrait by describing how student development theory informs our understanding of today's seniors. Rey Junco and Jeanna Mastrodicasa then discuss the technological changes in student culture and technology use by undergraduates, educators, and employers, encouraging the reader to embrace and integrate these changes when interacting with seniors.

In section II, Jillian Kinzie addresses how high-impact practices can be used to improve institutional efforts in supporting seniors. Jean Henscheid continues this discussion by examining the curricular context for enhancing the senior-year experience.

Section III focuses on the transition to the world of work. Heather Maietta turns our attention to the central topic of career development during this last year of college. A consideration of the gap between college preparation and the skills and knowledge needed in the world of work is addressed by Philip Gardner and April Perry.

Colleges and universities have many options for formalizing and ritualizing the transition out of college, and a number of possibilities are outlined by Peter Magolda and Michael Denton. Our institutions can be more intentional about trying to developing loyal alumni and future donors before the seniors leave us. Meredith Fakas and Mary Ruffin Childs offer strategies for doing just that.

In the concluding chapter, John Gardner and Mary Stuart Hunter provide a synthesis of the volume and suggest a set of recommendations for action steps that colleges and universities can take to meet the needs of seniors and improve their chances for success in an increasingly competitive world.

In summary, the implementation of a senior-year experience has benefits to students, institutions, and society. The senior year provides important opportunities for integration, closure and reflection, and transition (Gardner et al., 1998). In the same way that the first-year experience helps student navigate their transition into the institution, the senior-year experience provides students important opportunities to reflect on their experiences and facilitate the transition to postcollege life.

References

Association of American Colleges and Universities (AAC&U). (2007). *College learning for the new global century: A report from the National Leadership Council for Liberal Education and America's Promise*. Washington, DC: Author.

Arum, R., & Roska, J. (2011). *Academically adrift: Limited learning on college campuses.* Chicago, IL: University of Chicago Press.

Barefoot, B. O. (2000) The first-year experience: Are we making it any better? *About Campus, 4*(6), 12-18.

Bureau of Labor Statistics. (2010). *Number of jobs, labor market experience, and earnings growth: Results from a national longitudinal survey news release.* Retrieved from http://www.bls.gov/news.release/nlsoy.htm

Bureau of Labor Statistics. (2011, October). *Table 10: Employment status of the civilian non-institutional population by educational attainment, age, sex, race, and Hispanic or Latino and Non-Hispanic ethnicity.* Retrieved May 18, 2012 from http://www.bls.gov/news.release/empsit.t02.htm

Chickering, A. W., & Schlossberg, N. K. (1998). Moving on: Seniors as people in transition. In J. N. Gardner, G. Van der Veer, & Associates (Eds.), *The senior-year experience: Facilitating integration, reflection, closure, and transition* (pp. 37-50). San Francisco, CA: Jossey-Bass.

Collier, P. (2000). The effects of completing a senior capstone course on student identity. *Sociology of Education, 73*(4), 285-300.

Council of Graduate Schools (CGS), & Educational Testing Service (ETS). (2012). *Pathways through graduate school and into careers.* Washington DC: Authors.

Cuseo, J. (1998). Objectives and benefits of senior year programs. In J. N. Gardner, G. Van der Veer, & Associates (Eds.), *The senior-year experience: Facilitating Integration, Reflection, Closure, and Transition* (p. 21-36). San Francisco, CA: Jossey-Bass.

Dickinson, J. (1993). The senior seminar at Rider College. *Teaching Sociology, 21*(3), 215-218.

Durel, R. J. (1993). The capstone course: A rite of passage. *Teaching Sociology, 21*(3), 223-225.

Gaff, J. G., Ratcliff, J. L., & Associates. (1997). *Handbook of the undergraduate curriculum: A comprehensive guide to purposes, structures, practices, and change.* San Francisco: Jossey-Bass.

Gardner, J. N. (1999). The senior year experience. *About Campus, 4*(1), 5-11.

Gardner, J. N., Van der Veer, G., & Associates (1998). *The senior year experience: Facilitating integration, reflection, closure, and transition.* San Francisco, CA: Jossey-Bass.

Hart Research Associates. (2009). *Trends and emerging practices in general education.* Washington, DC: Association of American Colleges and Universities.

Hart Research Associates. (2010). *Raising the bar: Employer's views on college learning in the wake of the economic downturn.* Washington, DC: Association of American Colleges and Universities. Retrieved from www.aacu.org/leap/documents/2009_EmployerSurvey.pdf

Henscheid, J. M. (2000). *Professing the disciplines: An analysis of senior seminars and capstone courses* (Monograph No. 30). Columbia, SC: South Carolina University, National Resource Center for The First-Year Experience and Students in Transition.

Henscheid, J. M. (2008a). Institutional efforts to move students to and beyond college. In B. O. Barefoot (Ed.), *The first year and beyond: Rethinking the challenge of collegiate transition* (New Directions for Higher Education No. 144, pp. 79-87). San Francisco, CA: Jossey-Bass.

Henscheid, J. M. (2008b). Preparing seniors for life after college. *About Campus, 13*(5), 20-25.

Jay, M. (2012). *The defining decade: Why your twenties matter and how to make the most of them now.* New York, NY: Hatchette Book Group.

Keeling R. P., & Hersh, R. H. (2011). *We're losing our minds: Rethinking American higher education.* New York, NY: Palgrave Macmillan.

National Association of Colleges and Employers (NACE). (2012). *Job Outlook 2012.* Bethlehem, PA: Author.

Pistilli, M. D., Taub, D. J., & Bennett, D. E. (2003). Development of the senior concerns survey: An exploratory factor analysis. *Journal of The First-Year Experience & Students in Transition, 15*(1), 39-52.

Schneider, C. G. (2012). President's message where completion goes awry: The metrics for "success" mask mounting problems with quality. *Liberal Education, 98*(1). Retrieved from http://www.aacu.org/liberaleducation/le-wi12/president.cfm

Taub, D. J., Servaty-Seib, H. L., & Cousins, C. (2006). On the brink of transition: The concerns of college seniors. *Journal of The First-Year Experience & Students in Transition, 18*(2), 111-132.

Taylor, S. H. (2011). Engaging habits of mind and heart through integrative learning. *About Campus, 16*(5), 16.

van Gennep, A. (1960). *The rites of passage.* Chicago, IL: The University of Chicago Press.

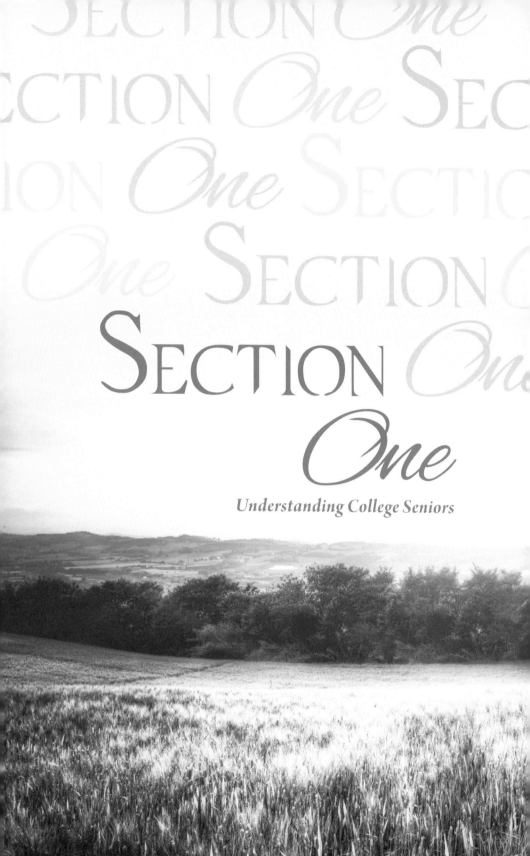

SECTION
One
Understanding College Seniors

CHAPTER One

Pathways and Portraits of Today's College Seniors

Jennifer R. Keup

James felt the chills of excitement when the first bars of "Pomp and Circumstance" played as he marched into the auditorium for his graduation ceremony. Although he could not see them, he could imagine his mother's tears and his father's proud expression as they witnessed the first member of their family earn a college degree. James smiled as he remembered trying to explain the transfer process to his immigrant parents and why he had to leave the local community college to travel halfway across the country to attend a four-year liberal arts institution, as well as his choice to study political science and become a college professor. That was an ongoing battle, but his summer internship in Washington, DC, during his junior year and recent admission to graduate school have helped ease the tension. So many different people have become important to him, including his first college roommate and best friend, an Afghanistan veteran currently serving in the Army reserves, and his friends from his work-study position and off-campus job. However, most important has been his faculty advisor, a fellow Chicano, who offered him the comfort of cultural similarity at a predominantly White institution. His advisor's tireless belief in him and encouragement to take advantage of every academic support structure and educational opportunity made all the difference as James transitioned to the institution and began to conceptualize his life beyond college. Now, it was the time to honor himself and all of the important people who supported him on his journey to become a college graduate.

Recent national attention has been focused on 21st century learning outcomes of college, which represent the skills and knowledge that students should acquire by graduation, including "knowledge of human cultures and the physical and natural world, intellectual and practical skills, personal and social responsibility, and integrative and applied learning" capabilities (AAC&U, 2011, p. 7). As the result of their educational and personal journeys through their undergraduate experience, college seniors should represent the mastery level of these skills that will help inform and motivate their personal, civic, and economic contributions to society. Further, college seniors are on the cusp of launching careers, starting graduate school, joining the ranks of campus alumni, and entering society as fully contributing citizens. Yet, despite the important characteristics of this critical juncture in the larger trajectory of individuals' educational and personal development, historically, our understanding of this group of students has been relatively contextual and institution specific.

Over the past several decades, the accountability movement in higher education has led to an increase in assessment activities of students at all points in their college career, with particular emphasis on the beginning and end of that journey. This move toward data-driven decision making and a culture of evidence has led to the proliferation of national survey instruments that focus on seniors as the unit of analysis. These instruments not only provide a broad overview of students' academic and campus life activities, as with the Cooperative Institutional Research Program's (CIRP) College Senior Survey, but also help illuminate specific aspects of seniors' educational engagement and participation in high-impact experiences (e.g., National Study of Student Engagement); career motivations, attitudes, and goals (Michigan State University's Collegiate Employment Research Institute's [CERI] recruiting and employment surveys); religious and spiritual development (College Student Beliefs and Values Survey); and civic engagement (Life After College: The Survey of Former Undergraduates). When combined with national trends on retention and degree completion as well as statistics from the U.S. Census Bureau and Department of Education, these data help create an aggregate picture of the demography of college seniors, identify how they engage intellectually and personally during their college experience, and provide evidence about their plans and expectations for life after college. While each of these issues will be further explored in subsequent chapters of this volume, the current chapter will provide an introduction, overview, and foundation on the topic of college seniors.

Senior: A Working Definition

Before embarking upon an extensive discussion of the various facets of the senior year, it is important to provide a definition of this construct. While many higher education scholars and practitioners intuitively know what a senior is, there is very little in the body of higher education literature that points to a unified and shared definition of this term. There is some reference to a senior as "a college student in the process of completing the final [quartile] of the baccalaureate degree" (Gardner, Van der Veer, & Associates, 1998, p. 4). Historically, senior status was often synonymous with the fourth year of the undergraduate experience. However, as both the students enrolling in college and the pathways through higher education have become more heterogeneous, the time it takes to earn a college degree has become a longer and less linear process. A definition of seniors that is based upon a four-year model fails to include "the growing number of students who matriculate into and out of two or more institutions, those who stop out, ... and those enrolled in programs that require more than four years to complete" (Henscheid, 2008, p. 80). Thus, it is far more accurate to use credits earned toward the bachelor's degree as the threshold for senior status than it is to rely upon a temporal model.

Given that many students take more than four years to earn a degree and often progress through many institutions, it is important to provide another subtle gradation to the working definition of senior, that of *graduating senior*. For the purposes of this chapter and volume, a senior is any student whose current institution recognizes that he or she has earned enough credits to be three quarters of the way to the conferment of an undergraduate degree. However, a graduating senior is a student who is currently enrolled in a program of coursework that, upon successful completion, would represent fulfillment of his or her final requirements toward degree attainment. Therefore, a student may have senior status for several years but is usually a graduating senior for only one or, if initially unsuccessful, two terms.

Finally, it is also important to recognize that the authors of this book will refer not just to students with senior status but also to the host of academic, social, and interpersonal activities and events that typically correspond with this final phase of the journey toward the baccalaureate. These experiences include coursework, curriculum, and capstone experiences; career development and anticipation of the transition to the workplace; preparation for graduate school; social networks and interpersonal relationships; and the transition of the relationship with the institution from student to alumni. Together, these and other developmental and personal milestones represent the *senior-year experience*. As noted by Gardner et al. (1998), the "senior year experience is a very flexible concept … [that] can be made to mean whatever its advocates, proponents, and developers want it to mean" (p. xiii). In addition, what is meant by this term often differs across institutions in order to reflect the college or university's characteristics, mission, culture, and student needs. Although many institutions will focus on one course, program, or initiative as the whole or crux of their senior-year experience, research and best-practice literature on other student transitions, such as the first-year experience (e.g., Barefoot et al., 2005; Koch & Gardner, 2006; Upcraft, Gardner, Barefoot, & Associates, 2005) and the sophomore year (e.g., Hunter et al., 2010; Tobolowsky, 2008; Tobolowsky & Cox, 2007), indicate that a multifaceted, comprehensive, integrated, and complementary approach to student transition and success programming yields the greatest institutional impact and student benefit. Thus, the most efficient and effective senior-year experiences will be those that integrate myriad curricular and cocurricular opportunities for students as they experience the culmination of their undergraduate years.

Demographic and Personal Characteristics of College Seniors

As mentioned previously, the proliferation of national assessment instruments over the past decade has assisted in the task of identifying characteristics and trends with respect to college students. Overall, college students have become more diverse in terms of race and ethnicity, socioeconomic status, disability status, and age (Aud et al., 2011; *Chronicle of Higher Education*, 2011-2012; Pryor, Hurtado, Saenz, Santos & Korn, 2007; Snyder & Dillow, 2011). These and other national data show that women continue to be overrepresented on college and university campuses across the country; first-generation students (i.e., neither parent has a college degree) represent a significant subpopulation of college students; 3-4% of college undergraduates have current or veteran military rank; and Hispanic, multiracial, and students who speak a language other than English at home are rapidly growing demographic categories among high school graduates and incoming college students (*Chronicle of Higher Education*, 2011-2012; Davis & Bauman, 2011; Shin, 2005; WICHE, 2008). Further, while the majority of undergraduates are attending public and four-year institutions, there has been a surge in enrollment in two-year colleges, and approximately 20% of these students eventually transfer to four-year institutions to earn a bachelor's degree (Davis & Bauman, 2011; NCES, 2008). Additionally, a small but growing proportion of undergraduates, approximately 9%, are attending private, for-profit institutions (Aud et al., 2011; *Chronicle of Higher Education*, 2011-2012).

While tempting, it is important not to draw conclusions specifically about seniors based on these general data regarding all undergraduates. Recently collected national data focused solely on college seniors help provide a current picture of students in the aggregate at this specific point in their educational journeys. Much like the data on all undergraduates, senior women outnumber their male counterparts on colleges and universities across the country at a rate of 55% to 45% (NSSE, 2011). With respect to racial and ethnic breakdowns, reports of national data range quite a bit. However, non-Hispanic, White students still represent a majority of seniors (64%), followed by Latino/a and African American students (9% each; NSSE, 2011). Seniors who identify as Asian/Pacific Islander in their race or ethnicity (7%) round out the top categories in this area of identity. Students who indicate that they are foreign, American Indian/Native American, or multiracial typically represent between one and two percentage points each in the racial and ethnic distribution of college seniors nationally (NSSE, 2011). In a related vein, data from the CIRP College Senior Survey indicate that more than 90% of college seniors report that English is their native language (Franke, Ruiz, Sharkness, DeAngelo, & Pryor, 2010), although an analysis of current high school students suggest that this statistic will decline as larger numbers of students from primarily Spanish-speaking households graduate from high school and matriculate to college (WICHE, 2008). As a final aspect of demography, the ages of college seniors still tend toward a traditional model of higher education with the majority of students at this point in their educational career reporting that they are 20-23 years old (61%) followed by those in the next age category of 24-29 (18%; NSSE, 2011).

Ability level is another important area of students' personal background, which can challenge students' progression towards college completion (Pryor et al., 2007; Pryor, Hurtado, DeAngelo, Palucki Blake, & Tran, 2010). This is particularly salient given the national increase in reported learning and developmental disabilities over the past few decades. While approximately 85% of seniors in the 2011 NSSE national norms self-reported that they did not have any disabilities, 3% indicated that they had a developmental disorder (e.g., ADHD, autism-spectrum disorder); 2% shared that they had a learning disability; and an additional 6% indicated one of the following disabilities (i.e., 2% for each category): mental health disorder, sensory impairment (e.g., vision or hearing), or a medical disability not represented in another category. Only 1% of the sample reported that they had a mobility impairment. The fact that this distribution is almost identical to the one calculated for first-year students with 2011 NSSE data suggests that students with disabilities seem to be successfully navigating the undergraduate experience to their senior year.

National data on seniors are also informative from a socioeconomic standpoint. While first-generation college students are often considered at risk for poor academic performance, adjustment, and retention, nearly half of seniors report that either their mother or father did not earn a college degree (Cataldi et al., 2011; NSSE, 2011). An examination of a recent cohort of more than 17,000 college graduates showed that greater than one third of them reported receiving a Pell Grant, 66% of them borrowed money to pay for college, and the average amount borrowed ranged from $20,500 for students at public, non-doctoral granting, four-year institutions to $36,800 at for-profit, four-year institutions (Cataldi et al., 2011). Other data indicate that "almost half of all college seniors (45%) rely on the help of family resources to pay for more than $10,000 of their educational expenses (including room, board, tuition and fees)" in a single year (Franke et al., 2010, p. 14), and many are using their own resources from work and personal savings to pay for college expenses. These same data revealed that 46% of students report working for pay off campus compared to 45% working for pay on campus. Although the proportion of students engaged in on- and off-campus employment is similar, it is important to note that students reporting that they worked off campus tend to work longer hours and miss class more frequently due to employment (Franke et al., 2010).

Together, these data paint a portrait of today's cohort of college seniors, which is largely representative of national data trends on undergraduate students. While there are a few indices that represent the persistence of more traditional students, most notably age, national data on college seniors illustrate a changing demographic on college campuses today. College seniors tend to be more racially and ethnically diverse and include growing representation of first-generation students, students with learning and developmental disabilities, and non-native English speakers than in previous decades. Further, higher education seems to be maintaining a continued commitment to an equity agenda as many seniors come from lower socioeconomic households. However, the combination of increased access in this segment of the college-going population and difficult economic times results in more college seniors who maintain student employment and accumulate significant debt to attend college.

Educational Experiences of College Seniors

National data indicate that college seniors spend a significant portion of their time on academic pursuits. More specifically, findings from analyses of 24,457 graduating seniors from 111 institutions who participated in the 2009 CIRP College Senior Survey (CSS) indicate that just under two thirds of the sample (64%) spent 10 or more hours per week attending classes or labs and more than half (56%) spent a similar amount of time on homework (Franke et al., 2010). In addition to studying, many of these same students report that they *frequently* discuss course content with fellow students outside of class (70%), studied with other students (45%), and worked on independent study projects (33%).

Interaction with faculty also represents a substantial measure of academic engagement for college seniors with more than 40% of 2009 CSS respondents indicating that they interacted with faculty during office hours for an hour or more per week while 32% communicated with faculty outside of class or office hours at least one hour per week (Franke et al., 2010). Other national data collected via the 2011 NSSE suggest the nature of these interactions with faculty both in and outside the classroom. Most commonly, seniors are discussing grades or assignments with their instructor, but slightly more than 40% of the 2011 NSSE senior sample reported that they *talked about career plans* with faculty *often* or *very often*, approximately one in four students indicated that they *discussed ideas from … readings or classes with faculty members outside of class*, and 23% *often* or *very often* worked with faculty on activities that were not course related, such as orientation, student life, and campus committees (NSSE, 2011).

Time diaries and frequency scales certainly provide an image of academic engagement among college seniors. However, most theories of involvement and engagement (e.g., Astin, 1999; Kuh, Schuh, Whitt, & Associates, 1991; Pace, 1980) point to the importance of the quality of involvement as well as the quantity of time spent in academic activities. As such, it is important to look to gauges of students' involvement in rigorous, integrated, and enriching educational experiences to indicate what students are doing with their time. For example, Table 1.1 shows the percent of seniors in the 2011 NSSE sample that engaged in coursework of increasingly complex levels of cognitive processes that are loosely organized around Bloom's Taxonomy (1956). It is heartening to note there is a positive relationship between cognitive complexity and the proportion of

Table 1.1
Emphasis of Coursework on Cognitive Processes

Coursework emphasizes:	Percent responding *quite a bit* or *very much*
Memorizing facts, ideas, or methods from your courses and readings	63
Synthesizing and organizing ideas, information, or experiences	77
Applying theories or concepts to practical problems or in new situations	82
Analyzing the basic elements of an idea, experience, or theory	86
Making judgments about the value of information, arguments, or methods	74

Note. Adapted from *NSSE 2011 U.S. Grand Frequencies: Frequency Distribution by Carnegie Classification*, by the National Survey of Student Engagement, 2011, p. 4. Copyright 2011 by the Indiana University Center for Postsecondary Research.

seniors reporting that their coursework emphasized these activities for the first four levels and informative to note that college seniors may not be getting enough opportunities to evaluate and make judgments about the value of ideas and information (i.e., the highest level) covered in their coursework (NSSE, 2011).

In addition, students' engagement in high-impact educational practices during their senior year is another index of the quality of their educational experience and provides support for their progress toward the integrative, inquiry, global, and civic learning processes that represent 21st century learning outcomes (AAC&U, 2011; Kuh, 2008; Leskes & Miller, 2006). Recent national data show that a substantial percentage of college students have engaged in such activities by spring of their senior year, including practica, internships, field experiences, or clinical assignments (50%); service-learning (48%); a culminating or capstone experience (32%); learning communities (27%); research with a faculty member (20%); and study abroad programs (15%) (NSSE, 2011). In addition, many institutions seem to be offering other high-impact practices to seniors, which have historically been the hallmark of lower-division student support programs. A recent national survey of institutional practices indicated that 93% of colleges and universities that offer student seminars provide one for seniors, a substantial proportion of seniors are still monitored by early warning systems, and 7% offer senior learning communities (Barefoot, Griffin, & Koch, 2012).

While these statistics are heartening measures of academic engagement among college seniors, the data also show patterns of academic disengagement. Nearly all students (96%) reported feeling bored in class at least occasionally and one in four said they were bored on a frequent basis (Franke et al., 2010). Further, 85% of respondents to this same survey *frequently* or *occasionally* missed class for reasons other than employment, approximately two thirds indicated that they came late to class at least occasionally, 52% reported that they failed to complete homework on time at least occasionally, and 38% acknowledged falling asleep in class (Franke et al. 2001). Additionally, male college seniors tend to be more academically disengaged than women and "American Indian, Asian/PI American, and African American students are more likely to have academic disengagement behaviors … than other racial/ethnic groups" (Franke et al., 2010, p. 6). Further, African American and Latino students were significantly less likely than their White peers to participate in study abroad programs, and student veterans were less likely to be academically engaged overall (NSSE, 2010). Finally, seniors' academic engagement and involvement tends to vary significantly by their major, which is the primary academic environment, area of affiliation, and source of opportunity during their time as an upper-division student (NSSE, 2010). For example, seniors in the hard sciences (e.g., biology, chemistry, physics) spent more time engaged in research with faculty; seniors in elementary or middle education and journalism majors more frequently reported studying abroad; engineering, nursing, physical education, and applied health fields more often engaged in internships and practica; and seniors studying history and political science tended to engage in senior culminating experiences at higher rates than their peers in other majors (NSSE, 2010).

Data from these same national surveys suggest that the result of students' academic involvement, interaction with faculty, and engagement in high-impact practices was favorable, and seniors are generally pleased with this aspect of their undergraduate experience. For instance, the vast majority of seniors feel their skills in several academic and intellectual areas—knowledge of a field or discipline, general knowledge, critical thinking, analytical and problem-solving skills—became stronger or much stronger since entering college (Franke et al., 2010); 86% indicated their educational experience was *good* or *excellent*; and 72% reported their institution provided the support they needed to succeed academically (NSSE, 2011). Further, most seniors indicated they were *satisfied* or *very satisfied* with several aspects of their academic experience, including class size (90%), library facilities (78%), and academic advising (63%). Finally, slightly more than half of students who used laboratory facilities, tutoring, and other academic assistance related high levels of satisfaction.

Personal and Interpersonal Experiences of College Students

As indicated in previous sections, academic pursuits and student employment represent significant aspects of seniors' collegiate experience. However, they are not the whole of students' lives. By their senior year, many undergraduates have become involved in the cocurricular life of campus, with more than half spending at least some time each week engaged in student clubs, organizations, and activities (NSSE, 2011). Specifically, more than half of the students responding to the 2009 CSS reported since entering college they had played club, intramural, or recreational sports; more than 20% participated in an ethnic or racial student organization; nearly 20% played intercollegiate athletics; and in excess of 15% had joined a social sorority or fraternity (Franke et al., 2010). Additionally, the majority of students devote at least some time toward more informal pursuits, such as relaxing and socializing; 70% of senior respondents to the 2011 NSSE indicated at least some time each week engaged in such activities. Further, a substantial proportion of these same survey respondents reported that they *often* or *very often* engaged in exercise or physical fitness (55%), participated in activities to enhance their spirituality (33%), and attended visual or performing arts events (23%) while in college (NSSE, 2011). Finally, as higher education has experienced growth among nontraditional, adult, and first-generation student populations, care for dependents living with the students (e.g., parents, children, spouse) has become a factor for many undergraduates. Approximately 40% of seniors reported that caregiver duties are a regular part of their weekly schedule, with 17% investing a minimum of 20 hours per week (NSSE, 2011).

College also represents a time when students begin to mature and develop in areas of citizenship and civic engagement. During college, traditional students typically reach voting age and both traditional and nontraditional students will likely hear, learn, and engage with ideas that may challenge and refine their sociopolitical beliefs. Further, college provides many outlets and opportunities for students to become involved in the local community to apply their beliefs and learning. Often a discussion of college student civic engagement conjures images of student activism of the 1960s, which represented protests and focused on national and global issues. However, college seniors today appear to exhibit a more local and service-minded ethos with respect to civic engagement. For instance, 15% of respondents to the 2009 CSS participated in political demonstrations or demonstrated for or against a war, but 71% of these same students performed volunteer work. In another example, only 12% worked on a local, state, or national political campaign while 83% indicated they discussed politics and 67% reported voting in a student election (Franke et al., 2010).

It is important to note, however, that this difference in the nature of civic engagement among college students does not necessarily represent a lack of social awareness or agency. National data show that all measures of social agency increase from the first year of college to the senior year, with statistically significant changes (i.e., six or more percentage-point increase by the senior year) occurring for students' commitment to keeping up-to-date with political affairs, influencing social values, helping others in difficulty, and participating in a community action program (Franke et al., 2010). These same students reported the highest increase across the undergraduate experience on a related measure of social and civic engagement: becoming involved in programs to clean up the environment, which had a 10 percentage-point increase. Also, "the undergraduate years appear to be a time of changing political preferences" with students adopting more liberal sociopolitical beliefs by their senior year (Franke et al., 2010, p. 34). Finally, one recent and important exception to the more localized character of civic involvement was voting in the 2008 presidential election, which followed a significantly long campaign and represented a watershed outcome in American history; 78% of CSS respondents indicated voting in that election (Franke et al., 2010).

College seniors' engagement with diversity and multiculturalism also represents another form of civic awareness and social involvement. Many seniors reported engaging in formalized curricula, programs, or organizations to enhance their understanding of a particular identity area or facilitate exposure to areas of difference during their time in college. These experiences included attending events sponsored by another racial or ethnic group (74%), taking an ethnic studies course (49%), attending a racial or cultural awareness workshop (33%), enrolling in a women's studies course (26%), and participating in an ethnic or racial student organization (22%) (Franke et al., 2010). However, the majority of seniors indicated that their experiences with diversity were informal and related to interpersonal interactions and relationships. More than 40% of seniors represented in the 2009 CSS results reported they had a roommate of a different race or ethnicity at some point during college, 55% had dined or shared a meal with students from another racial or ethnic group *often* or *very often*, and 44% frequently studied or prepared for class with students from a racial or ethnic group other than their own (Franke et al., 2010). Most times, the nature of these interactions was very positive, and more than two thirds of seniors indicated they had *meaningful and honest discussions about race/ethnic relations outside of class* (Franke et al., 2010). However, there were a few instances when cross-racial or ethnic interactions among these students became guarded

(13% reported *often* or *very often*), somewhat hostile (7% reported *often* or *very often*), or even threatening (6% reported *often* or *very often*) suggesting that educators cannot assume that students are equipped to fully handle cross-racial or intercultural interactions, even among seniors, without occasional guidance or facilitation. Additionally, students' engagement with diversity during college should not be focused solely on a racial or ethnic paradigm. Many college seniors represent significant progression from their first year on exploration and expression of sexual orientation, religiosity and spirituality, and culture with respect to their own identity (Astin, Astin, & Lindholm, 2010; Pascarella & Terenzini, 1991, 2005), and 89% of seniors reported having serious conversations with students who were very different from them in terms of their religious beliefs, political opinions, or personal values (NSSE, 2011).

Whether it is in the form of cocurricular involvement, leisure activities, civic engagement, or diversity interactions, interpersonal communication and relationships are the hallmark of cocurricular experiences during college. Socializing with friends was a fixture in nearly all seniors' time diaries and slightly greater than one third spent three or more hours per week participating in online social networks (Franke et al., 2010). Those students who persisted to the senior year were generally pleased with the nature of their relationships with other students. More specifically, 82% rated the quality of these relationships as friendly and supportive, which provides a sense of belonging (NSSE, 2011) and 88% were satisfied or very satisfied with their interactions with fellow students (Franke et al., 2010). As such, the majority of seniors felt favorably about the overall sense of community among students (Franke et al., 2010).

Career Plans and Pathways

As the vehicle to students' postgraduate plans for career and graduate school, seniors' majors are an interesting starting point in this discussion. Table 1.2 draws from data collected via the 2009 CSS to illustrate the top 10 primary majors (in aggregated categories) reported by this cohort of graduating seniors as well as the change in the percentage reporting this major from the first year of college. Most notably, majors in business, the social sciences, biological sciences, and history or political science are most popular, findings that were generally validated by seniors' responses to the 2011 National Survey of Student Engagement (NSSE, 2011). Conversely, fewer than 2% of the 2009 CSS respondent pool reported a major in mathematics or statistics, other technical areas, and agriculture. Some of the top majors represent the largest areas of disciplinary immigration, including

Table 1.2
Most Common Academic Majors Among Seniors

Major	Percent of seniors	Percent change from first year
Business	18.4	1.0
Social science	17.3	9.4
Biological science	10.3	0.8
History or political science	9.5	1.4
Humanities	8.1	3.9
Other nontechnical	6.7	0.8
Engineering	5.4	-1.4
English	5.0	2.0
Fine arts	4.7	0.4
Education	4.5	-2.0

Note. Adapted from *Findings from the 2009 Administration of the College Senior Survey (CSS): National Aggregates*, by R. Franke, S. Ruiz, J. Sharkness, L. DeAngelo, and J. Pryor, 2010, p. 91. Copyright 2010 by the Cooperative Institutional Research Program, University of California, Los Angeles.

English, humanities, and the social sciences. Perhaps not surprisingly, the largest emigration major from the first to the senior year, health professions (-7.3%), did not make the list of most popular majors.

Interestingly, current hiring practices for jobs do not always maintain a strong connection to major. In fact, an analysis of recruiting trends using data collected in 2010 and 2011 showed more than one third of employers were willing to seek qualified applicants for positions from a wide range of majors, and there has been an increase in employer interest for graduates from liberal arts majors (Gardner, Render, & Sciarini, 2010). Further, the competency areas of greatest interest to employers in "today's rapidly changing economy ... do not represent vocational traits or content but are indicators of higher-level cognitive skills and critical thinking" (Vakos, 2010, p. 15). In particular, employers seek initiative; interpersonal and professional relationship-building skills; the ability to analyze, evaluate, and interpret data; and the capacity to engage in lifelong learning (Vakos, 2010). However, many employers reported concern about the degree to which colleges are preparing students in these areas and most felt "colleges should place greater emphasis on a variety of learning outcomes developed through a liberal education" (Hart Research Associates, 2010, p. 1). Finally, employers expect a higher level of proficiency in the skills college graduates must possess. More specifically, "entry level jobs today are frequently requiring the same skill set as middle-management positions posted six to seven years ago," and the basic requirements of internships mirror the skills needed for entry-level jobs several years ago (Vakos, 2010. p. 16). Therefore, internships are not only a high-impact practice in the undergraduate experience but a critical step toward employability for a new college graduate.

Student responses to the 2009 CSS also provide some insight to the desired professional pathways of college seniors. Interestingly, the career category that generated the highest response rate was *other* (11.4%), suggesting the career paths for current graduates represent nontraditional or hybrid areas of the economic landscape. Otherwise, probable careers among these seniors included elementary or secondary teacher or administrator (10.2%), business executive (10.1%), physician (5.2%), lawyer (attorney) or judge (5.1%), accountant or actuary (4.5%), engineer (3.9%), and nurse (3.4%) (Franke et al., 2010). Given that many of these career paths require advanced degrees, it is not surprising that 83.1% of these seniors reported they plan to attend graduate school (Franke et al., 2010). However, it is important to note that it is unlikely these initial areas of career interest will be sustained over the lifespan of these students. Data drawn from the National Longitudinal Survey of Youth 1979 show individuals change jobs 11 times between the ages of 18 and 44 (U.S. Bureau of Labor Statistics, 2008).

Additionally, findings from other national surveys show the current cohorts of graduates maintain a significantly different attitude about work than previous generations. For example, the value of work as a central component of one's identity and the primary focus of one's time and energy is lower for today's young adults than for previous generations (Chao & Gardner, 2007a). Yet "job characteristics that are related to long-term career success [tend] to be ranked higher than job characteristics that are more short-term oriented," including "having interesting work, good benefits, job security, and chances for promotion" (Chao & Gardner, 2007b, p. 4). Despite the stereotype that millennials are more materialistic, status conscious, and self-centered, earning a high income was ranked eighth out of 15 job characteristics that were important to the job search process, and flexibility, the ability to work independently, and travel opportunities fell even lower in the rank order (Chao & Gardner, 2007b). These rankings of highly valued job characteristics were generally stable across gender, race, academic program, and age, although there were some differences by socioeconomic class with job security, flexibility in work hours, and limited stress being more important to young adults from low-income backgrounds (Chao & Gardner, 2007b). However, this focus on long-term career goals cannot be mistaken for organizational loyalty; nearly two thirds of respondents to a survey conducted by the Collegiate Employment Research Institute indicated "they would likely engage in job surfing behaviors during their early career" (Chao & Gardner, 2007c, p. 3), and 44% would back out on a job offer they had already accepted if they received a better offer thereafter.

Despite a more challenging economy, some expressions of pessimism among employers about graduate's readiness for the work force, and seniors' more relaxed commitment to work as a central component of their identity, graduating seniors are optimistic about their prospects for employment. In fact, this group's expectations about job offers has remained relatively consistent over the years. Approximately three quarters of students graduating from college in 2008 expected to receive two or more job offers upon graduation (Monster Worldwide, 2008).

Retention Data

While the senior year of college offers many opportunities for personal, academic, and professional development, the ultimate goal is to earn a degree and move beyond the university. Overall, 52% of students earn a degree within five years of entry (ACT, 2010). However, this statistic varies widely by institutional type, ranging from 39% at a public, master's-granting institution to 65% at a private, doctoral-granting institution (ACT, 2010). Time to degree is strongly associated with the institutional selectivity (ACT, 2011), but it is also likely representative of the structural and organizational elements that different types of colleges and universities are able to offer in support of student progress, success, and completion. Extending the degree completion timeline by one year captures additional students in the educational pipeline. According to data collected by the U.S. Department of Education, "approximately 57 percent of first-time students who sought a bachelor's degree or its equivalent and enrolled at a 4-year institution full time in fall 2002 completed a bachelor's degree or its equivalent at that institution within 6 years" (Aud et al., 2011. p. 72). However, this number is a conservative measure as it excludes students who transfer to another institution (either two- or four-year), which represents a more common pathway through higher education for students today.

Further analyses of degree attainment rates reveal not only significant differences by institutional type but also variation by student characteristics. For example, women not only outnumber men in the composition of undergraduates and seniors, but they also have higher completion rates than their male peers at both public and private institutions (Aud et al., 2011). In addition, among students seeking a bachelor's degree at a four-year institution, Asian American/ Pacific Islanders had the highest attainment rate (67%) followed by students who are White (60%), Hispanic (49%), Black (40%), and Native American/Alaska Native (38%). This racial or ethnic difference in postsecondary educational attainment remains a robust pattern regardless of institutional characteristics, and the disparities between historically underrepresented groups in higher education (i.e., most notably Blacks and Hispanics) and White students has increased from 1990 to 2005 (Aud et al., 2011). Finally, students who transferred between institutions tended to take longer to earn their degrees than students who attended only one institution (U.S. Department of Education, 2003).

There are numerous benefits of bachelor's degree attainment, and "college-educated individuals consistently rank higher than those with less education on a clear majority of the quality-of-life indicators" (Pascarella & Terenzini, 2005, p. 552). More specifically, individuals with a college education tend to be in better health as well as have healthier families; spend more time caring for offspring and engage in more developmentally enriching activities with their children; make more effective consumer choices; save and invest their income more efficiently; and participate in cultured leisure activities (Pascarella & Terenzini, 1991) and civic engagement (Pascarella & Terenzini, 2005) at higher levels than individuals without a college degree. Despite all of these benefits, none is arguably more fundamental to personal well-being and success than earning potential, and the positive association between educational attainment and median earnings is strong and has remained consistent over time. According to 2009 data, the median annual earnings for an individual with a bachelor's degree was $45,000 as compared to $36,000 for individuals with an associate degree, $30,000 for individuals with a high school diploma or equivalent degree, and $21,000 for individuals without a high school diploma or equivalent credential (Aud et al., 2011). In other words,

> young adults ages 25-34 with a bachelor's degree earned more than twice as much as young adults without a high school diploma or its equivalent, 50 percent more than young adult high school completers, and 25 percent more than young adults with an associate's degree. (Aud et al., 2011, p. 56)

Even when considering the earnings differential across areas of study or career paths and accounting for indebtedness from financial aid and other loans for college, it is clear that a college degree will have a substantial positive effect on a person's economic well-being over the course of a lifetime.

The consistent disadvantage of students of color, men, and transfers illustrated in degree-completion data represent important indices of at-risk students among college undergraduates. When coupled with the profound economic impact of earning a college degree, these statistics are a clarion call for policy and programming changes to achieve equity in bachelor's degree attainment.

Conclusion

Over the past several years, higher education has welcomed a more diverse cohort of students, including women, students of color, veterans, and students of different ability levels and from lower socioeconomic backgrounds to complement the more traditional student profile. Further, the assessment and accountability movement has generated more national data to track academic engagement, learning experiences, cocurricular involvement, and student development from entry through the senior year. As such, we are able to better understand seniors' positive academic experiences, such as their engagement in high-impact practices, interaction with faculty, and positive response to coursework emphasizing higher level cognitive processes. Conversely, it is now possible to identify specific areas of disengagement, such as feeling bored in or skipping class and prioritizing employment above academic obligations. These same data paint a clearer picture of students' life outside the classroom and show that a large proportion of college seniors work, participate in formal cocurricular activities, and engage in leisure activities. In addition, by their senior year, students undergo a great deal of personal development in the areas of civic engagement and agency, diversity interactions, and spirituality, which are fostered by both curricular and cocurricular activities. Finally and perhaps not surprisingly, many seniors are considering graduate school as well as career options, albeit with a degree of low commitment to personal work identity and an optimism that may not be commensurate with the current economy and job market. As higher education institutions strive to offer appropriate levels of challenge and support to students at all of the critical junctures in their educational journey, including the senior year, it is important to fully understand the characteristics and experiences of this population of students that national data tell us. Only then are college educators able to fashion an educationally purposeful senior-year experience that serves as a meaningful capstone to students' undergraduate experience, helps advance seniors' achievement of 21st century learning outcomes, and positions them for success in their life after college.

References

American College Testing, Inc. (ACT). (2010). *2010 Retention/completion summary tables.* Retrieved from http://www.act.org/research/policymakers/pdf/10retain_trends.pdf

American College Testing, Inc. (ACT). (2011). *National collegiate retention and persistence to degree rates.* Retrieved from http://www.act.org/research/policymakers/pdf/retain_2005.pdf

Association of American Colleges and Universities (AAC&U). (2011). *The LEAP vision for learning: Outcomes, practices, impact and employers' views.* Washington, DC: Author.

Astin, A. W. (1999). Student involvement: A developmental theory. *Journal of College Student Development, 40*(5), 518-529.

Astin, A. W., Astin, H. S., & Lindholm, J. A. (2010). *Cultivating the spirit: How college can enhance students' inner lives.* San Francisco, CA: Jossey-Bass.

Aud, S., Hussar, W., Kena, G., Bianco, K., Frohlich, L., Kemp, J., & Tahan, K. (2011). *The condition of education 2011* (NCES 2011-033). U.S. Department of Education, National Center for Education Statistics. Washington, DC: U.S. Government Printing Office.

Barefoot. B. O., Gardner, J. N., Cutright, M., Morris, L. V., Schroeder, C.C., Schwartz, S. W. . . . Swing, R. L. (2005). *Achieving and sustaining institutional excellence in the first year of college.* San Francisco, CA: Jossey-Bass.

Barefoot, B. O., Griffin, B. Q., & Koch, A. K. (2012). *Enhancing student success and retention throughout undergraduate education: A national survey.* Bevard, NC: John. N. Gardner Institute for Excellence in Undergraduate Education.

Bloom, B. (Ed.). (1956). *A taxonomy of educational objectives: The classification of educational goals, Handbook 1, The cognitive domain.* New York, NY: David McKay Company.

Cataldi, E. F., Green, C., Henke, R., Lew. T., Woo, J., Shepherd, B., & Siegel, P. (2011). *2008-09 Baccalaureate and Beyond Longitudinal Study (B&B:08/09): First look.* U.S. Department of Education. Washington, DC: National Center for Education Statistics.

Chao, G. T., & Gardner, P. D. (2007a). *How central is work to young adults* (White paper prepared for Monster TRAK.com). Retrieved from CERI website: http://ceri.msu.edu/publications/pdf/work_young_adults.pdf

Chao, G. T., & Gardner, P. D. (2007b). *Important characteristics of early career jobs: What do young adults want?* (White paper prepared for Monster TRAK.com). Retrieved from CERI website: http://www.ceri.msu.edu/publications/pdf/JobChar4-16.pdf

Chao, G. T., & Gardner, P. D. (2007c). *Today's young adults: Surfing for the right job* (White paper prepared for Monster TRAK.com). Retrieved from CERI website: http://ceri.msu.edu/publications/pdf/YAdults-16.pdf

Chronicle of Higher Education. (2011-2012). Almanac Issue 2011-12. *Chronicle of Higher Education, 57*(1).

Davis, J. W., & Bauman, J. (2011). *School enrollment in the United States: 2008.* Washington, DC: U.S. Department of Commerce, U.S. Census Bureau.

Franke, R., Ruiz, S., Sharkness, J., DeAngelo, L., & Pryor, J. (2010). *Findings from the 2009 administration of the College Senior Survey (CSS): National aggregates.* Los Angeles, CA: Cooperative Institutional Research Program at the Higher Education Research Institute.

Gardner, J. N., Van der Veer, G., & Associates (1998). *The senior year experience: Facilitating integration, reflection, closure, and transition.* San Francisco, CA: Jossey-Bass.

Gardner, P., Render, I., & Sciarini, N. (2010). *Recruiting trends 2010-2011: 40th anniversary edition.* East Lansing, MI: Michigan State University, The Collegiate Employment Research Institute (CERI) and The MSU Career Services Network.

Hart Research Associates. (2010). *Raising the bar: Employers' views on college learning in the wake of the economic downturn.* Washington, DC: Association of American Colleges and Universities. Retrieved on November 4, 2011, from www.aacu.org/leap/documents/ 2009_EmployerSurvey.pdf

Henscheid, J. M. (2008). Institutional efforts to move seniors through and beyond college. In B. O. Barefoot (Ed.), *The first year and beyond: Rethinking the challenge of collegiate transition.* (New Directions for Higher Education, No. 144, pp. 79-87). San Francisco, CA: Jossey-Bass.

Hunter, M. S., Tobolowsky, B. F., Gardner, J. N., Evenbeck, S. E., Pattengale, J. A., Schaller, M. A., Schreiner, L. A., & Associates (2010). *Helping sophomores succeed: Understanding and improving the second-year experience.* San Francisco, CA: Jossey-Bass.

Koch, A. K., & Gardner, J. N. (2006). The history of the first-year experience in the United States: Lessons from the past, practices in the present, and implications for the future. In A. Hamana & K. Tatsuo (Eds.), *The first-year experience and transition from high school to college: An international study of content and pedagogy.* Tokyo, Japan: Maruzen Publishing.

Kuh, G. D. (2008). *High-Impact educational practices: What they are, who has access to them, and why they matter.* Washington, DC: Association of American Colleges and Universities.

Kuh, G. D., Schuh, J. H., Whitt, E. J., & Associates (1991). *Involving colleges: Successful approaches to fostering student learning and development outside the classroom.* San Francisco, CA: Jossey-Bass.

Leskes, A., & Miller, R. (2006). *Purposeful pathways: Helping students achieve key learning outcomes.* Washington, DC: Association of American Colleges and Universities.

Monster Worldwide, Inc. (2008). *MonsterTRAK's annual entry-level job outlook reveals 2008 graduates are optimistic, while employers hedge hiring expectations.* Retrieved on November 4, 2011 from http://about-monster.com/content/monstertraks-annual-entry-level-job-outlook-reveals-2008-graduates-are-optimistic-while-empl.

National Center for Educational Statistics. (NCES). (2008*). Descriptive summary of 2003-04 Beginning Postsecondary Students: Three years later* (NCES Report 2008-174). Washington, DC: U.S. Department of Education. Retrieved from http://nces.ed.gov/pubsearch/pubsinfo.asp?pubid=2008174

National Survey of Student Engagement (NSSE). (2010). *Major differences: Examining student engagement by field of study — annual results 2010.* Bloomington, IN: Indiana University Center for Postsecondary Research.

National Survey of Student Engagement (NSSE). (2011). *NSSE 2011 U.S. grand frequencies: Frequency distribution by Carnegie classification.* Bloomington, IN: Indiana University Center for Postsecondary Research.

Pace, C. (1980). Measuring the quality of student effort. *Current Issues in Higher Education, 2,* 10-16.

Pascarella, E. T., & Terenzini, P. T. (1991). *How college affects students.* San Francisco, CA: Jossey-Bass.

Pascarella, E. T., & Terenzini, P. T. (2005). *How college affects students, volume 2: A third decade of research.* San Francisco. CA: Jossey-Bass.

Pryor, J. H., Hurtado, S., Saenz, V. B., Santos, J. L., & Korn, W. S. (2007). *The American freshman: Forty year trends.* Los Angeles, CA: Higher Education Research Institute, UCLA.

Pryor, J. H., Hurtado, S., DeAngelo, L., Palucki Blake, L., & Tran, S. (2010). *The American freshman: National norms fall 2010.* Los Angeles, CA: Higher Education Research Institute, UCLA.

Shin, H. B. (2005). *School enrollment — Social and economic characteristics of students: October, 2003.* Washington, DC: U.S. Department of Commerce, U.S. Census Bureau.

Snyder, T. D., & Dillow, S. A. (2011). *Digest of education statistics 2010* (NCES 2011-015). Washington, DC: National Center for Education Statistics, Institute of Education Sciences, U.S. Department of Education.

Tobolowsky, B. F. (2008). Sophomores in transition: The forgotten year. In B. O. Barefoot (Ed.), *The first-year and beyond: Rethinking the challenges of collegiate transition* (New Directions for Higher Education, No. 144). San Francisco, CA: Jossey-Bass.

Tobolowsky, B. T., & Cox, B. E. (2007). *Shedding light on sophomores: An exploration of the second college year* (Monograph No. 47). Columbia, SC: University of South Carolina, National Resource Center for The First-Year Experience & Students in Transition.

Upcraft, M. L., Gardner, J. N. Barefoot, B. O., & Associates (2005). *Challenging and supporting the first-year student: A handbook for improving the first year of college.* San Francisco, CA: Jossey-Bass.

U.S. Bureau of Labor Statistics. (2008). *National Longitudinal Survey of Youth 1979: Average number of jobs started by individuals from age 18 to age 44 in 1978-2008 by age and sex.* (Report No. NLSY79, Round 23) Retrieved on November 4, 2011 from http://www.bls.gov/nls/y79supp.htm

U.S. Department of Education. (2003). *Postsecondary institutions in the United States: Fall 2003 and degrees and other awards conferred: 2002-2003, Indicator 21.* Washington, DC: National Center for Education Statistics.

Vakos, T. (2010). An interview with Philip Gardner: Workforce readiness of recent college graduates. *E-Source for College Transitions, 8*(1), 14-18.

Western Interstate Commission for Higher Education (WICHE). (2008). *Knocking at the college door—March, 2008: Projections of high school graduates by state and race/ ethnicity 1992-2022.* Boulder, CO: Author.

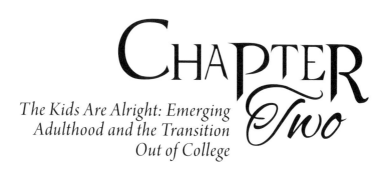

Chapter Two

The Kids Are Alright: Emerging Adulthood and the Transition Out of College

Tracy L. Skipper

Near the end of the semester in an upper-level English course that included many seniors, the discussion turned to preparing for the transition out of college. The professor asked the class to reflect briefly on the meaning of adulthood as it related to this transition. Many of the students defined adulthood in terms of instrumental goals (i.e., a means to another end, such as financial independence) or traditional markers (e.g., marriage, parenthood). As Tanya noted, "I feel that once I get my 'big girl job' and my 'big girl paycheck' I will finally believe myself to be an adult." Yet for other students, such roles and goals alone were insufficient markers of adulthood. One student who had a nine-month-old son noted parenthood did not make her feel like an adult because her parents still took care of her. Some students, and perhaps many of their family members, seemed to view college completion as the magical entry point to adulthood. Leslie envisioned "becoming an adult" as she crossed the stage at graduation. Other students described goals suggesting the achievement of developmental rather than, or in addition to, instrumental goals. For example, Thomas defined being an adult as "understanding one's place in life and finding contentment in that place," while Kelley suggested it meant "knowing who you are and fully embracing that personality." By the end of the discussion, the professor realized, regardless of the individual definitions of adulthood, helping students achieve these instrumental and developmental milestones would be critical to their future personal and professional success.[1]

Traditionally, adulthood has been characterized by the achievement of a set of culturally sanctioned, instrumental goals, such as stable employment, marriage, and parenthood. Between 1950 and 1970, U.S. college graduates (and other young people in the population) achieved these goals in their early 20s. Yet, the time between graduation and attaining the external markers of adulthood has increased dramatically in the last three decades. In 1970, the average age at which women married was 20.8, with the birth of the first child following within one year; by 2000 the average age for marriage was 25 with a corresponding rise in age at birth of first child (Mathews & Hamilton, 2009; U.S. Census Bureau, 2003). Men follow a similar pattern, with the average marriage age of 23.2 in 1970 rising to 26.8 in 2000.

In response to this protracted journey toward adulthood, Arnett (2004) has theorized the advent of a distinct life stage between adolescence and adulthood. *Emerging adulthood* is characterized as a time of identity exploration, instability, intense self-focus, the sense of being in between, and possibility. Further, Arnett (2004) suggests "the American college is the emerging adult environment par excellence" (p. 140), designed to allow for unfettered personal exploration in a relatively safe and contained space. Indeed, Arnett's description of emerging adulthood evokes several theories that commonly shape our understanding of and approach to students in the senior year of college, particularly those that speak to identity development, interpersonal relationships, and cognitive development. Such theories point to the developmental rather than the instrumental foundations for adulthood. For example, Baxter Magolda (2001) defines adulthood as "the ability to construct our own visions, to make informed decisions in conjunction with coworkers, to act appropriately, and to take responsibility for those actions" (p. 14). Similarly, adults understand "relationships in a complex way that allows [them] to assess and contrast individual and family needs, determine a course of action in connection with, but not subsumed by, other family members, and take responsibility for those actions" (p. 15).

---

[1] Student comments here and throughout the chapter were taken from a brief survey the author administered to students enrolled in an upper-level English course in spring 2011. Of the 25 students who responded, 15 were in their senior year. The age of students enrolled in the course ranged from 19 to 32, with an average age of 22.2. Students' names have been changed to protect their privacy.

Helping students achieve both the instrumental and developmental goals associated with adulthood are central to the mission of higher education. The focus on these goals may become particularly intense as students prepare to graduate from college. Many stakeholders (e.g., legislators, parents and family members, the students themselves) may place the highest value on achieving instrumental goals of adulthood—most notably, stable employment that allows for independent living. Yet, these achievements are intertwined with development. If we want college graduates to attain the instrumental goals of adulthood, then we must pay attention to and help structure the developmental work making that possible.

To that end, this chapter describes some of the most common theories guiding educational practice in the senior year (e.g., Chickering and Reisser's vectors of psychosocial development, Perry's scheme of intellectual and ethical development, King and Kitchener's reflective judgment model, and Baxter Magolda's journey toward self-authorship). Rather than dealing with each theory separately, the discussion is organized around the major areas of individual development—epistemological, intrapersonal, and interpersonal—to draw a concise portrait of the major developmental tasks of each dimension.[2] While such a treatment highlights the holistic nature of development, it does not allow for the description of any one theory in depth. Readers are encouraged to turn to the primary sources for a full treatment.

The chapter opens with a brief description of Arnett's theory of emerging adulthood. While Arnett's contention that emerging adulthood represents a new stage of development has been challenged, his work provides a useful reminder of the context in which development in the late teens and early 20s occurs. The bulk of the chapter puts theoretical flesh on the bones of the emerging adulthood concept, drawing on a range of theories of college student development and offering insight into the kinds of challenges faced and supports needed in the senior year. It concludes by acknowledging some of the limitations of these theories in guiding our work with college students.

Emerging Adulthood: A Portrait of Today's Graduating Seniors

The hallmark of adulthood, according to Arnett (2004) is self-sufficiency, characterized as (a) taking responsibility for one's actions, often balanced by

---

[2] I am indebted to Marcia Baxter Magolda's holistic description of development in *Making Their Own Way: Narratives for Transforming Higher Education to Promote Self-Development* for this framework.

responsibility to others; (b) making independent decisions; and (c) becoming financially independent. Young people making the journey toward self-sufficiency in America today have been characterized as anxious, depressed, and unwilling to grow up (Arnett, 2007). Yet Arnett (2007) challenges the accuracy of this depiction, suggesting people ages 18 to 25 are engaged in a unique period of development that is largely misunderstood because of its recent advent. He labels this period emerging adulthood and suggests it has five key features:

1. *Identity exploration*. Arnett (2006) contends this exploration has shifted from adolescence (ages 10 to 18) to the late teens and early 20s. During this period, emerging adults experience a lessening of parental control, but they are not yet "committed to a web of adult roles" affording them "an exceptional opportunity to try out different ways of living and different possible choices in love and work" (p. 8).

2. *Instability*. Emerging adulthood may also be a particularly unstable time. Arnett (2004) suggests "Emerging adults know they are supposed to have a Plan with a capital P. . . . However, for almost all of them, the Plan is subject to numerous revisions," as might be expected with all their explorations (p. 10). Instability in emerging adulthood is also evidenced in the extreme mobility of individuals during this period (Arnett, 2004, 2006).

3. *Self-focus*. While emerging adults are frequently portrayed as selfish and self-absorbed, Arnett (2006) suggests this is a normal and healthy part of identity exploration: "being self-focused allows emerging adults the psychological space to contemplate the 'who am I?' questions that are at the heart of identity and to pursue opportunities in love, work, and education that will promote their self-knowledge" (p. 10).

4. *Feeling in-between*. When asked whether they felt like adults, 60% of those Arnett (2004) surveyed responded, "yes and no." This may be particularly true for emerging adults enrolled in higher education who might still be supported by parents or do not feel part of the "real" working world outside of college.

5. *Possibilities*. Because many emerging adults have yet to make stable commitments to relationships and careers, this time period offers multiple possibilities. Arnett (2007) notes "to many emerging adults becoming an adult means the end of possibilities, the end of spontaneity, the compromise of their dreams" (p. 27).

The theoretical basis of Arnett's work has been challenged (e.g., Côté & Brynner, 2008; Hendry & Kloep, 2007). While few debate Arnett's assertion that the age of achieving the traditional markers of adulthood (e.g., marriage, parenthood, stable employment, financial independence) has been steadily increasing in the United States and other Western nations over the last three decades, most take exception to his characterization of this trend as the advent of a new developmental stage. Côté and Brynner argue the delay in reaching adulthood has more to do with evolving social norms and shifting labor markets than it does with changes in individual development.

Similarly, Hendry and Kloep (2007) charge that Arnett's concept of emerging adulthood is narrowly defined with respect to socioeconomic status. Examining the experiences of 18- to 30-year-olds in Wales, they identified a group of individuals who were "disadvantaged by their lack of resources, skills, and societal opportunities" (p. 77), yet who nonetheless exhibited some similarities with their more affluent peers—that is, living at home with their parents and working intermittently. Hendry and Kloep conclude, "Rather than being in a state of emerging adulthood, they were more likely in a state of 'prevented adulthood' and in 'unhappy stagnation'" (p. 77). Arnett's theory seems to ignore or, at the very least, downplay the ways in which oppression may shape the experience of emerging adulthood and recycles the myth of the American Dream: anyone can succeed through hard work and determination. Yet, it fails to account for the ways that gender, race, ethnicity, social class, sexual orientation, or other marginalized statuses may shape the opportunities available to emerging adults and undercut individual efforts.

Despite these shortcomings, Côté and Brynner (2008) note emerging adulthood provides a useful metaphor for describing the experiences of a particular segment of the population: 18 to 30-year-olds who are enrolled in or who have graduated from college. As such, emerging adulthood is offered here not as a complementary theory of development in young adulthood but as shorthand for a range of developmental tasks that coincide with the transition out of college (e.g., critical thinking, identity development, career decision making, emotional maturity, self-sufficiency).

Epistemological Development

At the core of epistemological development is answering the question, how do I know, which is shaped by people's assumptions about the nature of knowledge and their strategies for justifying what they believe (King & Kitchener, 1994). Perry's (1968/1999) scheme of ethical and intellectual development

(Figure 2.1) is perhaps the most frequently referenced theory of epistemological development in the college years. Based on a longitudinal study of a group of Harvard and Radcliffe undergraduates in the late 1950s, the scheme has served as the impetus for other large-scale studies designed to more clearly describe women's epistemological development (Belenky, Clinchy, Goldberger, & Tarule, 1986), postrelativistic thinking (King & Kitchener, 1994), and gender-related differences in development (Baxter Magolda, 1992). This section draws on Perry's scheme and King and Kitchener's reflective judgment model (Figure 2.2) to describe the basic trajectory of epistemological development during college and the range of developmental positions that are reached by graduation.

Most traditional-aged students enter college believing there are answers (in most cases, one right answer) to all questions and that authorities (e.g., teachers, parents, religious leaders) know those answers. Perry (1968/1999) refers to this as

---

Scheme of Ethical and Intellectual Development

Position 1: Basic Duality
- All questions have one right answer. Authorities know the answers and are responsible for teaching them to others.

Position 2: Multiplicity Prelegitimate
- Diverse opinions arise from poorly qualified authorities or those who want students to discover answers on their own.

Position 3: Multiplicity Legitimate but Subordinate
- Individuals accept that some knowledge is temporarily uncertain.

Position 4a: Multiplicity Coordinate
- Where all answers are unknown, all opinions are equally valuable.

Position 4b: Relativism Subordinate
- Individuals seek to understand how authorities arrived at certain answers.

Position 5: Relativism
- Rather than absolute answers, theories are structures that help evaluate information within a given context.

Position 6: Commitment Foreseen
- Beliefs, opinions, and values begin to be grounded internally rather than externally.

Position 7-9: Evolving Commitments
- Individuals learn to establish priorities in order to balance competing commitments.

Figure 2.1. Perry's scheme of ethical and intellectual development (Perry, 1968/1999, 1981).

Reflective Judgment Model

Pre-Reflective Thinking
> Real problems for which there are no answers do not exist. Evidence is not used to reach conclusions.
> - Stage 1. Knowledge is concrete, absolute, and predetermined.
> - Stage 2. Knowledge is certain, though it may not be available.
> - Stage 3. Some knowledge is temporarily uncertain. In areas of uncertainty, personal beliefs or opinions are equally valid.

Quasi-Reflective Thinking
> Some problems are ill-structured. Knowledge claims about these problems contain elements of uncertainty.
> - Stage 4. Knowledge is increasingly abstract, uncertain, and ambiguous. Evidence is used to confirm previously held beliefs.
> - Stage 5. Knowledge is contextual and subjective. Multiple, legitimate interpretations of a problem exist.

Reflective Thinking
> Knowledge claims are contextual and must be actively constructed.
> - Stage 6. Knowledge is uncertain and context-bound. Authorities are valued experts.
> - Stage 7. Knowledge is constructed by analyzing and synthesizing evidence and opinions into coherent explanations.

Figure 2.2. Reflective judgment model (King & Kitchener, 1994).

dualism, while King and Kitchener (1994) define this as pre-reflective thinking, which assumes that knowledge is absolutely certain though it may not be immediately available. Pre-reflective thinkers' beliefs are frequently unexamined and justified based on their alignment with an external authority figure. As students encounter divergent beliefs in their environment (e.g., residence halls, intramural fields, classrooms), their views about the nature of knowledge begin to moderate. They may start to accept that some knowledge is uncertain, though they believe that authorities will eventually find the answer to questions that are currently unknown. Yet, they have few tools for dealing with this emerging uncertainty and rely on personal beliefs, which are still largely defined by external others, to make decisions until absolute knowledge becomes available (King & Kitchener, 1994). This late pre-reflective thinking parallels Perry's multiplicity, where students view the introduction of diversity and complexity (i.e., uncertainty) as either a failure of authorities to play "their mediational role" (p. 81) or as a mere instructional tool designed to help students learn to think for themselves.

In late multiplicity, students make "a grudging concession" to the uncertainty of knowledge, but as Perry (1968/1999) notes this "does not affect the nature of truth itself (only man's relation to it!)" (p. 99). This late multiplicity corresponds with the entry into quasi-reflective thinking (King & Kitchener, 1994), where individuals assume knowledge is largely uncertain and evidence used to justify claims is mainly idiosyncratic. Perry suggests the problem occupying students at this point in their epistemological development is how to judge the answers to questions: "Where even Authority doesn't know the answer yet, is not any answer as good as another?" (p. 99). While King and Kitchener find students begin to use evidence and reasons to justify their beliefs, they do so inconsistently, selecting evidence that confirms previously held opinions. The hold of those prior beliefs is so strong that even though "individuals may see that evidence contradicts their own opinion [they] still hold to the opinion without attempting to resolve the contradiction" (p. 59). Perry also notes the continued pull of external authorities during this period, suggesting students begin to weigh different opinions because this is the way authorities want them to think. Students begin to think in relativistic terms, but they see this "as a special way of thinking about certain problems" rather than adopting it as a universal approach to making sense of the world (Perry, p. 122).

As students wrestle with the uncertainty of knowledge, they may come to the realization knowledge is contextual. In late quasi-reflective thinking, individuals begin to justify beliefs within a particular context using context-specific rules for inquiry and interpretation. Yet, knowledge remains context-bound because quasi-reflective thinkers have not "developed the ability to relate several abstractions into a system that allows comparisons across different contexts" (King & Kitchener, 1994, p. 62). As individuals develop this capacity, they move into reflective thinking, where knowledge is seen as the result of a process of reasoned inquiry and solutions to problems are constructed using the best available evidence from a range of perspectives and contexts. These solutions are also open to re-evaluation as new evidence becomes available.

Perry's (1968/1999) relativism seems to bridge the quasi-reflective and reflective thinking described by King and Kitchener (1994). He emphasized the contextual nature of knowledge while suggesting relativism provided individuals "an alternate context" or "ground for detachment and for objectivity" (p. 140). Perry described the shift from multiplicity to relativism as a dramatic, but quiet, revolution, noting that while it marked a major upheaval in epistemology, none of the subjects in his research discussed it as a conscious event.

Research on the reflective judgment model (King & Kitchener, 2002, 2004) suggests epistemological development in college plateaus about Stage 4, early quasi-reflective thinking. In fact, students only appear to gain about a half a stage in the move from pre-reflective to quasi-reflective thinking from the first-year of college to the senior year. A good bit of this growth may happen early in the college years. Perry saw evidence of multiplistic thinking in his sample near the end of the first college year, and research by Kitchener, Lynch, Fischer, and Wood (1993) found some evidence of developmental spurts around age 19 (i.e., traditionally the first and second year of college). King and Kitchener (2002) note the move to quasi-reflective thinking is a small, but significant developmental milestone because of the qualitatively different set of assumptions individuals are able to engage.

The upshot is few, if any, students leave college as reflective thinkers. Yet, King and Kitchener (2004) note "intense study in a discipline may provide the leading edge for the development of more complex epistemic cognition and true reflective thinking" (p. 47). Thus, upper-level courses in the major may lay the groundwork for seniors to think reflectively about problems in their field of study, though they may not yet be able to apply those skills to problems arising in other contexts. Students who are better prepared to employ reflective thinking across contexts are likely to be those who have been involved in interdisciplinary study, especially when an intensive capstone experience is required. Writing about the thesis requirement at Miami University, Haynes (2004) noted students in the interdisciplinary program showed greater evidence of interdisciplinary perspectives and integration than students in traditional majors. They were also more likely to reflect self-consciously on the limitations and merits of particular approaches and demonstrate an awareness of how different disciplines would approach a topic.

While seniors may not have achieved reflective thinking, they may recognize it as an important component of achieving adulthood. Julie, a senior at the University of South Carolina, describes adulthood as "process[ing] information and mak[ing] educated decisions based on what you've found." Seniors may not yet demonstrate the levels of cognitive complexity desired by institutions of higher education and future employers, but their ability to recognize it when they see it may indicate the initial approaches to reflective thinking.[3]

---

[3]King and Kitchener (2004) note that people are typically able to recognize reasoning about one stage level higher than what they are capable of producing.

Intrapersonal Development

If the question driving epistemological development is, What do I believe, the question at the center of intrapersonal development is, Who am I? The answer to that question encompasses vocation or career, social group membership (i.e., race or ethnicity, gender, sexual orientation), social roles (i.e., parent, spouse or significant other), and the intersection of these factors to form a core identity. While students grapple with the answer to this question throughout college, planning for life after graduation makes issues related to identity particularly salient for seniors. Chickering and Reisser's (1993) vectors of psychosocial development is one of the most commonly referenced theories of intrapersonal development for college students, but the later positions in Perry's scheme also provide some insight into how students answer the who-am-I questions

Three of Chickering and Reisser's (1993) vectors seem to have direct bearing on intrapersonal development, especially near the end of college: (a) establishing identity, (b) developing purpose, and (c) developing integrity (Figure 2.3). According to Chickering and Reisser, establishing identity involves navigating a number of interrelated tasks, including developing comfort with one's body and appearance; comfort with one's gender and sexual orientation; a sense of self in social, historical, and cultural contexts; clarification of self-concept through roles and lifestyle; sense of self in response to feedback from valued others; self-acceptance and self-esteem; and personal stability and integration. The development of a sense of self in context has been widely explored by researchers (e.g., Josselson, 1996; Torres, Howard-Hamilton, & Cooper, 2003; McCarn & Fassinger, 1996). However, theories of identity development tend to look at social identity in isolation, compartmentalizing the development of gender identity from racial or ethnic identity, for example.

To address this gap in understanding, Jones and McEwen (2000) conceptualized the model of multiple dimensions of identity. They suggest an individual's various social identities as defined by gender, race, sexual orientation, social class, and religion form a series of interconnected spheres around the core personal identity delineated by individual attributes and characteristics. The individual's context (i.e., family background, sociocultural conditions, current experiences, career decisions, and life planning) determines, in part, the salience that different social identities may have for the core at any given moment. For example, as seniors make decisions about careers, different identities may demand greater attention. Women may have to grapple with questions related

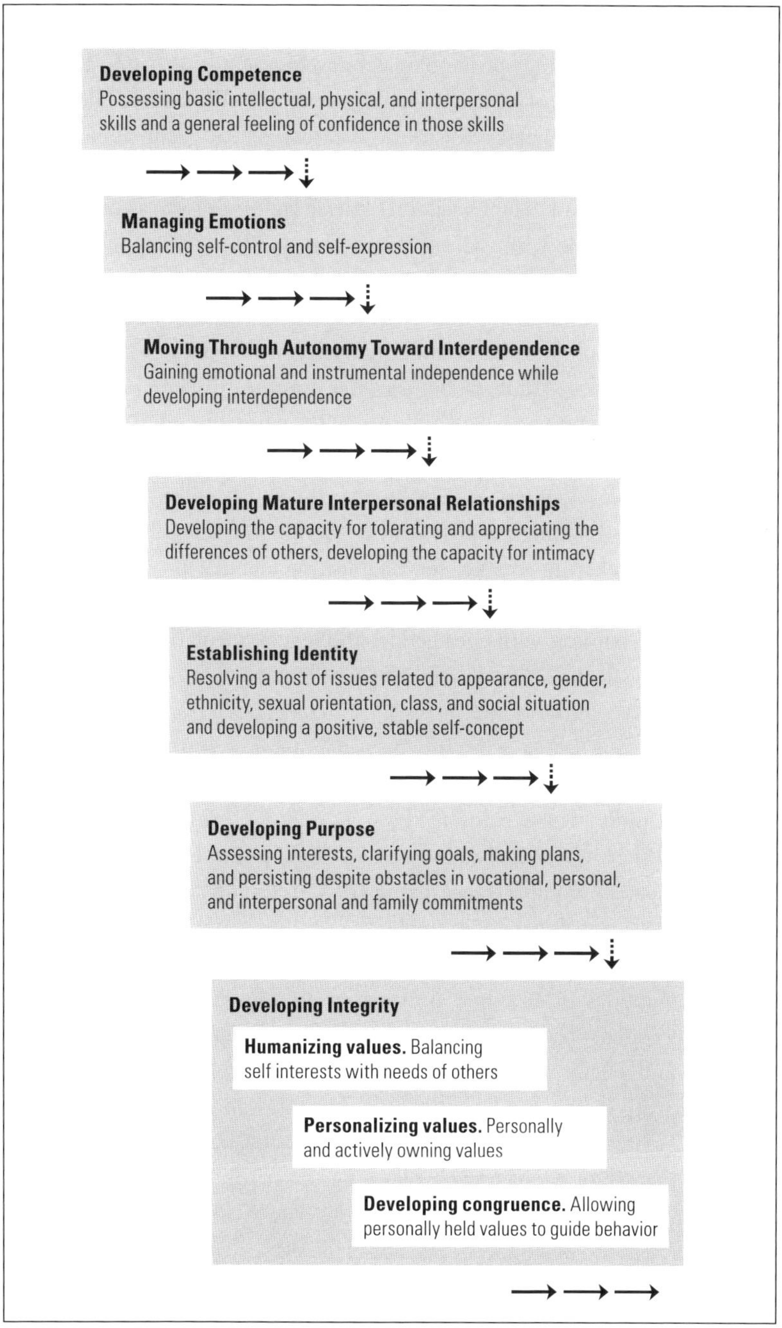

Developing Competence
Possessing basic intellectual, physical, and interpersonal skills and a general feeling of confidence in those skills

$\longrightarrow \longrightarrow \longrightarrow \downarrow$

Managing Emotions
Balancing self-control and self-expression

$\longrightarrow \longrightarrow \longrightarrow \downarrow$

Moving Through Autonomy Toward Interdependence
Gaining emotional and instrumental independence while developing interdependence

$\longrightarrow \longrightarrow \longrightarrow \downarrow$

Developing Mature Interpersonal Relationships
Developing the capacity for tolerating and appreciating the differences of others, developing the capacity for intimacy

$\longrightarrow \longrightarrow \longrightarrow \downarrow$

Establishing Identity
Resolving a host of issues related to appearance, gender, ethnicity, sexual orientation, class, and social situation and developing a positive, stable self-concept

$\longrightarrow \longrightarrow \longrightarrow \downarrow$

Developing Purpose
Assessing interests, clarifying goals, making plans, and persisting despite obstacles in vocational, personal, and interpersonal and family commitments

$\longrightarrow \longrightarrow \longrightarrow \downarrow$

Developing Integrity

Humanizing values. Balancing self interests with needs of others

Personalizing values. Personally and actively owning values

Developing congruence. Allowing personally held values to guide behavior

$\longrightarrow \longrightarrow \longrightarrow$

Figure 2.3. Seven vectors of psychosocial development (Chickering & Reisser, 1993).

to gender if they have settled on a nontraditional career field, and GLBTQ students may have to decide whether they will be out in the job search as they craft résumés and personal statements and prepare for job interviews.

Initially, Jones and McEwen (2000) suggested externally imposed identities would not be "seen as integral to the core" (p. 40), but subsequent research (Abes, Jones, & McEwen, 2007) indicates an individual's cognitive capacity may mediate those external influences (Figure 2.4). For individuals who engage in what they call formulaic meaning making, akin to Perry's dualism, "contextual influences and perceptions of identity are closely connected" (Abes et al., p. 7). Thus, externally imposed expectations about identity (e.g., appropriateness of career choice, expectations for marriage and family) may be assigned greater salience by the individual. As the meaning-making filter increases in complexity, individuals have a "greater ability to determine the relationship between context and perceptions of identity" (p. 11). In other words, the salience of social identities is determined by internal rather than external influences. Further, as Chickering and Reisser (1993) suggest, an individual's way of thinking, learning, and making decisions appears to shape his or her movement through the vectors, especially with respect to establishing identity. For college seniors who are adopting quasi-reflective ways of thinking, the balance in determining the salience of social identities may be shifting from external to internal factors.

Reisser (1995) suggests establishing identity is the core of their theory and "encompasses all of the other vectors" (p. 509). Its relationship to developing purpose and developing integrity, for example, is immediately apparent. Developing purpose "entails an increasing ability to be intentional, to assess interests and options, to clarify goals, to make plans, and to persist despite obstacles" (Chickering & Reisser, 1993, p. 50) and encompasses three major elements: (a) vocational plans and aspirations, (b) personal interests, and (c) interpersonal and family commitments—all issues that move to the fore as students to prepare to graduate from college.

In the final vector, developing integrity, Chickering and Reisser (1993) theorize development proceeds through three sequential, but overlapping stages. In the first stage, humanizing values, there is a shift "away from automatic application of uncompromising beliefs and using principled thinking in balancing one's own self-interest with the interest of one's fellow human beings" (p. 51). In the second stage, personalizing values, individuals consciously affirm "core values and beliefs while respecting other points of view" (p. 51). Finally, individuals develop congruence, as they begin to match their "personal values

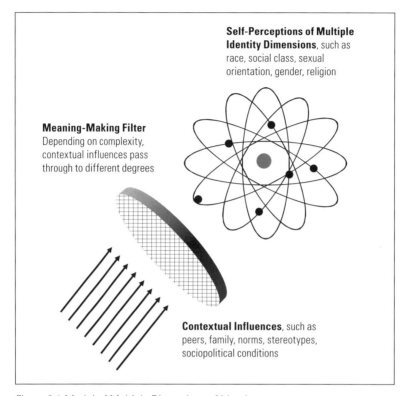

Figure 2.4. Model of Multiple Dimensions of Identity.

Adapted from "Reconceptualizing the Model of Multiple Dimensions of Identity: The Role of Meaning-Making Capacity in the Construction of Multiple Identities," by E. S. Abes, S. R. Jones, & M. K. McEwen, 2007, *Journal of College Student Development, 48*(1), p. 7. Copyright 2007 by the American College Personnel Association. Reprinted with permission.

with socially responsible behavior" (p. 51). As students move away from absolutism toward multiplicity and relativism near the end of college, they undoubtedly use a different lens to examine their own values. Although seniors may engage in all aspects of developing integrity, their efforts to apply their values in more considered ways may be most readily apparent.

While Perry's (1968/1999) scheme is most frequently examined from the standpoint of epistemological development, the later positions of his model provide insight into intrapersonal development during emerging adulthood, aligning in many ways with Chickering and Reisser's (1993) descriptions of developing purpose and developing integrity. Perry suggests relativism poses a threat to identity: "If one comes to look upon all knowing and all valuing as contingent on context, and if one is then confronted with an infinite universe of potential contexts for truth and care, one is threatened with loss of identity" (p. 149). One way to ameliorate this threat to identity is to make commitments or conscious choices about where to invest one's energy.

Commitments are defined both by their content (e.g., career, marriage, religion, politics, friendships, social endeavors, general values) and style, which represents strategies for balancing the external and internal tensions related to choices about the content of a particular commitment. While Perry (1968/1999) suggests individuals may foresee commitments as the resolution to the problems presented by relativism, they may also experience "'having to choose' ... as a narrowing, a loss of freedom defined as the freedom to choose" (p. 153). Such apprehensions persist among undergraduates and recent college graduates today. For example, Julie, like many college seniors, decides to postpone making a commitment—perhaps to avoid having to make difficult decisions: "I think the wisest decision for myself is to put off getting a 'real' job for a while. I have the rest of my life to join the workforce, but I can only be spontaneous for so long."

For other students, uncertainty about how to proceed may lead to feelings of anxiety. Among the subjects in Perry's (1968/1999) study who were on the verge of making commitments (e.g., deciding on a career, whether to marry, relocation for a job or graduate school), they felt the need for action but were unsure how to begin. They acknowledged taking the "first steps may require an almost arbitrary faith, or even a willing suspension of disbelief" (p. 154).

Perry (1968/1999) suggests the final three positions of his scheme—those focusing on commitments—do not represent three distinct stages as much as degrees of ripening. He notes Position 7 tends to be focused on the content of commitment and, thus, may be closely aligned with issues of identity and purpose: it "describes the state in a student's life in which he has undertaken to decide on his own responsibility who he is, or who he will be, in some major area of life" (p. 170). In the senior year of college, the most salient area of life probably revolves around the question of career, though at the time of Perry's study marriage and family also figured prominently. If Position 7 focuses on the content of the commitment, Position 8 highlights the style of commitment, and Position 9 "describes a maturity in which a person has developed an experience of 'who he is' in his Commitments both in their content and his style of living them" (p. 171). In this way, the final position of Perry's scheme seems aligned with the congruence stage of Chickering and Reisser's (1993) developing integrity. Individual ratings of the interviews among Perry's subjects suggest juniors and seniors are clearly beginning to concentrate on the content of their commitments (Position 7) and that many seniors are also considering how they will balance the challenges they perceive are presented by making commitments in particular areas of their lives (Position 8).

Interpersonal Development

Closely related to how-do-I-know and who-am-I questions is the question, How do I want to relate to other people? Two of Chickering and Reisser's (1993) vectors—moving through autonomy toward interdependence and developing mature interpersonal relationships—provide insight into the tasks facing college seniors in relation to this question. Chickering and Reisser suggest the successful resolution of questions surrounding autonomy means "learning to function with relative self-sufficiency, to take responsibility for pursuing self-chosen goals, and to be less bound by others' opinions" (p. 47). As noted earlier, self-sufficiency is a key marker of adulthood, and college seniors are likely to equate this with instrumental and emotional independence, taking responsibility for their own actions and the ability to rely on themselves. As individuals gain emotional independence, they experience "freedom from continual and pressing needs for reassurance, affection, or approval" from parents, peers, and occupational or institutional reference groups (p. 47). Yet, some research (Murphy, Bluestein, Bohlig, & Platt, 2010) suggests emotional connection "is crucial in mediating individuals' transition from college to career, their expectations of their first jobs, and ultimately their well-being" (p. 179). Thus, rather than creating emotional distance, some college students may rely more heavily on their social support networks (i.e., family, friends, significant others) as they approach the end of college

At the most basic level, instrumental independence is the ability to manage the tasks of daily living, but Chickering and Reisser (1993) also emphasize its connection to epistemological development, suggesting it entails problem-solving skills or the ability to think critically and translate thought into action. As evidenced by the comments of students at the beginning of this chapter, college seniors will likely struggle to establish instrumental independence. They may be relatively free of parental control but continue to be dependent on their parents for financial support. And, as noted above, they may still need their emotional support. It is important to recognize that interdependence—"respecting the autonomy of others and looking for ways to give and take with an ever-expanding circle of friends" (Chickering & Reisser, p. 48)—rather than independence, marks the successful resolution of this developmental task. As such, advisors, counselors, and others working with students in the senior year need to help them find a healthy balance between relying on important others and moving toward self-sufficiency.

Closely connected to realizing autonomy (and theorized as building on it developmentally) is establishing mature interpersonal relationships, which Chickering and Reisser (1993) suggested encompass both tolerance for and appreciation of differences and the capacity for intimacy. Women may focus on, and have a greater capacity for mature relationships, earlier than men do. Foubert, Nixon, Sisson, and Barnes (2005) found "women not only were more tolerant than men throughout their college experience, but women also were more tolerant at the beginning of their college experience than men were after 4 years of development during college" (p. 469).

The increasing age of first marriage may suggest relationships are less of a concern for students in the senior year than they once were. While students may not be contemplating marriage, they may still struggle with issues related to significant relationships. Concerns about maintaining relationships after college will no doubt cause stress for many students.

A Holistic Understanding of Development

The preceding discussion examined three domains of development in emerging adulthood. Yet development in one domain shapes the course of development in the others. Though Baxter Magolda's early work (e.g., Baxter Magolda, 1992) focused on students' intellectual development in college, her subsequent research has evolved to a holistic understanding of development (e.g., Baxter Magolda, 2001, 2009), encompassing all three domains. As such, it serves as a useful synthesis to the foregoing discussion and as a counterpoint to Arnett's theory of emerging adulthood. Baxter Magolda (2001) describes the developmental trajectory of emerging adulthood, based on interviews with participants in her longitudinal study during their 20s. She suggests they moved through four phases on the journey toward self-authorship—a loose progression of stages that took nearly a decade for them to traverse.

1. *Following external formulas*. As Arnett found, the emerging adults in Baxter Magolda's (2001) study frequently had plans for their lives, but these were often "predetermined scripts for success in adult life … gleaned from others around them" (p. 71). Many college seniors will find themselves in this position as graduation approaches. Thus,

they may move into adult roles, such as stable employment or committed relationships, without a real sense of active, internal decision making, and discover external formulas for success do not always work. When participants in Baxter Magolda's study came to this realization, it did not necessarily lead them to the conclusion the formula might need to be abandoned. Some may have simply assumed they needed to ease into these roles. This attitude is illustrated by Daniel, a graduating senior at the University of South Carolina with plans to teach but only after mentoring or tutoring first: "I believe that I am not ready personally to teach full time for I am afraid that it will burn me out too quickly." Somewhat wary of a career in public education, he is still reluctant to abandon his initial plan.

Subsequent research (Baxter Magolda, 2009) suggests individuals may move through following external formulas in a series of microsteps. In the early part of this stage, there is a strong reliance on authority for the right answers, a definition of self based on external expectations, and deference to others in relationships. In the middle period, people begin to experience uncertainty, which may lead to feelings of discomfort and confusion. There remains a strong pull to live up to external expectations. In the late part of the stage, individuals begin to be more open to uncertainty and to recognize there may be conflicts between others' expectations and their own. There is also a dawning "recognition of the need to be oneself" (p. 629). For college seniors, movement through such a process might look something like this: A student may enter the late college years with a fairly stable career choice, but one that may be shaped by parental or social expectations. While learning more about the career (e.g., through internships or recruiting visits), the student may begin to question that initial choice, especially as personal values and interests solidify. There may be a desire to honor emerging self-interests, but external expectations continue to exercise a strong pull, and a career decision the student is no longer certain about may remain in place as graduation approaches.

2. *The crossroads*. As individuals move into the late period of external formulas, they begin to realize the formulas are no longer working or that they are insufficient. They recognize the need for internal definitions but do not have a clear plan for getting there (Baxter Magolda, 2001). As Baxter Magolda (2009) notes, "Part of the discomfort of the crossroads stems from the knowledge that one needs to construct

one's own beliefs and values yet at the same time one has not formed internal criteria to use to do so" (p. 630). In terms of career, Baxter Magolda (2001) noted participants struggled with balancing their own emerging voices, their approaches to work, and "parental or societal expectations about successful work lives" (p. 108). Emerging adults in this study were also frustrated in their attempts to please themselves by attempting to please others. For college seniors, this might mean basing decisions about graduate school or jobs on the geographic proximity to significant others. Yet, "most participants came to the realization that the only way to resolve tensions between their own and others' voices was to act in ways that were true to their own voices while mutually negotiating how needs are met" (p. 111). As such, two central tasks of this stage are beginning to listen to the internal voice and cultivating that voice so it can be used to find internal criteria for decision making (Baxter Magolda, 2009). For many college students, the senior year can mark the emergence of the internal voice, and issues related to the development of identity and autonomy may determine the level of trust students place in that voice.

3. *Becoming the author of one's own life.* In subsequent research, Baxter Magolda (2009) has collapsed this stage with internal foundation into the single phase of self-authorship. This combined stage has three core elements: (a) learning to trust the internal voice, (b) building internal foundations, and (c) securing commitments. Becoming the author of one's own life essentially focuses on the first of these. During this time, Baxter Magolda's (2001) participants were engaged in intense self-reflection as they tried to make "the best decisions possible in particular contexts, but were aware of on-going uncertainty in a contextual world" (p. 149). Here, participants began to actively engage the internal voice in decision making and seemed comfortable with those decisions even when they were at odds with previously held beliefs or expectations. While external influence remained present, "the internal voice, or self, became the coordinator and mediator of external influence" (Baxter Magolda, 2001, p. 119).

Although the internal voice may emerge for some students, many seniors will struggle with this. In examining career decision making late in college, Allen and Taylor (2006) suggested some students (i.e., tourist pathmakers) followed specific plans "designed to avoid uncertainty and ambiguity" in response "to external pressures" (p. 606). Other students (i.e., lost searchers) were waiting for "someone to rescue them" (p. 599) by providing a set career direction. In both cases, these students' career decision-making strategies were defined by an inability to identify and listen to their inner voices. As such, advising and career interventions for some college seniors may need to focus less on setting specific academic and career goals and more on cultivating the inner voice (e.g., more opportunities for self-reflection or moving from task orientation to greater reflection and analysis). This seems to mirror earlier observations made by Baxter Magolda (2001) who suggested the values clarification that undergirds much career decision making often "occurs in the context of external self-definition, pressure to choose a major, and societal pressure regarding career success" (p. 310). To counteract this, Baxter Magolda suggests values clarification activities be coupled with direct experience and that major and career decisions made early in college be revisited in the junior or senior year when emerging internal voices may now be in conflict with earlier choices.

4. *Internal foundation*. This stage expresses both a stable sense of self and a core set of beliefs that form the basis for decision making. Few of the participants in Baxter Magolda's (2001) study achieved internal foundations before the age of 30. As such, it remains an aspirational state for most college seniors. As Baxter Magolda (2001) noted, this internal belief system was consistent, yet "open to expansion" as individuals had new experiences and "was not threatened by new experience [making] participation in mutual relationships possible" (p. 161). Participants also released notions of being able to control the external world, recognizing, instead, they could only control the meaning they made of it. This realization gave participants greater confidence in being able to manage their own lives. In short, achieving internal foundation or self-authorship is the developmental basis for adulthood. In most cases, colleges—despite the opportunities for self-exploration—do little to provide students with this foundation. Speaking of the participants in her study, Baxter Magolda (2001) noted, "They would have been better prepared for [adult] roles, and have struggled less, had the conditions for self-authorship been created during their college experience." (p. xxii).

In fact, current educational pathways encourage students to follow external formulas rather than cultivate their inner voices. Yet, Baxter Magolda (2001) argues the entire educational experience (e.g., the curriculum, campus jobs, residence life, leadership and service experiences, career and academic advising) can be reframed to support self-authorship. Because later chapters of this book will touch on strategies for engaging students in several of these areas, here it will suffice to note the central components of Baxter Magolda's framework for promoting self-authorship are that knowledge is complex and socially constructed, that the self plays a central role in knowledge construction, and that expertise is mutually shared. These ideas are enacted through three principals that support student development: (a) validating learners as knowers, (b) situating learning in learners' experiences, and (c) defining learning as mutually constructing meaning. However, embracing the challenge of helping students achieve self-authorship would mean changing our core assumptions about the educational mission. Historically, education has been understood as transmitting a body of knowledge in a specific discipline, which students were expected to master. Using such a framework to organize our work with students throughout their educational journey would stand these traditional assumptions on their head, but it would also better prepare college seniors to navigate the challenges of emerging adulthood.

Limitations of Theories Describing Emerging Adulthood

While the theories described in this chapter provide a useful framework for understanding the developmental challenges facing students during the college years and for designing supports to help them navigate those challenges, several limitations to their usefulness exist. First, the theories described above were largely derived from research on White, middle-class populations. While they have been refined by subsequent researchers and theorists, it is important to keep in mind the role gender, race, ethnicity, or social class may play in the experience of emerging adulthood. For example, in their review of literature on identity development for women and racial or ethnic nonmajority students, Baxter Magolda, Abes, and Torres (2009) suggested lower levels of cognitive complexity were associated with pre-encounter identity statuses, meaning these students were more likely to privilege and conform to expectations set by the majority culture. In other words, an adherence to external formulas may hinder the development of key aspects of their identity. At the same time, they note some researchers have found "students with low privilege lacked external formulas for succeeding in college and tended to develop self-authorship earlier than those with high privilege" (p. 203). This finding is similar to Arnett's (2004, 2006) argument that emerging adulthood affords people from troubled or less privileged backgrounds the possibility to re-invent themselves. That is, because the external formulas never applied to them, they may have an easier time identifying and listening to their own internal voices.

While some nonmajority students and others from dysfunctional backgrounds may experience limited freedoms from external formulas, it would be wrong to assume this will be the case for all students. For students from low SES backgrounds, the cost of college may be an impetus to adhere to predetermined pathways (Allen & Taylor, 2009). For them, the possibilities to be discovered through exploration are simply luxuries they feel they cannot afford. Moreover, nonmajority students are also at risk from damaging external messages about issues such as their ability to become educated or the kinds of careers that are suitable to pursue. Baxter Magolda et al. (2009) note "part of constructing a learning partnership with students in this situation involves introducing alternative messages to change negative external messages to positive internal messages" (pp. 210-211).

Second, the context within which many of these theories arose was one where students enrolled in college—typically a four-year college or university—immediately after high school and, if they completed a four-year degree, they most likely did so at the institution of initial enrollment. As such, these theories frequently presume a traditional-aged college population and may provide less insight into the experiences of adult learners. Yet, both Arnett's theory of emerging adulthood and Baxter Magolda's longitudinal research suggests the journey toward adulthood may extend to age 30 for many people. For older students, college enrollment may be prompted by attempts to resolve questions of identity or purpose—one of the revisions to the plan that Arnett describes. Older students are also likely to have experience balancing competing obligations (e.g., work, family commitments) with their own needs. For this reason, they may be more attuned to the inner voice than their traditional aged-counterparts. As educators, it is important to understand how the developmental experiences of adult learners may be similar to their younger peers and the ways in which they may differ. In these cases, life-span development models (e.g., Levinson, 1986; Neugarten & Neugarten, 1987) may be important supplements to theories of college student development.

Conclusion

King (2009) states while students make "clear and steady progress in learning to think reflectively in college, few college graduates evidenced the ability to make reflective judgments" (p. 604). Similarly, Baxter Magolda (2001) notes few participants in her longitudinal study had made significant progress toward achieving self-authorship while in college. Even earlier generations of students—who might have begun to think about the kinds of commitments they wanted to make as adults—had not yet built the internal structure for balancing those commitments against external demands (Perry, 1968/1999). Thus, it is no wonder emerging adults might be seen as floundering and that their delay in making progress on these fronts might be misinterpreted as selfishness or a refusal to grow up. Students' lack of progress toward both developmental and instrumental goals of adulthood has also been used as an indictment of the relevance of higher education. And, as Baxter Magolda has argued, colleges and universities must provide students with the kinds of experiences that will move them toward self-authored adulthood by college graduation earlier in their educational experience. For while the developmental tasks we have explored here may be particularly salient in the senior year of college, they cannot be resolved in that timeframe if we have not helped students achieve the necessary structures for doing so.

References

Abes, E. S., Jones, S. R., & McEwen, M. K. (2007). Reconceptualizing the model of multiple dimensions of identity: The role of meaning-making capacity in the construction of multiple identities. *Journal of College Student Development, 48*(1), 1-22.

Allen, J. K., & Taylor, K. (2006). The senior year transition: Women undergraduates search for a path. *Journal of College Student Development, 47*(6), 595-608.

Arnett, J. J. (2004). *Emerging adulthood: The winding road from the late teens through the twenties.* New York, NY: Oxford University Press.

Arnett, J. J. (2006). Emerging adulthood: Understanding the new way of coming of age. In J. J. Arnett & J. L. Tanner (Eds.), *Emerging adults in America: Coming of age in the 21st century* (pp. 3-19). Washington, DC: American Psychological Association.

Arnett, J. J. (2007). Suffering, selfish, slackers? Myths and reality about emerging adults. *Journal of Youth and Adolescence, 36*, 23-29.

Baxter Magolda, M. B. (1992). *Knowing and reasoning in college: Gender-related patterns in students' intellectual development.* San Francisco, CA: Jossey-Bass.

Baxter Magolda, M. B. (2001). *Making their own way: Narratives for transforming higher education to promote self-development.* Sterling, VA: Stylus.

Baxter Magolda, M. B. (2009). The activity of meaning making: A holistic perspective on college student development. *Journal of College Student Development, 50*(6), 621-639.

Baxter Magolda, M., Abes, E., & Torres, V. (2009). Epistemological, intrapersonal, and interpersonal development in the college years and young adulthood. In M. C. Smith & N. DeFrates-Densch (Eds.), *Handbook of research on adult learning and development* (pp. 183-219).

Belenky, M. F., Clinchy B. M., Goldberger, N. R., & Tarule, J. M. (1986). *Women's ways of knowing: The development of self, mind, and voice.* New York, NY: Basic Books.

Chickering, A. W., & Reisser, L. (1993). *Education and identity* (2nd ed.). San Francisco, CA: Jossey-Bass.

Côté, J., & Brynner, J. M. (2008). Changes in the transition to adulthood in the UK and Canada: The role of structure and agency in emerging adulthood. *Journal of Youth Studies, 11*(3), 251-268.

Foubert, J. D., Nixon, M. L., Sisson, V. S., & Barnes, A. C. (2005). A longitudinal study of Chickering and Reisser's vectors: Exploring gender differences and implications for refining the theory. *Journal of College Student Development, 46*(5), 461-471.

Haynes, C. (2004). Promoting self-authorship through an interdisciplinary writing curriculum. In M. Baxter Magolda & P. M. King (Eds.), *Learning partnerships: Theory and models of practice to educate for self-authorship* (pp. 63-90). Sterling, VA: Stylus.

Hendry, L. B., & Kloep, M. (2007). Conceptualizing emerging adulthood: Inspecting the emperor's new clothes? *Child Development Perspectives, 1*(2), 74-79.

Jones, S. R., & McEwen, M. K. (2000). A conceptual model of multiple dimensions of identity. *Journal of College Student Development, 41*(4), 405-414.

Josselson, R. (1996). *Revising herself: The story of women's identity from college to midlife.* New York, NY: Oxford University Press.

King, P. M. (2009). Principles of development and developmental change underlying theories of cognitive and moral development. *Journal of College Student Development, 50*(6), 597-617.

King, P. M., & Kitchener, K. S. (1994). *Developing reflective judgment: Understanding and promoting intellectual growth and critical thinking adolescents and adults.* San Francisco, CA: Jossey-Bass.

King, P. M., & Kitchener, K. S. (2002). The reflective judgment model: Twenty years of research on epistemic cognition. In B. K. Hofer & P. R. Pinrich (Eds.), *Personal epistemology: The psychology of beliefs about knowledge and knowing* (pp. 37-61). Mahwah, NJ: Lawrence Erlbaum Associates.

King, P. M., & Kitchener, K. S. (2004). Reflective judgment: Theory and research on the development of epistemic assumptions through adulthood. *Educational Psychologist, 39*(1), 5-18.

Kitchener, K. S., Lynch, C. L., Fischer, K. W., & Wood, P. K. (1993). Developmental range of reflective judgment: The effect of contextual support and practice on developmental stage. *Developmental Psychology, 29*(5), 893-906.

Levinson, D. J. (1986). A conception of adult development. *American Psychologist, 41,* 3-12.

Mathews, T. J., & Hamilton, B. E. (2009). *Delayed childbearing: More women are having their first child later in life.* (NCHS Data Brief, No 21). Hyattsville, MD: National Center for Health Statistics.

McCarn, S. R., & Fassinger, R. E. (1996). Revisioning sexual minority identity formation: A new model of lesbian identity and its implications for counseling and research. *Counseling Psychologist, 24,* 508-534.

Murphy, K. A., Blustein, D. L., Bohlig, A. J., & Platt, M. G. (2010). The college-to-career transition: An exploration of emerging adulthood. *Journal of Counseling & Development, 88,* 174-181.

Neugarten, B. L., & Neugarten, D. A. (1987). The changing meanings of age. *Psychology Today, 21,* 29-33.

Perry, W. G., Jr. (1981). Cognitive and ethical growth: The making of meaning. In A. W. Chickering and Associates, *The modern American college: Responding to the new realities of diverse students and a changing society* (pp. 76-116). San Francisco, CA: Jossey-Bass.

Perry, W. G., Jr. (1999). *Forms of ethical and intellectual development in the college years: A scheme.* San Francisco, CA: Jossey-Bass. (Original work published 1968)

Reisser, L. (1995). Revisiting the seven vectors. *Journal of College Student Development, 36*(6), 505-512.

Torres, V., Howard-Hamilton, M. F., & Cooper, D. L. (2003). *Identity development of diverse populations: Implications for teaching and administration in higher education* (ASHE-ERIC Higher Education Report 29.6). San Francisco, CA: Jossey-Bass.

U.S. Census Bureau. (2003). *Annual social and economic supplement: 2003 current population survey* (Current Population Reports, Series P20-553). Washington, DC: Author.

CHAPTER *Three*

The Impact of Technology on Learning, Development, and Communication

Reynol Junco and Jeanna Mastrodicasa

Sara updates her Facebook status constantly, often using mobile technology to do so. She sometimes gets into passionate disagreements with friends on the Internet, responding to posts that offer opinions different from her own. She often multitasks online, toggling between school work, social media, and entertainment websites and prefers to text rather than to contact others via telephone, e-mail, or instant messaging—getting short bursts of responses almost instantly. During Sara's four years in college, her Facebook profile showcased several different versions of her true self: the football fan, the party girl, the unattached heterosexual in search of a mate, the Latina who likes to cook, the serious girl-friend to a fraternity member, and the dedicated volunteer at a local elementary school. Overall, Sara represents the traditional college student whose identity development is expressed and mediated by her technology use.

Today's college student faces developmental challenges similar to those of earlier generations, but his or her management of those tasks is played out in a very public way, reflected in photos, comments, status updates, and wall postings on online social media sites. Further, students' use of technology is rapidly evolving and differs considerably from that of their predecessors. Not surprisingly, the changing relationship to technology impacts college students in a number of areas, including identity development and expression, student engagement and learning, and interpersonal communication. Research is ongoing in several areas to understand the myriad influences of technology on students' experiences and to provide higher education administrators a better sense of how to challenge and support students during their undergraduate years.

In combination, technology access, use, and influence create a different universe in which students interact and learn. While many of the issues technology raises are not unique to seniors, the final year of the undergraduate experience represents a significant milestone in students' facility with these tools and their impacts. Further, the senior year signifies both the culmination of students' experiences in a technologically rich college environment as well as the springboard for their responsible use and application of skills gained in college, including those directly related to technology or informed by it, in their personal and professional lives as adults. This chapter will describe newer social technologies; how students use them; and their impact on student development, learning, multitasking, communication, and career planning.

While Chickering and Gamson's (1987) research on student engagement was completed before the widespread use of the Internet, e-mail, and social media, their framework remains relevant. In fact, their seven engagement principles—(a) student-faculty contact, (b) cooperation among students, (c) active learning, (d) prompt feedback, (e) time-on-task emphasis, (f) communication of high expectations, and (g) respecting diversity— were later expanded upon to include a focus on technology (Chickering & Ehrmann, 1996). We will revisit these concepts throughout the chapter.

Access to Social Media and Information Technology

Today's college students are avid users of technology. Indeed, they have never known a time when computers did not exist. As such, they are more likely to use computers, Internet technology (e.g., wireless access), and online services (e.g., games, blogs, classifieds) than students from older generations (Zickuhr, 2010). Early in its development, the Internet was used for isolated and isolating tasks, such as reading news, playing games, and participating in asynchronous message boards. With the advent of the social web, the focus of the Internet is now on communication, connection, and engagement. Students are no strangers to these technologies, being rapid adopters and consumers of *social media*—a category of online websites, applications, services, and practices that afford users the opportunity to connect to each other and create, share, and collaborate on content. Social media websites (e.g., Facebook, Twitter, LinkedIn, YouTube, MySpace, Skype) provide a wide range of ways to connect and share.

Indeed, these services represent an exponential leap forward in how the Internet is used and include options for creating profiles, sharing media in a variety of forms, and communicating with groups of friends. As of this writing, Facebook is the social media website with the highest penetration rate among college students (Junco, 2012a). The most recent large-scale survey on college student social media use conducted by the EDUCAUSE Center for Applied Research (ECAR) shows 90% of students use social networking websites, with 97% of those saying they used Facebook (Smith & Caruso, 2010). Recent data also reveal students devote a lot of time to Facebook, spending an average of more than 1 hour and 40 minutes a day on the site (Junco, 2009).

It may be expedient to say all college students are avid and skilled users of technology; however, data show persistent differences in technology ownership and use based on background characteristics (Cooper & Weaver, 2003; DiMaggo, Hargittai, Celeste, & Shafer, 2004; Hargittai, 2008a; Junco, Merson, & Salter, 2010; Kaiser Family Foundation, 2004). While almost all of the research on digital inequalities focuses on Internet and communication technologies in general, Hargittai (2008b) conducted the only published study of gender, ethnic, and socioeconomic differences between users and nonusers of social networking sites. She found Latino students were less likely to use Facebook than White students, and students whose parents had a college degree exhibited greater usage than students with parents without a degree. These findings suggest not all students use Facebook and that nonusers may share one or more common characteristics.

Further, Hargittai (2010) found persistent differences in Internet-use skills among college students. Similar to her earlier research, she found students whose parents have more formal education, male students, and those who are White or Asian American have higher levels of Internet skills than others. Digital inequalities are seen with other information and communication technologies (ICT), as well. For instance, Junco et al. (2010) found that while White and male students were more likely to own a cell phone, female and African American students spent more time talking and texting on their phones.

Based on their socioeconomic background, students do not have the same access to and skills related to technology when they enter college. Research on high school students (Brown, Higgins, & Hartley, 2001; Milone & Salpeter, 1996; Pisapia, 1994; Warschauer, Knobel, & Stone. 2004) found students in public schools in lower socioeconomic areas were more likely to use computers for academic practice and quizzing, while students in higher socioeconomic areas were more than three times as likely to learn how to program computers.

This differential use has been attributed to the ways teachers encourage students, their access to technology, and the focus of schools in different socioeconomic areas. Given these findings, it is important to understand that as students transition into and through college to their senior year, they may not start, nor continue to be, on a level playing field when it comes to technology access, use, and skills.

Mobile Devices and Newer Technologies

In addition to regular and frequent use of social media, there is a growing desire for people to be able to work, learn, and study whenever and wherever they choose, and the number of technologies that support such activities is increasing. *Cloud computing* delivers and shares information and resources through a service over the Internet that can be accessed anywhere irrespective of computer type or operating system, creating a more portable information environment that connects to the individual, not the computer itself. Data in the cloud reside in cyberspace, accessible only by a web-enabled device (Johnson, Smith, Willis, Levine, & Haywood, 2011; Smith & Caruso, 2010).

Recent data on longitudinal trends of emerging technologies in higher education argue that both electronic books and mobile devices will become widely used by institutions in the immediate future (Johnson et al., 2011). The fastest growing area of technology adoption as of this writing is the use of wireless mobile devices to access the Internet, which often take the form of a cell phone or tablet (e.g., iPad) that allows connection without any hardwiring (Smith & Caruso, 2010). Mobile connectivity has been found to help equalize access to the Internet for minority populations; therefore, focusing on supporting mobile technologies in higher education can serve to minimize digital inequalities (Junco et al., 2010; Smith, 2010). Indeed, cell phones are both less expensive than computers and are also seen as essential by students who may not be able to afford a computer (Junco et al., 2010). Smith and Caruso (2010) state,

> There is no doubt that mobile technology will continue its dramatic expansion as a consumer technology and will experience widespread adoption and usage among our students. Devices such as iPads, iPhones, e-book readers, and Android-powered phones (and tablets …) will erode distinctions between computer and mobile device and will see ownership levels equaling or exceeding those that laptops enjoy today on campus. (p. 22)

Mobile devices to access information and communicate continue to rise in popularity with all adults, especially college-aged students. As of 2010, cell phones were owned by 95% of those in the youngest adult age group of 18-34. In addition to serving as a telephone, the vast majority of those phones are used to take photos (91%) and send or receive text messages (94%; Zickuhr, 2010). More than half of adults use cell phones to retrieve information, and 40% have used them in an emergency situation, in addition to 42% reporting they have used them to stave off boredom (Smith, 2011). Further, 63% of undergraduate students owned an Internet-capable handheld device (compared to 84% and 46% ownership of a laptop or desktop computer, respectively; Smith & Caruso, 2010). Not only has the possession of these handheld devices increased, but the usage has as well. In 2010, 55% of the owners used them daily to access the Internet, up from 45% of daily users in 2009 (Smith & Caruso, 2010).

The use of mobile devices by undergraduates can be viewed as a maturing technology, as demonstrated by an increase in *power users* (i.e., students who use their devices to access the Internet weekly or more often) and a decrease in nonusers from 2009 to 2010. In 2010, 85% of mobile-device owners used them to seek information (e.g., news, weather, sports, specific facts), and 81.7% used them to check e-mail. Approximately three-quarters (76.9%) of owners accessed social networking websites from their devices, and the remaining uses (i.e., instant messaging; conducting personal business, such as banking or shopping; downloading or streaming music or videos) all fell within the range of 30-40% each (Smith & Caruso, 2010).

Similarly, The Pew Internet and American Life Project found 70% of all adults aged 18-29 used their cell phones or tablet computers to get local news and information, and those young adults are also more likely to access all types of information via mobile devices as compared to other age groups (Purcell, Rainie, Rosensteil, & Mitchell, 2011). In response to the increased usage of mobile devices to access the Internet, websites are being optimized to provide information in compatible formats. In addition, the proliferation of new applications for mobile devices encourages greater use.

Cloud-based tools for productivity are predicted to have the most rapid increase in usage in the near future (Smith & Caruso, 2010). Rather than using e-mail attachments or saving data to a thumb drive, cloud computing allows users to make changes to a file that can be synchronized on both work and home computers. In addition, one can collaborate on documents with colleagues or share video clips and photos with friends, saving them in virtual personal file cabinets. The 2010 ECAR benchmarking survey about undergraduate technology use reported more than one third of college students are using cloud applications (e.g., Google Docs) for collaborative sharing. Further, 75% were using at least one cloud-based service in a course (e.g., wikis, social networking, blogging, video sharing; Smith & Caruso, 2010). The popularity and growth of this type of technology is evidenced by Dropbox, a cloud-based data storage site, which reported 25 million users uploading 300 million files per day (Kopytoff, 2011).

As Chickering and Gamson (1987) recommended, giving prompt feedback is essential for cognitive development and psychosocial growth, and mobile technologies seem to make instant response not only easier, but also of a higher priority. Grades can now be posted online and viewed from any location with Internet or cellular access. Papers can be reviewed and comments inserted electronically and returned to a student. Faculty can use mobile technologies in the classroom to poll students and provide immediate formative feedback.

It is challenging to write about technology and its future as the services, products, and uses change rapidly and constantly. However, technology will remain a crucial part of the college student's life and influence various aspects of student learning and development.

Impact on Student Learning and Engagement

Not only are college students substantial consumers of technology, but technology has also transformed how students learn. Internet and communication technologies have provided a medium for students to communicate, learn, engage, and connect differently compared to previous generations. By the time students are in their senior year, they should have acquired proficient discipline-specific technological skills to be competitive in their fields as well as more general skills needed to secure a position (e.g., conduct an online job search, attach a file to e-mail, write professional electronic communication).

The use of technology, though, goes beyond the job search process. In recent studies focusing on Facebook, researchers found a relationship between social media and *student engagement*, defined as the amount of time and effort students invest in academic and cocurricular educational activities that are empirically linked to desired college outcomes (Heiberger & Harper, 2008; HERI, 2007; Junco, 2012b). For instance, there was a significant positive relationship between time spent on Facebook and time spent engaging in campus activities (Junco, 2012b). In addition, Facebook tasks, such as creating or RSVPing to events, commenting on content, and viewing photos, were positively related to student engagement outcomes. There was also a positive relationship between Facebook usage and forming and maintaining *social capital*—"the resources accumulated through the relationships among people" (Ellison, Steinfield, & Lampe, 2007, p. 1145)—as evidenced by the results from a HERI (2007) study that found high-frequency users reported more daily interactions offline with close friends with whom they developed strong connections. Finally, there is also evidence that Facebook use is positively related to civic engagement (Valenzuela, Park, & Kee, 2009).

However, this social media-student engagement relationship is not always positive. Junco (2012b) found some Facebook uses (e.g., playing games such as Mafia Wars and Farmville) were significantly negative predictors of engagement on a 19-item scale based on the National Survey of Student Engagement (NSSE). This and other studies suggest that by the senior year students have used Facebook in ways that both enhance and detract from their academic and cocurricular engagement. Interestingly, seniors spent the least amount of time on Facebook compared to juniors, sophomores, and first-year students (Junco, 2011).

While students have generally navigated their online social world with little help, if any, from higher education professionals, the classroom presents an opportunity for faculty and staff to use social technologies to positively shape students' learning and engagement and prepare them for their transition beyond graduation. Chickering and Gamson (1987) made the case for the effectiveness of active-learning techniques, many of which can easily incorporate technology For instance, digital, electronic, or online response tools can be used for discussion or quizzes, or the Facebook groups feature can be employed to create an interactive virtual class environment on a platform that is popular with students. Data from Junco (2012a) show students prefer to use Facebook for course management features over other technologies, including learning management systems (LMSs), and they readily engage with each other in active learning through the use of the group wall and chat feature.

Additionally, social media technologies allow faculty to emphasize time on task and facilitate students' engagement with the material outside of class (Chickering & Gamson, 1987). For instance, class conversations can extend beyond the typical three to four hours of weekly in-class contact by using social media. Indeed, Junco, Heiberger, and Loken (2011) attribute part of their success in using Twitter to engage students and improve their grades to the fact they were able to maximize time on task by continuing class discussions via Twitter. Students not only easily adopted the technology, but they reflected on course content and readings in deeper and more critical ways than is typical for students at their level. Further, collaborative learning is an important skill graduating seniors need to have. Social technologies (e.g., Facebook, Twitter) support collaboration among students, allowing them to cooperate in ways not previously thought possible (Junco et al., 2011).

Chickering and Gamson (1987) also listed contact between students and faculty as a good practice to improve learning. In the digital age, it is important to support as many avenues for student-faculty communication as possible, whether that is through social media or offline interactions. In addition to increasing student contact, faculty and staff should model appropriate ways to communicate via social media to help students develop their online social skills as they transition through their senior year.

Technology and Multitasking

We define *multitasking* as divided attention and nonsequential task switching for ill-defined tasks; for example, when a student is text messaging a friend while studying for an examination. By the senior year, students have accumulated hours of practice multitasking. The trickle of information available online a decade ago has turned into a deluge of data funneled through social and mobile technologies. We have cell phones that ensure we can be reached anywhere; text messages to answer during the in-between times; e-mail inboxes that are constantly full; continuous feeds streaming headlines by the hour, or even minute; Facebook accounts where friends are asking for our attention; and Twitter accounts that inundate us with new data, news, and commentary. These are just a few of the pulls of our advanced technological society, in addition to traditional media, such as television, newspapers, magazines, and radio. Multitasking can be (and often is used as) a way to manage the voluminous flow of information encountered daily (Chun, Golomb, & Turk-Browne, 2011). As such, it becomes a survival strategy that helps students pick out bytes of information while attending to other important tasks.

As a rule, multitasking is adaptive for low-risk and low-stakes activities (e.g., talking on the phone while doing laundry) and is maladaptive for high-risk and high-stakes activities (e.g., texting during a lecture or while driving). Faculty interest in this area is warranted given the detrimental effects of multitasking on learning. Mayer and Moreno's (2003) research-based cognitive theory of learning and information overload demonstrates that humans have a finite amount of cognitive processes available at any one time. When these processes become overloaded, deeper processing and learning may be inhibited. In addition, research has shown that Facebooking or texting while trying to study is clearly related to difficulties in encoding information and deeper learning and results in lower grade point averages (Junco & Cotten, 2012; Rosen, Lim, Carrier, & Cheever, 2011; Wood et al., 2012)

Students seem to be aware of multitasking's negative impacts even while actively engaged in it. This disconnect is evidenced in findings from a recent study by Junco and Cotten (2010), which found 93% of instant messaging (IM) users reported chatting online when doing schoolwork while 57% of the same study participants also self-reported that doing schoolwork while IMing had a detrimental effect on their work. It is, therefore, incumbent upon those who engage with seniors to help them differentiate types of multitasking that are harmful as they transition beyond college. Interestingly, recent data suggest doing social activities (e.g., Facebook, texting) while trying to learn has a detrimental effect on learning outcomes while doing academic-type tasks does not (e.g., e-mailing, searching for non-course-related content; Junco & Cotten, 2012). Therefore, faculty and staff can help students recognize the ways socializing via emerging technologies can impede the learning process, while also honoring the fact that students will (and should) multitask in other ways. One strategy would be to help students consider when they might "turn off" their socializing so they may focus on studying and the processes necessary for deeper learning; this can be done much in the same way that we encourage students to set aside blocks of study time in a distraction-reduced environment to use their time most efficiently.

Student Identity Development and Expression

As students present their images to others through profiles and applications on social networking sites, they are participating in a form of identity exploration called *impression management*, a concept that can be traced back to the work of Goffman (1959) and which has been examined in various iterations from the establishment of the Internet and personal homepages to profiles on social networking sites (Dominick, 1999; Kramer & Winter, 2008; Pempek, Yermolayeva, & Calvert, 2009). College students today are consciously and unconsciously working to influence the impressions they make on others in online spaces as part of their journey through identity development. Yet, little research has focused on the impact of computers, technology, and social media use on development. Psychosocial theories of development provide some basis for analysis of this process in a digital context. Chickering and Reisser's (1993) seven vectors of college student development include two—establishing identity and developing purpose—that are directly impacted by an online presence. These will be discussed in greater detail later in this section.

Just as previous generations of students established their identities in physical spaces (e.g., Chickering & Reisser 1993; Erickson, 1963), today's college senior also has to develop his or her identity online. Social networking sites provide a public communication venue to showcase one's ideal identity by updating statuses, posting to walls, sharing photos, and making comments on each other's pages (boyd & Ellison, 2007; Hum et al., 2011; Kramer & Winter, 2008; Pempek et al., 2009). Further, students choose to indicate membership in certain subgroups as defined by race, gender, sexual orientation, or subculture (e.g., music, movies) in constructing their online identity (Hum et al. 2011; Pempek et al., 2009). As college students develop their online identities, they accumulate, use, and manage social capital, including emotional support, new information, and different ideas (Ellison, Steinfeld, & Lampe, 2007, 2011). The analysis of the impact of social networking is important as the usage of these sites and tools permeate students' everyday lives.

Digital photos are one way students can manage how others perceive them online. Hum and colleagues (2011) found there was no difference by gender in the content or quantity of photos. The majority of the college student's Facebook profile photographs were inactive, posed, appropriate, and contained only the subject, indicating the participants may be aware of the importance of constructing such an identity via their main photograph. The majority of the study participants' profiles contained 20 or more images in their albums, suggesting students are choosing to provide multiple identity clues to other Facebook users via their profile pictures.

As noted earlier, Junco (2011) found first-semester students and sophomores spent more time on Facebook than juniors and seniors. This is likely an indicator of students using Facebook differently as they navigate different developmental milestones. More specifically, new students may need to continue their connection with their circle of high school friends; however, as they move through developmental stages towards interdependence, they rely less on the social capital afforded by Facebook use. Our experience and interviews with hundreds of students have shown that later in their college careers, students are more interested in keeping their Facebook content private from potential employers or graduate schools, suggesting some understanding of how their online identities impact others.

As students continue to develop their identity using an online presence, some work harder to maximize their personal brand. Creating and promoting a brand for a product aims at a target audience and showcases why the product is unique and a good one to choose; the same principle can be applied to a *personal brand*. Being able to sell one's self; market one's own brand; and control an image to present to a future employer, dating partner, or friend is something important to many college students, especially seniors. Tactics to showcase a personal brand include publishing blogs and personal websites, creating and maintaining profiles within social media, and optimizing search engine results about oneself (Labrecque, Markos, & Milne, 2011; Shepherd, 2005).

A study by Labrecque and colleagues (2011) examined how people managed their online personal brands. All participants stated they intentionally controlled information to maintain their brand identity, but they also realized others contributed to that brand by providing content in comments and photo tagging. By deciding what to share and not to share online, participants not only made intentional choices but sometimes also included information that could be or was misconstrued. Smith and Kidder (2010) stated the "greatest misdirected branding" (p. 46) occurs when wall posts or photos provide negative commentary or images that might be viewed by professional audiences. Unfavorable or inaccurate posts or tags can also be circulated without knowledge or consent of the individual. Further, platforms to showcase one's brand continue to evolve as new technologies either provide more synergistic tools or as the terms of service of the platform change to the detriment of branding strategies (Labrecque et al., 2011).

The creation and maintenance of a personal brand takes on increasing importance in the senior year as students enter the job market or apply for graduate school, internships, or service opportunities (e.g., the Peace Corps). It has become a widely accepted practice that potential employers will recruit and assess applicants based on their social networking profiles (CareerBuilder.com, 2009; NACE, 2011; Smith & Kidder, 2010). A Careerbuilder.com survey of hiring managers in 2009 found 45% used social media to research potential candidates. Of this group, 35% reported they did not hire a candidate based on what they found. The top three reasons for employers to disregard a candidate reflected the poor judgment of that individual and included (a) candidate posted provocative or inappropriate photographs or information (53%); (b) candidate posted content about personally using alcohol or drugs (44%); and (c) candidate bad-mouthed their previous employer, coworkers, or clients (35%). Thus, career development professionals, advisors, and others helping students make the transition out of college need to provide guidance on how to manage students' personal brand.

Several empirical studies have recently been published to examine self-presentation on social networking sites based on the content of profiles and have focused on the psychological constructs of self-esteem, narcissism, shyness, social class consciousness, motivation, extraversion, and overall well-being (e.g., Cotten, 2008; Hum et al., 2011; Kramer & Winter, 2008; Kolek & Saunders, 2008; Mehdizadeh, 2010). Once again, the identity development theories of Chickering and Reisser (1993) and Erickson (1963) help to frame how students create profiles, build social capital, and develop identity over their college career. While elements of social media use could be applied to all seven vectors in Chickering and Reisser's psychosocial development model, the two vectors described below are most directly relevant. For a more complete discussion of this theory, see chapter 2.

Establishing Identity

This developmental task builds on the work of earlier vectors and is central to the model. When students establish identity, they have created a (generally) stable sense of self, which encourages the development of self-esteem. Social media profiles reflect the student's sense of both perceived self and his or her communicated self. As college students develop and reach this stage, their online postings, sharing of information, and profiles would reveal stability in self-presentation and communications.

Developing Purpose

This vector is most closely associated with the senior year in that students have created a stable sense of self and now look toward the future and wonder, Who am I going to be? As students transition into and through the senior year, they are more intensely focused on what their vocational goals will be and how they will reach those goals. They may have already started to think about how their social media profiles may affect their ability to obtain a job. For example, they may ensure their profiles look professional and do not contain information that may disqualify them in a job search. They may also consider how they can network with current friends and potential employers.

One area of concern related to college students is a perceived increase in narcissism, which is generally defined as an unhealthy focus on the self. Campbell and Twenge (2010) discuss changes in narcissism assessment scores among college students over time, and they believe the rise of social networking is one of the major contributors. Highly narcissistic students require the most attention from faculty and staff at a college or university, as they tend to demand special treatment, cheat, have conflicts with others, drink, gamble, and engage in numerous short-term sexual relationships as well as to be the perpetrators of violent crimes on campus when those extreme activities occur (Campbell & Twenge, 2010). Arnett's (2000) work on emerging adulthood noted that the 20s and early 30s are a time of "change and exploration" (p. 471). He counters the argument that emerging adults are essentially selfish. While taking the time to concentrate on oneself may be perceived as narcissism, Arnett suggests it is a natural part of identity development during early adulthood.

Social Media and Civil Discourse

Using ICTs for social connections and communications comes with its downsides for civil discourse. In face-to-face or phone interactions, most people are able to pick up subtle cues in communication (e.g., body language, vocal tone, volume, eye contact, gestures) that frame a conversation. In face-to-face interactions when verbal and nonverbal messages conflict, the nonverbal message is given greater weight. As blocks of communication get shorter and provide fewer contextual cues, as with social media, the ability to correctly perceive tone diminishes. This can make it easier for disagreements to spiral into serious confrontations. Further, Epley and Kruger (2005) found "expectancies influence impressions formed over e-mail more than those formed over the telephone" (p. 417) and as a result, racial stereotypes are strengthened when interacting over e-mail. Their findings suggest it is much easier for the receiver of an electronic communication to project his or her own stereotypes and expectations on the other person because of the ambiguity of the medium. This can often lead to unintended misunderstandings.

In addition, online interactions can be muddled by the *online disinhibition effect*—the propensity for individuals to say things in online communications they would not say in face-to-face communications. While such disinhibition can be helpful for academic communications where the student is reticent to participate, it can be damaging when students say hurtful things on purpose, spread negative information in deliberate attempts at cyberbullying, or have their words misinterpreted because of the receiver's inability to tell tone online. Therefore, it is important to encourage and teach students how to use social technologies in ways that engender civil discourse and also promote collaboration (Junco & Chickering, 2010).

Yet, social media offer students unprecedented opportunities for collaboration. Elavsky, Mislan, and Elavsky (2011) and Junco, Elavsky, and Heiberger (2012) demonstrated social media can be used to effectively create virtual communities to support student learning. Furthermore, Junco et al. (2011) found students will engage in productive collaboration through social media going so far as to support each other emotionally as well as with course projects. These studies show students can be taught and encouraged to use social media to collaborate for educational benefit. Consequently, throughout the undergraduate experience, students should be presented with curricular and cocurricular opportunities to collaborate online, gaining important skills for graduate school and the workplace.

Postgraduation Competencies

For postgraduate success, it is critical that college students have a minimum of technology-related competencies. While there are obvious competencies on which we must focus (e.g., using e-mail and word processing applications), here we discuss those that are not commonly taught as part of the curriculum and yet are essential to succeeding in today's digital society.

- *Privacy*. We make an important distinction between the *technological* and *philosophical* aspects of online privacy. Technological aspects are related to Internet skills and revolve around the understanding of how to modify privacy settings on social media. Philosophical aspects are related to the broader understanding that information that is shared online can almost never be considered private since control has been relinquished to a second party (and possibly even others). While many seniors use social media privacy settings to protect their information from those who they would not want seeing it, other students have lower levels of sophistication when it comes to this issue. Social networking sites themselves add to these difficulties as they often change default privacy settings without notice or announcement, which can make unwilling and unwitting users share more of their information than they intend. Therefore, it is essential that those who work with seniors not only familiarize themselves with both the technical and philosophical aspects of online privacy but also that they teach students how to manage their online presence.

- *Online civil discourse*. While civil discourse is often encouraged in the classroom, educators rarely, if ever, teach or model civil discourse in online spaces. Faculty and staff are generally reticent to use social media with students and, therefore, have little opportunity to help with both direct teaching of civil discourse and modeling of said discourse. In light of the online disinhibition effect, growing media reports of cyberbullying, and the inability to discern tone online, it is important to encourage graduating students to reflect on their online communications and the impact they may have on the recipients. These competencies are especially important as students enter the workforce where they will need to maintain collegial relationships with colleagues both offline and online. We can help students mold their communication into more appropriate statements by setting high expectations—letting students know civil discourse is expected and that their comments about class material should show levels of critical thinking congruent with their developmental level.

- *Managing digital identity*. In addition to the impact one's digital identity has on a potential job search, the basic transitions of college students during those formative years are now being chronicled online for others to view. On an elementary level, it is critical to help students consider how their social media profiles will be viewed by others. While the topic of search engine optimization (SEO) is beyond the scope of this chapter, it is important for graduating students and the professionals who work with them to have an understanding of how online content affects search page ranks and their visibility when they are being checked out by potential employers or anybody else on the Internet.

Summary

For almost a decade, social media have provided students new, technologically enhanced ways to socialize. More recently, research has shown the technologies favored by college students can be used in ways that enhance their experience, aid in their psychosocial development, and improve the learning process. Senior-year experience professionals must not only be aware of these technologies and how they impact students but should also work actively to integrate social technologies in educationally relevant ways.

References

Arnett, J. J. (2000). Emerging adulthood: A theory of development from the late teens through the twenties. *American Psychologist, 55,* 469-480.

boyd, d. m., & Ellison, N. B. (2007). Social network sites: Definition, history, and scholarship. *Journal of Computer-Mediated Communication, 13*(1). Retrieved from http://jcmc.indiana.edu/vol13/issue1/boyd.ellison.html

Brown, M., Higgins, K., & Hartley, K. (2001). Teachers and technology equity. *Teaching Exceptional Children, 33,* 32-39.

Campbell, W. K., & Twenge, J. M. (2010, Winter). The narcissism epidemic on campus. *NASPA Leadership Exchange,* 26-29.

CareerBuilder.com (2009). *Forty-five percent of employers use social networking sites to research job candidates, CareerBuilder survey finds.* Retrieved June 10, 2011, from http://www.careerbuilder.com/share/aboutus/pressreleasesdetail.aspx?id=pr519 &sd=8%2F19%2F2009&ed=12%2F31%2F2009

Chickering, A. W., & Ehrmann, S. C. (1996, October). Implementing the seven principles: Technology as lever. *AAHE Bulletin,* 3-6.

Chickering, A. W., & Gamson, Z. F. (1987, March). Seven principles for good practice in undergraduate education. *AAHE Bulletin,* 3-7.

Chickering, A. W., & Reisser, L. (1993) *Education and identity,* (2nd ed.). San Francisco, CA: Jossey-Bass.

Chun, M. M., Golomb, J. D., & Turk-Browne, N. B. (2011). A taxonomy of external and internal attention. *Annual Review of Psychology, 62,* 73-101.

Cooper, J., & Weaver, K. D. (2003). *Gender and computers: Understanding the digital divide.* Mahwah, NJ: Erlbaum.

Cotten, S. (2008). Students' technology use and the impacts on well-being. In R. Junco & D. M. Timm (Eds.), *Using emerging technologies to enhance student engagement.* (New Directions for Student Services, No. 124, pp. 55-70). San Francisco, CA: Jossey-Bass.

DiMaggio, P., Hargittai, E., Celeste, C., & Shafer, S. (2004). Digital inequality: From unequal access to differentiated use. In K. Neckerman (Ed.), *Social inequality* (pp. 355-400). New York, NY: Russell Sage Foundation.

Dominick, J. (1999). Who do you think you are? Personal home pages and self-presentation on the World Wide Web. *Journalism and Mass Communication Quarterly, 76,* 646-658.

Elavsky, C. M., Mislan, C., & Elavsky, S. (2011). When talking less is more: exploring outcomes of Twitter usage in the large-lecture hall. *Learning, Media and Technology, 36*(3), 215-233. doi: 10.1080/17439884.2010.549828

Ellison, N. B., Steinfield, C., & Lampe, C. (2007). The benefits of Facebook "friends:" Social capital and college students' use of online social network sites. *Journal of Computer-Mediated Communication, 12*(4), 1143-1168.

Ellison, N. B., Steinfield, C., & Lampe, C. (2011). Connection strategies: Social capital implications of Facebook-enabled communication strategies. *New Media & Society, 13*(6), 873-892. doi: 10.1177/1461444810385389

Epley, N., & Kruger, J. (2005). When what you type isn't what they read: The perseverance of stereotypes and expectancies over e-mail. *Journal of Experimental Social Psychology, 41,* 414–422.

Erikson, E. H. (1963). *Childhood and society.* New York, NY: Norton.

Goffman, E. (1959). *The presentation of self in everyday life.* Garden City, NY: Doubleday.

Hargittai, E. (2008a). Whose space? Differences among users and non-users of social network sites. *Journal of Computer-Mediated Communication, 13*(1), 276-297.

Hargittai, E. (2008b). The digital reproduction of inequality. In D. Grusky (Ed.), *Social stratification,* (pp. 936-944). Boulder, CO: Westview Press.

Hargittai, E. (2010). Digital na(t)ives? Variation in internet skills and uses among members of the "net generation." *Sociological Inquiry, 80*(1), 92-113.

Heiberger, G., & Harper, R. (2008). Have you Facebooked Astin lately? Using technology to increase student involvement. In R. Junco & D. M. Timm (Eds.), *Using emerging technologies to enhance student engagement.* (New Directions for Student Services, No. 124, pp. 19-35). San Francisco, CA: Jossey-Bass.

Higher Education Research Institute (HERI). (2007). *College freshmen and online social networking sites.* Retrieved from http://www.gseis.ucla.edu/heri/PDFs/pubs/briefs/brief-091107-SocialNetworking.pdf

Hum, N. J., Chamberlin, P. E., Hambright, B. L, Portwood, A. C., Schat, A. C., & Bevan, J. L. (2011). A picture is worth a thousand words: A content analysis of Facebook profile photographs. *Computers in Human Behavior, 27,* 1828-1833.

Johnson, L., Smith, R., Willis, H., Levine, A., & Haywood, K., (2011). *The 2011 Horizon Report.* Austin, TX: The New Media Consortium.

Junco, R. (2009). *Teaching teens to Twitter: Supporting engagement in the college classroom.* Presented at Harvard University's Berkman Center for Internet and Society. Retrieved from http://cyber.law.harvard.edu/events/luncheon/2009/12/junco

Junco, R. (2011, May). *First semester students and sophomores spend more time on Facebook.* Retrieved from http://blog.reyjunco.com/first-semester-students-and-sophomores-spend-more-time-on-facebook

Junco, R (2012a, January). *College students prefer to use Facebook in their courses.* Retrieved from http://blog.reyjunco.com/college-students-prefer-to-use-facebook-in-their-courses

Junco, R. (2012b). The relationship between frequency of Facebook use, participation in Facebook activities, and student engagement. *Computers & Education, 58*(1), 162-171. doi: 10.1016/j.compedu.2011.08.004

Junco, R. & Chickering, A. W. (2010, September/October). Civil discourse in the age of social media. *About Campus, 15*(4), 12-18.

Junco, R., & Cotten, S. R. (2010). Perceived academic effects of instant messaging use. *Computers & Education, 56*, 370-378.

Junco, R. & Cotten, S. R. (2012). No A 4 U: The relationship between multitasking and academic performance. *Computers & Education, 59*(2), 505-514.

Junco, R., Elavsky, C. M., & Heiberger, G. (2012). Putting Twitter to the test: Assessing outcomes for student collaboration, engagement, and success. *British Journal of Educational Technology.* doi: 10.1111/j.1467-8535.2012.01284.x

Junco, R., Heiberger, G., & Loken, E. (2011). The effect of Twitter on college student engagement and grades. *Journal of Computer Assisted Learning, 27*(2), 119-132.

Junco, R., Merson, D., & Salter, D. W. (2010). The effect of gender, ethnicity, and income on college students' use of communication technologies. *Cyberpsychology, Behavior, and Social Networking, 13*(6), 619-627.

Kaiser Family Foundation. (2004, August). *The digital divide survey snapshot.* Retrieved from Kaiser Family Foundation website: http://www.kff.org/entmedia/loader.cfm?url=/commonspot/security/getfile.cfm&PageID=46366

Kolek, E. A., & Saunders, D. (2008). Online disclosure: An empirical examination of undergraduate Facebook profiles. *NASPA Journal, 45*(1), 1-25.

Kopytoff, V. G. (2011, June 6). Data grows, and so do storage sites. *New York Times,* p. B1.

Kramer, N. C., & Winter, S. (2008). Impression management 2.0: The relationship of self-esteem, self-efficacy, and self-presentation within social networking sites. *Journal of Media Psychology, 20*(3), 106-116.

Labrecque, L. I., Markos, E., & Milne, G. R. (2011). Online personal branding: Processes, challenges, and implications. *Journal of Interactive Marketing, 25*, 37-50.

Mayer, R., & Moreno, R. (2003). Nine ways to reduce cognitive load in multimedia learning. *Educational Psychologist, 38*(1), 43-52.

Mehdizadeh, S. (2010). Self-presentation 2.0: Narcissism and self-esteem on Facebook. *Cyberpsychology, Behavior, and Social Networking, 13*(4), 357-364.

Milone, M. N., & Salpeter, J. (1996). Technology and equity issues. *Technology and Learning, 16*(4), 38-47.

National Association of Colleges and Employers (NACE). (2011). *Social media in the job search: LinkedIn, Twitter outpace Facebook as tools.* Retrieved from NACE website: http://www.naceweb.org/s06082011/social_media_job_search/

Pempek, T. A., Yermolayeva, Y. A., & Calvert, S. L. (2009). College students' social networking experiences on Facebook. *Journal of Applied Developmental Psychology, 30*, 227-238.

Pisapia, J. (1994). *Technology: The equity issue.* Richmond, VA: Metropolitan Educational Research Consortium.

Purcell, K., Rainie, L., Rosensteil, T., & Mitchell, A. (2011). *How mobile devices are changing community information environments.* Retrieved from Pew Internet: American Life Project website: http://pewinternet.org/~/media//Files/Reports/2011/PIP-Local%20mobile%20survey.pdf

Rosen, L. D., Lim, A. F., Carrier, L. M., & Cheever, N. A. (2011). An empirical examination of the educational impact of text message-induced task switching in the classroom: Educational implications and strategies to enhance learning. *Psicologia Educativa, 17*(2), 163-177.

Shepherd, I. (2005). From cattle and coke to Charlie: Meeting the challenge of self-marketing and personal branding. *Journal of Marketing Management, 21,* 589-606.

Smith, A. (2010). *Mobile access 2010.* Retrieved from Pew Internet: American Life Project website:http://www.pewintenet.org/~/media//Files/Reports/2010/PIP_Mobile_Access_2010.pdf

Smith, A. (2011). *Americans and their cell phones.* Retrieved from Pew Internet and American Life Project website: http://pewinternet.org/Reports/2011/Cell-Phones.aspx

Smith, S. D., & Caruso, J. B. (2010). *ECAR study of undergraduate students and information technology.* (Research Study, Vol. 6). Retrieved from EDUCAUSE Applied Research website: http://www.educause.edu/Resources/ECARStudyofUndergraduateStuden/217333

Smith, W. P., & Kidder, D. L. (2010). You've been tagged! (Then again, maybe not): Employers and Facebook. *Business Horizons, 53,* 491-499.

Valenzuela, S., Park, N., & Kee, K. F. (2009). Is there social capital in a social network site? Facebook use and college students' life satisfaction, trust, and participation. *Journal of Computer-Mediated Communication, 14*(4), 875-901.

Warschauer, M., Knobel, M., & Stone, L. (2004). Technology and equity in schooling: Deconstructing the digital divide. *Educational Policy, 18*(4), 562-588.

Wood, E., Zivcakova, L., Gentile, P., Archer, K., De Pasquale, D., & Nosko, A. (2012). Examining the impact of off-task multi-tasking with technology on real-time classroom learning. *Computers & Education, 58*(1), 365-374.

Zickuhr, K. (2010). *Generations 2010.* Washington, DC: Retrieved from Pew Internet: American Life Project website: http://pewinternet.org/~/media//Files/Reports/2010/PIP_Generations_and_Tech10.pdf

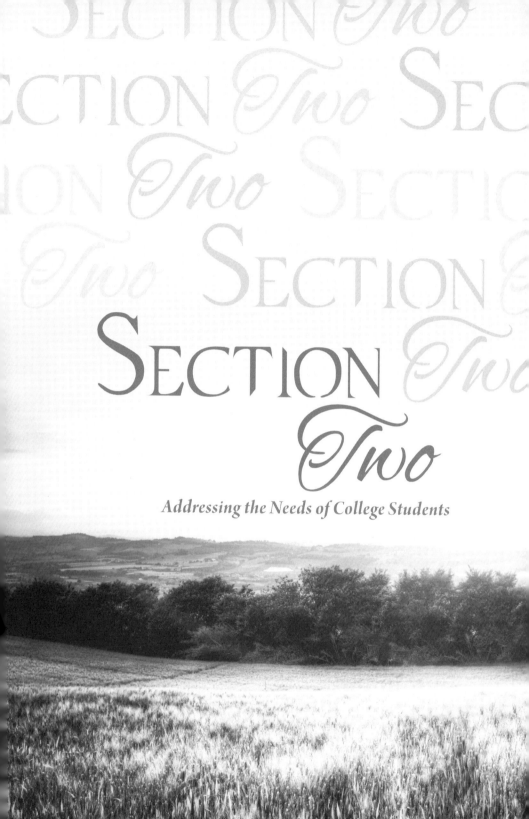

SECTION
Two

Addressing the Needs of College Students

CHAPTER Four

Optimizing High-Impact Educational Practices and the Senior Year

Jillian Kinzie

When I think about the highlights of my education, I have to start with my first-year seminar. It was important in my transition to college both personally and academically, but even more, it was the first step of many in becoming an independent person. I openly embraced my seminar topic and began to ask some hard questions about myself and the world, questions that helped inform my studies. My class was small, and my professor was also my advisor. He got to know me, my writing, and my educational goals and was able to give me useful feedback and challenge my ideas. I volunteered with a couple of youth-serving organizations during college, but it was not until my service-learning course that I was able to combine my interest in gender and science in a project that explored girls' middle-school science experiences. I helped the local Girls Club address girls' science inhibitions and interests and then earned credit that summer when I interned with the Club and presented my project at their regional meeting. The experience really opened my eyes and made me feel like I could make a difference with what was going on around me. The high point of my education was probably my senior year when everything kind of came together. I had good relationships with several professors who knew me and what I was capable of and who were ready to mentor me with my senior project. When it came time to pick a topic, I felt ready because I learned how to do research in my methods class and had direct experience in the field through my service-learning project. The senior project provided me the opportunity to see firsthand how the research I had been reading for most of my college career was actually conducted, and it provided me a great introduction to the kind of work I expect to do in graduate school. —Jenny H., graduating senior at Midwestern University

The senior year in college offers students a final opportunity to bring together the pieces of their undergraduate education into a coherent whole and realize the culmination of their educational career. Intentionally sequenced coursework, meaningful curricular and cocurricular experiences, and timely advising can foster such coherency and culmination. Rigorous coursework in the major, for example, that demands students apply what they know to solve novel or real problems in the field and the workplace, or leadership experiences that put students in charge of complex campus or community events, can provide substantive experiences that transform students and prepare them for life beyond college. As briefly illustrated in Jenny's vignette, these sorts of transformative experiences (a) engage students at high levels in purposeful tasks, (b) put them at the center of their own active and reflective learning experiences, and (c) are critical to enhancing their learning and development.

Decades of research on student learning and development indicates learning is a cumulative process shaped by challenging events and experiences, inside and outside the classroom. Although various educational experiences can foster substantive and transformative learning, certain ones appear to have a greater likelihood of contributing to desired college outcomes. These experiences have been dubbed *high-impact* because when done well, they engage students at levels that boost their performance across a variety of educational activities and desired outcomes, such as (a) persistence, graduation, and academic success; (b) deep levels of learning (i.e., reflective and integrative); (c) higher rates of student–faculty interaction; (d) intellectual and practical skills, including written communication, critical thinking, and personal and social responsibility; (e) greater appreciation for diversity and intercultural understanding; and (f) enhanced content knowledge and application (Brownell & Swaner, 2010; Pascarella & Terenzini, 1991, 2005).

A report by the Association of American Colleges and Universities (2007) identified 10 promising high-impact practices (HIPs) for their contribution to essential 21st century learning outcomes. They include

- first-year seminars and experiences,
- common intellectual experiences,

- collaborative assignments and projects,
- learning communities,
- service-learning,
- writing intensive courses,
- undergraduate research,
- study abroad and other experiences with diversity,
- internships, and
- capstone courses and projects.

These HIPs engage college students to a greater extent than traditional classroom-based instruction alone and are associated with strong positive effects across a host of desirable educational outcomes. Even more, the practices are particularly effective for historically underserved students, suggesting a compensatory effect on grades and retention for an important segment of the undergraduate population (Kuh, 2008). HIPs appear to offer great benefit to students. Yet, not all HIPs are fully taken advantage of to foster the learning they permit or to be maximally transformative. In addition, the extent to which the experiences are widespread or accessible to and engaged in by underserved students is less than optimal.

HIPs epitomize the transformative educational experiences we want for all students, and this chapter explores that potential. More specifically, it examines what makes HIPs so effective and how they might be implemented more intentionally to provide maximum opportunities for students, especially in creating a coherent, integrated, and transformative senior-year experience. First, the characteristics of HIPs are discussed, followed by an elaboration of their value and benefits. Then, several approaches to embedding HIPs are briefly highlighted to demonstrate ways to expand access. Finally, considerations for ensuring quality and more widespread participation in these transformative experiences are discussed.

Characteristics of HIPs

At their core, high-impact practices are educational activities grounded in the principles of experiential learning. First theorized by David Kolb (1984), and based on the work of John Dewey (1997) and other educational theorists including Jean Piaget, experiential learning involves the transformation of experience into knowledge via carefully crafted activities. These activities are structured to require the learner to act, make decisions, take initiative, interact, reflect, analyze, and make meaning of and apply new ideas from the experience. HIPs (e.g., service-learning, internships and field experiences, undergraduate research) are clear examples of experiential learning.

Several HIPs, including learning communities, first-year seminars, study abroad, and senior capstones, are obvious curricular structures for experiential learning. These programs have been available on a good many campuses for a long time and are generally familiar to students and educators. For example, the University of South Carolina's first-year seminar, University 101, is internationally known for its effectiveness in helping new students make a successful transition to the University. While learning communities (i.e., courses that are linked or clustered, often around a theme, and enroll a common cohort of students) are less common, the program at The Evergreen State College is considered a model curricular structure. Kalamazoo College made study abroad, internships, and independent study formal elements of the curriculum known as the K-Plan. Students at Kalamazoo take a rigorous liberal arts education supplemented by one or more terms abroad and internship opportunities as well as a required senior individualized project, which may take the form of a thesis, an artistic performance, or other work-intensive activity. These intentionally structured curricular experiences provide staged opportunities for experiential learning, and in some cases, like at Kalamazoo, are required for all students.

Certain HIPs feature a blend of curricular and cocurricular experiences. For example, the University of Missouri's freshman interest groups (FIGs) are learning communities made up of 15-20 first-year students housed in the same residence hall who share similar academic or career interests, take three core courses together, and attend events related to shared interests. The curricular structure of FIGs is complemented by the residential living component and optional events. The cooperative experience at Northeastern University in Boston, which alternates semesters of academic study with semesters of full-time employment in positions related to students academic or career interests, has been affording students professional experiences with employers across the United States and in countries around the world for more than 100 years. Finally, a variety of well-established mentored undergraduate research opportunities, including summer research and paid research experiences, available at The College of Wooster provide valuable experiences in advance of the required independent study (IS) project and seminar that helps students integrate and synthesize all they have learned in one piece of scholarly work. These examples illustrate the complementary opportunities for experiential learning.

As shown in the aforementioned institutional examples, HIPs can cut across the curriculum and cocurriculum, be required for graduation or simply available, and exist at a range of institutional types. Although most HIPs have a common purpose (e.g., emphasizing experiential learning), and some have similar structure (e.g., a required seminar), they are variously designed and implemented. The variation in design, combined with evidence of their educational effectiveness, suggests the positive impact of HIPs is more about what they demand of students and institutions rather than how they are named or structured. The effectiveness of HIPs can be attributed to the emphasis on the central principles of experiential learning and the increased likelihood that students will

- invest time and effort,
- interact with faculty and peers about substantive matters,
- experience diversity,
- receive more frequent feedback,
- discover relevance of their learning through real-world applications, and
- engage in a coherent, academically challenging curriculum.

These six conditions are the essence of what makes HIPs powerful practices for increasing student learning and development (Kuh, 2008; NSSE, 2007). Illustrating these conditions in the context of specific high-impact practices provides additional insight into their importance and also demonstrates their key features.

First, educational experiences that demand students devote considerable amounts of time and effort are essential to ensuring high levels of learning. HIPs generally provide this experience in spades since their structure calls for students' attention and deepens their investment in the activity as well as commitment to their academic program and the institution. For example, a learning community that is team-taught by two faculty members and has an integrative element connecting material across courses (i.e., in discussion groups, class assignments, and activities) demands that students dedicate time to exploring the intersections of these courses. The explicit attention to integrative experiences and assignments in the learning communities at The Evergreen State College compels students to put forth more effort, and in turn, invest more in the process of learning.

Second, HIPs put students in circumstances that necessitate interaction with faculty and peers about substantive matters, typically over extended periods of time. Culminating experiences, including capstones or senior projects, may demand seniors work individually with a project faculty advisor at least once a week and complete an oral or poster presentation to a wider campus audience. The senior year at the College of Wooster includes a two-semester individual IS seminar that meets weekly, providing a regular time and place for the student and faculty advisor to discuss progress and setbacks in the research process. It culminates in a day-long Senior Research Symposium featuring performances, presentations, and exhibits of senior work, in which the entire campus participates.

Third, HIPs tend to place students in situations in which they will engage in substantive interactions with individuals different from themselves, encouraging greater cultural awareness and understanding. Study abroad or other cross-cultural immersion experiences are obvious opportunities for this to occur. Service-learning can provide more local contact with diverse populations when they are intentionally structured to foster sustained interaction across multiple differences. For example, the University of Michigan Community Scholars Program (MCSP), a residential learning community emphasizing deep learning, meaningful civic engagement and service-learning, and intercultural understanding and dialogue, offers students a chance to lead and serve in the community, reflect, and engage in intentional dialogue with peers who share a commitment to social justice and democracy. Moreover, longitudinal data in the Wabash National Study of Liberal Arts Education (Salisbury & Goodman, 2009) showed students who reported high levels of interaction around diversity in service-learning and study-abroad experiences realized greater gains in intercultural competence.

Fourth, frequent feedback is also a key element of HIPs. Internship and cooperative experiences in which students' performances are evaluated by the site supervisor and the supervising faculty are rich with opportunities for immediate informal and formal feedback. Writing-intensive courses and undergraduate research experiences can also provide critical opportunities for frequent feedback. Although undergraduate research can take many forms (e.g., embedded in a course, part of a special summer opportunity, individual or small-group project), it should be developed and executed under the mentorship of engaged faculty members since the most critical aspect of the experience is for students to have multiple and frequent opportunities to receive feedback about their work. When research is conducted in the context of a course or a senior capstone, feedback can occur among students and from the faculty member.

Fifth, participating in these activities provides opportunities for students to apply what they are learning in different settings, on and off campus. Study abroad and other global education experiences offer students a world context for their scholarship. Internships and field placements are other venues for students to test what they are learning in unfamiliar situations. Cooperative experiences help students discover avenues to intellectual and personal growth by adding depth to classroom studies; providing exposure to career paths and opportunities; and inspiring students to delve deeper, sharpen their focus, and pursue greater academic challenges. With these connections, students continue to gain valuable work experience and develop a broader view of the world in which they live and work. Co-op placements offer students first-hand experiences with real, unscripted problems and provide the opportunity to link coursework to learning beyond the campus.

Finally, it can be life changing to study abroad, participate in service-learning, conduct research with a faculty member, or complete an internship or other field experience (e.g., student teaching). However, when one or more of these activities are completed in the context of a coherent, academically challenging curriculum incorporating active, collaborative, and meaningful learning and opportunities, the odds are increased that students' participation in HIPs will amount to more than just an accumulation of interesting experiences. This final point is significant because it indicates the importance of the total learning environment and curriculum in the effectiveness of HIPs. In short, high-impact practices can simply be disconnected, brief educational activities if they are not thoughtfully integrated into the undergraduate program.

These six elements are necessary conditions for achieving the total benefits of HIPs. Even more, HIPs must be done consistently well and regularly evaluated to ensure effectiveness.

The Value and Benefits of HIPs

Ideally, college should be a transforming experience. Kegan (2000) distinguishes between *transformational* and *informational learning*, arguing transformational learning involves epistemological change, or the construction of a new way of knowing or new frame of reference, whereas informational learning is simply collecting content knowledge. Transformational learning has an effect on the mind itself; it changes ways of knowing and can be discomforting and life changing. It is this kind of transformational learning that is the outcome most broadly associated with participation in high-impact practices. Glimmers of the transformative aspects of HIPs are reflected in the opening vignette: Jenny's story highlights the challenges and new ways of knowing she experienced through several high-impact practices. Indeed, HIPs have the potential to be life changing and transformative.

Although transformative learning is the broad goal, most high-impact practices arrived on the campus scene for a variety of practical reasons. Some experiences, such as first-year seminars, emerged in the field as an intentional way to help orient new students, facilitate their transition to college, and improve retention rates. Participation in a first-year seminar is positively associated with persistence and grades in the first year and is also credited with increasing student-faculty interaction, active learning, greater knowledge of and use of campus resources, and more participation in campus events and peer interaction (Keup & Barefoot, 2005; Pascarella & Terenzini, 2005). First-year seminars are considered nearly ubiquitous (Barefoot, 2000) and are one of the more purposeful and well-studied HIPs.

Another HIP, community-based research or service-learning, which has its roots in the 1960s Civil Rights, Peace Corps, and VISTA movements, became a recognized pedagogical practice in the 1980s with a national initiative to promote service among undergraduate students (Jacoby, 1996). Service-learning demands students learn and develop through active participation in thought-fully organized service experiences in the community, which are integrated into the academic curriculum and provide structured time for student reflection. Service-learning is associated with increased civic responsibility, gains in moral reasoning and intercultural understanding, greater commitment to the welfare of others, increased commitment to service-oriented careers, and increased ability to apply class learning to real-world situations (Brownell & Swaner, 2010; Jacoby). It also provides students personal benefits, including a feeling of well-being and giving back, and opportunities to develop close connections with peers, faculty, and community members with similar interests that ultimately may help students persist in college and graduate.

In 2007, the National Survey of Student Engagement (NSSE), an annual survey to assess student and institutional investment in effective educational practices, began reporting findings related to student participation in high-impact practices and the relationship between HIPs and student engagement.

HIPs were associated with greater student engagement overall and several were moderately related to deep learning subscales, especially integrative and reflective learning as well as self-reported gains. Notably, participation in HIPs varied by a range of institution and student characteristics. Variation in participation by student characteristics raises some concern about access to HIPs and suggests certain students (e.g., first-generation students and particular racial-ethnic groups) are underrepresented in some high-impact practices. Further discussion about access and equity will be taken up later in this chapter.

Several issues of the NSSE reports (2007, 2008, 2009, 2010, 2011) highlight results from more in-depth examinations of HIPs to understand the features that make the experiences effective. For example, after controlling for several student and institution characteristics in the 2007 NSSE, it was found that the study-abroad experience was moderately related to higher order, integrative, and reflective learning as well as self-reported gains in general education and personal-social development. Study-abroad participants were more engaged in educationally purposeful activities upon their return and reported gaining more from college compared to nonparticipants. Interestingly, the length of time of the experience did not make a difference in self-reported gains or the frequency with which students used deep learning approaches back on their home campuses; however, where the students lived while abroad did affect gains. Specifically, students who lived with host nationals (e.g., home stays) demonstrated greater integrative and reflective learning benefits and personal and social gains. These results suggest the amount of time of the study-abroad placement is not as important as whether a student has such an experience. This finding has particular implications for students who may be challenged for financial and personal reasons to spend a semester or longer abroad. In short, it supports the value of short-term abroad experiences. Even more, the benefits of study abroad are salient for the senior year. For instance, students who study abroad would benefit from additional opportunities to connect those global lessons to course work and senior-year experiences.

High-impact experiences particularly germane to the senior year include senior capstone courses, culminating projects, or comprehensive exams. Many institutions offer some form of senior culminating experience (e.g., thesis, comprehensive exam, field placement) so that students have a structured opportunity to connect what they have learned in courses with on- and off-campus activities and to integrate, synthesize, and apply knowledge. NSSE results regarding student participation in a senior culminating experience (of which about a third of students report having completed) show a net positive relationship for students who do such experiences after controlling for a host of student and institutional variables (NSSE, 2007). These students had higher scores on NSSE's benchmarks of effective educational practice and the deep approaches to learning scales as well as greater self-reported gains in learning and development (NSSE, 2007, 2009).

In addition, students reported the culminating experience contributed substantially (*quite a bit* or *very much*) to their abilities in a number of areas. The patterns of student-attributed gains differed, however, depending on the type of culminating activity (NSSE, 2007). For example, after controlling for student background and institutional characteristics, the comprehensive exam, a final project or thesis, and a presentation were linked to gains, such as writing, thinking critically and imaginatively, and synthesizing; however, there was no relationship between these activities and gains in understanding key concepts in the major. The time students invested in the senior project and extent to which faculty provided feedback made important contributions to the quality of the culminating experience. Quite simply, students whose culminating experiences required greater investments of time reported greater gains than students who devoted less time to the activities. In addition, students who met more frequently with their supervising faculty member and received clearly explicated expectations for the activity and helpful feedback reported greater gains. Finally, students whose culminating experience required a final product or performance gained more in desired areas compared with their peers who did not.

Senior capstone experiences were explicitly explored in the 2009 NSSE Annual Results via an appended set of questions administered to students from all types of majors and institutions who indicated participation in this type of programming. A large majority (87%) of these students had completed or were currently enrolled in a senior seminar or capstone course. It was most common for such courses to be taken in the student's major field or department (83.8%) and to be a requirement for graduation (93.5%). Participation in a senior capstone project had the strongest impact on the extent to which students interacted with faculty, including high levels of interaction in and out of class and time spent discussing ideas as well as getting feedback. Students varied in the amount of knowledge and skills they say they gained from seminars or capstone courses. For example, seniors most commonly reported their seminar or capstone course contributed to their growth in thinking critically and analytically, learning effectively on their own, developing intellectual curiosity, and making decisions and judgments based on evidence or reasoning. On the other hand, fewer students (though still a majority) claimed these classes helped them in their ability to make ethical choices, understand global issues, and acquire work-related knowledge and skills. Overall, seniors felt their capstone courses fostered a range of desirable learning outcomes.

Every HIP is associated with specific values and benefits. It also appears there is a cumulative benefit for involvement in several HIPs. Students who participate in multiple HIPs are more engaged overall. However, while NSSE results show participation in HIPs and other measures of engagement are positively related, the direction of the effect is difficult to determine. It is possible that students who are more engaged to begin with are also choosing to take advantage of HIPs. Notably, a report from California State University Northridge (Huber, 2010) highlights the differential value that seniors derived from participating in selected high-impact practices: service-learning, internships, senior experience, research with faculty, and study abroad. The findings indicate participation in multiple HIPs of different kinds provides greater benefit to students than participation in only one type. In addition, results suggest HIP participation serves to enhance student performance and persistence in several important ways, with traditionally underserved and low-income students often benefitting disproportionately.

Another advantage of involvement in several HIPs is these activities convey educationally productive experiences that can influence the quality and outcomes of subsequent activities leading up to and including the senior year. For example, students who have participated in undergraduate research, study abroad, or internships prior to a required senior-year project have had learning experiences that likely put them in a different developmental place than students who did not have these experiences. Likewise, students who, for example, had profound service-learning experiences in which they completed a significant community-based research project and worked with the organization to take action on the findings, might be underwhelmed if senior-year courses offer no opportunities to take their project to the next level or deepen their learning. Similarly, students who study abroad might need to reconnect with other study-abroad peers to deepen their reflection or connect to campus-based diversity initiatives to extend the transformative potential of their experience. The extent to which students have participated in HIPs is worthy of consideration in advising sessions to ensure maximum exposure and to plan for optimum educational benefit.

In sum, HIPs convey many benefits. The power of these practices to boost learning and development and provide students life changing experiences led Kuh (2008) to prescribe that every student participate in at least two *high-impact activities* during their undergraduate program—one in the first year and one later related to their major field. The obvious choices for the first year are first-year seminars, learning communities, and service-learning. In the later years of college, study abroad, internships and other field placements, and a culminating experience are all desirable. Even more, the cumulative effect of participation in multiple HIPs has the potential to contribute to achieving a coherent, transformative senior year.

HIPs and the Senior Year: Institutional Approaches

While some HIPs, such as senior capstones and internships, can plainly be implemented in the senior year as a way to cap off the degree, greater educational effect is possible when HIPs are thoughtfully sequenced throughout the undergraduate experience. Moreover, intentional staging of HIPs in the undergraduate program prior to the senior year can offer greater transformative potential. This section explores approaches to implementing HIPs to afford educational advantage in the senior year.

HIPs have developmental sequencing, with early experiences serving to introduce students to a community of learners and fostering active engagement in experiential learning early in their academic career. HIPs may be tailored to address the characteristics of entering students and special student populations or to introduce signature experiences aligned with institutional mission. Experiences in the sophomore year might emphasize connections to the academic major or to the community via service-learning, take on the challenge of cocurricular leadership, or focus on the development of particular learning outcomes (e.g., writing via writing-intensive courses). Junior year is the logical time for applied learning experiences, such as study abroad and internships. HIPs in the senior year include obvious opportunities for field experience, independent research, capstone courses, and senior projects.

Involvement in high-impact practices can offer important introductory experiences and have a cumulative effect over the course of students' educational careers. For example, Eastern Oregon University's (EOU) two-quarter first-year seminar, which includes an undergraduate research requirement, exposes the predominately first-generation student body to a supportive, but intense, academic experience early on (AAC&U, 2011). Although the primary purpose for EOU's adoption of the seminar and research experience was to employ a set of high-impact practices that encouraged retention, academic achievement, and a sense of belonging, the selection of these particular practices was also to bookend the capstone and practicum courses that were already embedded into the third and fourth years. Structuring a significant experience like this early in the students' program can successfully introduce them to the value of HIPs, better prepare them for high-impact experiences in later years, and prompt them to seek out other opportunities to participate in meaningful educational experiences in subsequent terms.

Similarly, by the time students at Indiana University-Purdue University Indianapolis (IUPUI) reach their senior year, most have participated in the institution's longstanding first-year seminars or learning communities, many of which incorporate an undergraduate research or service-learning theme. Building on their commitment to experiential learning, IUPUI formalized participation in HIPs by challenging students to include at least two of four designated RISE (research, international, service-learning, experiential learning) experiences into their degree programs. Each RISE category incorporates qualified experiences, integration of knowledge, reflection, and assessment, and is documented on students' transcripts. RISE experiences have proliferated across schools and departments to address curricular interests related to experiential learning in the disciplines as well as in general education and to assist in preparing students for careers, citizenship, and graduate school. To help guide students through their educational plan, foster goal commitment, and create meaningful opportunities to discuss curricular coherence, IUPUI implemented an advising process, the Personal Development Plan (PDP), that is introduced in the first-year seminar, to enable students to understand, implement, and mark progress toward a degree and career goal by creating and following a personalized plan that is open to revision and reevaluation every semester in collaboration with an academic advisor or faculty member.

Education at Mount Holyoke College is based in the liberal arts tradition and a long history of experiential education. To deepen these roots and build on the value of high-impact practices, Mount Holyoke strengthened opportunities for internships by embedding them within a curricular pathway called Nexus: Curriculum to Career (a 16-credit minor) that facilitates students' integration of academic and professional knowledge (Pierson & Troppe, 2010). Students in Nexus participate in a sequence of coursework, experiential learning, and critical reflection, including two introductory academic courses (four credits each) relevant to a selected track theme; one two-credit pre-experience course (Ready for the World) or a suitable social science methods course; an experiential component, such as an internship, research project, or summer job; a public presentation at the annual fall symposium; one two-credit postexperience course (Tying it all Together) to integrate their professional experience into their academic pathway; and one 300-level, four-credit course in a relevant topic. Mount Holyoke also strives to make internships accessible to all students by offering financial assistance available through a centralized funding process administered by the Career Development Center. Students may apply for merit-based internship or research fellowships issued annually from the college. All students participating in these high-impact practices can present at the fall symposium, which provides students returning from summer internship and research projects an opportunity to reflect critically on how their learning experiences outside the classroom connect to their coursework. The intentional sequencing and investment in internships and undergraduate research has not only made high-impact practices more available and meaningful for students, but it has also fostered greater opportunities for integrating content knowledge and experience, and coherency in the senior year.

The implementation of a significantly revised general education program in the mid-1990s at Portland State University (PSU), designed to engage students actively in their education and to emphasize student-faculty interactions throughout the program, placed increased emphasis on high-impact practices for all students (White, 1994). The core components of PSU's University Studies are the Freshman Inquiry course, thematic course clusters for sophomore through senior levels, and the senior capstone experience. A strength of this model is in its staged approach, beginning with the required year-long Freshman Inquiry course and culminating in the capstone class, which consists of teams of students from different majors working together to complete a project addressing a real problem in the Portland metropolitan community. The senior capstone provides an opportunity for students to apply the expertise learned in the major to real issues and problems while cultivating crucial life abilities, including establishing connections within the larger community, developing strategies for analyzing and addressing problems, and working with others trained in different fields.

As the discussion about capstone courses in chapter 5 illustrates, there are many ways to operationalize capstone experiences, including as an independent study, a course required for the major, an interdisciplinary experience, a comprehensive exam, or a field-based project. Although capstone courses are generally designed to foster integration, synthesis, and application as well as facilitate the transition to life after college, they should be carefully tailored to ensure the experience reflects the institution's academic mission and builds on students' prior experiential learning and, particularly, the HIPs in which the institution has invested. Thus, adding a senior capstone course without scaffolding experiences to lead up to it, or failing to take into account students earlier experiences with HIPs, falls short of advantaging the cumulative power of high-impact practices.

Senior culminating experiences provide great benefits to students in terms of capping off their undergraduate experience. In addition, these experiences can offer a natural opportunity for educational assessment. The culminating aspects of capstone courses and projects provide an occasion for departments and units to learn more about the overall quality of the educational program. For example, institutions can make use of student work produced in senior capstone courses to assess institutional learning outcomes, such as writing, critical thinking, or integrative learning. Examining institutional learning outcomes across majors may also provide an opportunity to exchange effective teaching and learning approaches. Academic departments may wish to use a rubric to assess specific skills and content knowledge evident in senior papers or projects. These assessment results could be used to document quality in the undergraduate experience or to identify areas in need of improvement. For instance, a department that is disappointed in the level of integrative learning demonstrated in senior projects may decide to introduce intentionally blended or linked assignments and experiences in required sophomore- and junior-year courses to provide students early integrative learning experiences. Results of student performance in the capstone should be used to improve the pathway leading to the capstone.

High-impact practices hold great promise for enriching quality in undergraduate education and providing students meaningful educational experiences upon which to build and grow. Yet, if high-impact practices are to become part of more students' undergraduate experience, then colleges and universities, departments, and general education units need to establish more intentional structures and appropriate sequencing for HIPs.

Considerations for HIPs

HIPs offer transformative learning opportunities for all students. Nevertheless, if left to their own devices, many students and faculty members will simply not participate in HIPs. To encourage greater involvement, institutions must create roadmaps and incentives to induce purposeful behavior toward these ends. The University of Wisconsin Madison (n.d.), for example, published a summary of HIPs available in the first year (i.e., First-Year Interest Groups, Undergraduate Research Scholars), throughout the college (i.e., study abroad, aspects of the general education requirements related to writing and diversity), and in the final years (i.e., capstones, senior thesis) to help foster greater awareness among faculty and advisors about their availability. Some institutions have made experiences unavoidable by assigning all students to a first-year seminar; requiring two or more writing-intensive courses across the majors; or expecting students to do some form of culminating senior experience (e.g., field placement, internship, capstone project or paper). More students would take advantage of HIPs if they were well-planned or required.

As indicated earlier, examinations of students' participation in HIPs suggests some systematic variation by student and institutional characteristics. For example, transfer students are less likely to participate in all HIPs; African American students participate in study abroad at half the rates of White students; business majors have very low rates of participation in undergraduate research; and students at baccalaureate liberal arts colleges are more likely to participate in a range of HIPs than students at all other institutional types (NSSE, 2010). These disparities indicate uneven access to HIPs and suggest greater efforts must be made to remove barriers and ensure underrepresented student participation.

Although aggregate differences in participation exist, colleges and universities can learn more about the promise of HIPs by examining participation within their own institutions. For example, California State University Northridge (CSUN) discovered access to HIPs does not vary by the socioeconomic background of their diverse students, but that students from disadvantaged backgrounds benefit disproportionately by participating in multiple high-impact practices (Huber, 2010). CSUN's report concluded insofar as academic departments already offer an array of courses encompassing HIPs, encouraging their majors to engage in different types may require only small curricular changes and might yield a significant increase in student success and persistence. The University of Wisconsin Eau Claire is using its NSSE data to examine underserved students' (i.e., first-generation and/or low-income) access to high-impact practices and is striving to remove barriers to their participation. Looking at institutional data about students' involvement in HIPs is an important first step to determining access and equity. Even more, evidence HIPs convey greater benefits to students historically underrepresented in higher education makes it imperative to ensure access.

While participation in high-impact practices can be a powerful contributor to learning, achieving this outcome requires careful structuring and supervision of the students' experience. Poorly structured service-learning, undergraduate research, or internship programs that are not well integrated with the academic curriculum, or that fail to optimize the six conditions known to make HIPs effective, will make less of a contribution to student learning even though they may help students develop in other ways (Eyler, 2009; Kuh, 2008; Vogelgesang & Astin, 2000). Internship or service-learning programs may claim to connect experience and learning but fail to provide the reflective experiences to make this happen. In addition to the vagaries of individual implementation, some models for HIPs are more likely than others to include the six conditions and other important features that make a particular HIP educationally effective. For example, structured reflection in service-learning and faculty mentoring in undergraduate research are vital aspects of these experiences. Assessing the extent to which the six conditions and the critical features of specific HIPs are prominent is important to assuring high-quality experiences.

Institutions seeking to maximize the promise of HIPs might consider the following questions to examine access, equity, and quality:

- What curricular structures (i.e., PSU's revised general education program) or educational practices (i.e., IUPUI's Personal Development Plan) could best foster students' participation in HIPs?

- Are HIPs sequenced to encourage cumulative benefit? To what extent are students advised into experiences, and how are HIPs used in the senior year?

- How widespread and available are HIPs? Are some student populations (i.e., racial and/or ethnic groups, low-income or transfer students) or major fields systematically underrepresented?

- What barriers exist to greater participation in HIPs? How might these be eliminated?

- How is the quality of HIPs monitored? How prominent are the six conditions and other critical features of specific HIPs? Are HIPs providing maximum educational impact?

- How might senior culminating experiences be advantaged as an opportunity to assess learning outcomes and provide departments and units information about educational quality? What needs improvement in the pathway leading to the capstone? What mechanisms exist to facilitate this feedback loop?

High-impact practices have the potential to provide transformative learning experiences that position students well for their final college year and for life after college. HIPs are effective because they harness conditions that support and challenge students and put them in situations in which they are in charge of their active and reflective learning. Yet, to leverage the full transformative power of HIPs, colleges and universities must intentionally optimize the experiential learning opportunities available to students leading up to and including the senior year.

References

Association of American Colleges & Universities (AAC& U). (2007). *College learning for a new global century: A report from the National Leadership Council for Liberal Education and America's Promise*. Retrieved from http://www.aacu.org/advocacy/leap/documents/GlobalCentury_final.pdf

Association of American Colleges & Universities (AAC& U). (2011, January/February). Engaging students with high-impact practices at Eastern Oregon University. *AAC&U News: Insights and Campus Innovations in Liberal Education*. Retrieved from http://www.aacu.org/aacu_news/AACUNews11/February11/feature.cfm

Barefoot, B. O. (2000) The first-year experience: Are we making it any better? *About Campus, 4*(6), 12-18.

Brownell, J. E., & Swaner, L. E. (2010). *Five high-impact practices: Research on learning outcomes, completion, and quality*. Washington, DC: Association of American Colleges & Universities.

Dewey, J. (1997). *Experience and education*. New York, NY: Simon & Schuster.

Eyler, J. (2009). *Effective practice and experiential education* (Paper commissioned for the conference on Liberal Education and Effective Practice). Retrieved from http://www.clarku.edu/aboutclark/pdfs/EYLER%20FINAL.pdf

Huber, B. J. (2010). *Does participation in multiple high-impact practices affect student success at Cal State Northridge? Some preliminary insights*. Retrieved from http://calstate.edu/app/compass/documents/CSUN-Participation-Multiple-High-Impact-Practices.pdf

Jacoby, B. (1996). Service-learning in today's higher education. In B. Jacoby & Associates, (Eds.), *Service-learning in higher education: Concepts and practices* (pp. 3-25). San Francisco, CA: Jossey-Bass.

Kegan, R. (2000). What "form" transforms?: A constructive-developmental approach to transformative learning. In J. Mezirow (Ed.) & Associates, *Learning as transformation* (pp. 3- 34). San Francisco, CA: Jossey-Bass.

Keup, J. R., & Barefoot, B. O. (2005). Learning how to be a successful student: Exploring the impact of first-year seminars on student outcomes. *Journal of The First-Year Experience & Students in Transition, 17*(1), 11-47.

Kolb, D. A. (1984). *Experiential learning as the source of learning and development.* Englewood Cliffs, NJ: Prentice Hall.

Kuh, G. D. (2008). *High-impact educational practices: What they are, who has access to them, and why they matter.* Washington, DC: American Association for Colleges & Universities.

National Survey of Student Engagement (NSSE). (2007). *Experiences that matter: Enhancing student learning and success: NSSE 2007 annual report.* Bloomington, IN: Indiana University.

National Survey of Student Engagement (NSSE). (2008). *Promoting engagement for all students: The imperative to look within—2008 results.* Bloomington, IN: Indiana University Center for Postsecondary Research.

National Survey of Student Engagement (NSSE). (2009). *Assessment for improvement: Tracking student engagement over time: Annual results 2009.* Bloomington, IN: Indiana University Center for Postsecondary Research.

National Survey of Student Engagement (NSSE). (2010*). Major differences: Examining student engagement by field of study: Annual results 2010.* Bloomington, IN: Indiana University Center for Postsecondary Research.

National Survey of Student Engagement (NSSE). (2011*). Fostering student engagement campuswide: Annual results 2011.* Bloomington, IN: Indiana University Center for Postsecondary Research.

Pascarella E. T., & Terenzini, P. T. (1991). *How college affects students: Findings and insights from twenty years of research.* San Francisco, CA: Jossey-Bass.

Pascarella E. T., & Terenzini, P. T. (2005). *How college affects students: A third decade of research* (Volume 2). San Francisco, CA: Jossey-Bass.

Pierson, M., & Troppe, M. (2010). Curriculum to career. *Peer Review, 12*(4). Retrieved from the Association of American College and Universities website: http://www.aacu.org/peerreview/pr-fa10/pr-fa10_curriculum.cfm

Salisbury, M., & Goodman, K. (2009). Educational practices that foster intercultural competence. *Diversity & Democracy, 12*(2), 12-13.

Vogelgesang, L., & Astin, A. W. (2000), Comparing the effects of community service and service-learning. *Michigan Journal of Community Service Learning, 7,* 25-34.

University of Wisconsin Madison. (n.d.*). High-impact educational practices at UW-Madison.* Retrieved from https://tle.wisc.edu/node/1034

White, C. R. (1994). A model for comprehensive reform in general education: Portland State University. *The Journal of General Education, 43*(3), 168-237.

CHAPTER
Five

Senior Seminars and
Capstone Courses

Jean M. Henscheid

Given options for their final project, a group of seniors majoring in landscape architecture and enrolled in a year-long senior capstone course chose to complete their project at a community service site many of them had visited in their first year—Roosevelt High School. The inner-city school had recently received a grant from the district to turn a blighted corner of the campus into a green space, and the university students wanted to help design and build it. The capstone instructor had connected with a creative writing faculty member in periodic cross-disciplinary capstone design conversations, and from discussions with the campus service-learning coordinator, they learned the high school's students had voted to have the green space include a permanent exhibit of Roosevelt Heroes, stories of exceptional individuals who had graduating from the school since its opening in 1901. The two instructors collaborated in planning their capstone courses to allow students in both capstones to work together designing and building the space and researching and writing the profiles of the Roosevelt Heroes. Assignments were created to help the students demonstrate learning as it related to the university's vision for undergraduate education and the institution-wide learning outcomes. Activities allowed students to become increasingly autonomous. By the end of the year, the students were fully in charge of all aspects of the project. The Roosevelt Heroes Green Space, built collaboratively by the university students and several high school students, was officially opened during a public ceremony attended by hundreds of Roosevelt High alumni and students, the university students, the university president, members of the school board, and the mayor of the city.

Effective senior seminars and capstone courses provide students at the end of their undergraduate experience opportunities to demonstrate they are prepared to apply the knowledge and skills gained in college to tasks they and others value. These model, culminating classroom experiences are designed around activities that encourage the highest engagement of students, including field placements, time-intensive projects, work in groups, meetings with supervising faculty, and assignments with clear expectations (Kinzie, McCormick, & Nelson Laird, 2010). The research of learning theorists (Paige, 2010; van Merriënboer, Kirschner, & Kester, 2003) and reports from students (Kinzie et al., 2010) suggest these are the types of experiences that lead to both engagement and the greatest gains in complex cognitive and social skills.

This chapter explores a process for designing and delivering senior seminars and capstone courses. This process and its variations, used especially for fostering complex learning, are based in the growing recognition that creating effective senior seminars and capstone courses includes the thoughtful and coordinated planning of courses students complete prior to their senior year in both general education and the academic major. Underlying this process is the assumption that the level of learning evidenced as students end college is directly related to the quality of scaffolding for learning built prior to the final year. The processes used to design and deliver complex learning experiences for seniors are built on a second assumption that a community of educators has committed to a set of methods for helping students achieve desired levels of learning. A third assumption is that what counts as learning for these students is decided, and acted, on by a community of educators.

The chapter begins by making the case that the current outcomes-based education movement has been most important in prompting institutions to turn to the kind of course design process that elevates the importance of senior seminars and capstone courses. The ironic twist to this argument is that the design of effective culminating courses does not begin with intense perseveration on outcomes but with agreement on the kinds of activities resulting in overall student learning and development. These activities are the course-based equivalent of high-impact practices (HIPs) described in chapter 4. This chapter will then turn to institutional examples illustrating how the process for designing effective senior seminars and capstone courses works. While others may use alternate terms to describe the methods they employ to develop culminating courses for seniors, the process outlined in this chapter fairly represents current practices in the design of courses that support the kind of complex learning identified as the hallmark of a college education (AAC&U, 2007). Whether implicitly or explicitly, then, senior seminars and capstone courses are increasingly designed by

- establishing values and products of the course,
- selecting methods for learning,
- establishing the role of the instructor,
- building in increasing complexity and student independence,
- committing to depth of study,
- committing to collaboration, and
- determining individual and group learning assessment and feedback procedures.

The process, referred to as *senior-level course design*, is both descriptive of current practices and prescriptive. As laid out here, it may be useful as a guide for designing or retooling existing senior seminars and capstone courses and, equally important, the courses that precede them.

Increasing Importance of Seniors Seminars and Capstone Courses

From the inveterate professor teaching her 25th senior capstone in physics to the provost preparing for a reaffirmation of accreditation site visit, college educators at every level and of every stripe are increasingly training their attention on answering three questions: (a) What do we want students to learn? (b) How can we help them learn it? and (c) How will we know if they have learned it? The reasons these questions undergird most current conversations about and in higher education are legion and exhaustively documented elsewhere (e.g., Arum & Roksa, 2011; Deresiewicz, 2011; Fischer, 2011). In brief, these questions are more widely asked now because recent advances in cognitive science have put scholars and educators in a better position to explore possible answers. Questions like these are also increasingly raised by critics with suspicions (and some evidence) that higher education is not structured well enough to answer them or to care enough about the answers. From both fronts, these questions about student learning are the basis for the latest calls for outcomes-based education, an approach that requires students to demonstrate they have learned desired content and skills. In 2002, a singular event prompting institutions in the United States to relook at outcomes-based education came with the release of an Association of American Colleges and Universities (AAC&U) report regarding the role of higher education today and in the future, including central aims and essential practices. Many of the action steps writers of this report suggested had direct and profound implications for courses intended to culminate the undergraduate experience, where final learning outcomes should be demonstrated. Along with the specific recommendation that all seniors at every institution should complete an integrative, capstone experience, the report called for institutions to build toward these capstone experiences by

- producing standards and assessments that focus on intellectual capacities and reflect the complex nature of learning and learning styles;

- basing institutional accountability on demonstrated student success in achieving liberal education outcomes;

- setting explicit goals for individual student learning so academic department and general education outcomes can align with them;

- implementing curricula to develop student knowledge and intellectual capacities cumulatively and sequentially, drawing on all types of courses (e.g., general education, the major, electives) and noncourse experiences;

- having faculty members across disciplines and departments assume collective responsibility for the entire curriculum to ensure every student an enriching liberal education; and

- requiring faculty members to focus on important student outcomes, regularly assess student progress, base teaching on research about learning, and raise expectations of student achievement.

Notably, the capstone is the only course specifically identified in the 2002 AAC&U report for inclusion in the curriculum of every institution. The opportunity, and burden, for designers of these courses is to organize student experiences around activities that allow them to demonstrate what they have learned throughout college. Gardner and Van der Veer were prescient in 1998 when they predicted the senior seminar or capstone would increasingly become the seat for determining how and whether students had learned in college. They may or may not have predicted that, a few years later, a national call would go out recommending every college and university create a course with this as its central purpose.

Designing Courses for Complex Learning

While colleges and universities continue to build curricula by first distinguishing between courses students will complete in general education from those they will complete in the academic major, these distinctions are becoming less salient under outcomes-based education. The more important conversation centers on collectively determining the levels and types of skills and knowledge students will attain in college and designing curricular and cocurricular pathways for students to achieve these desired outcomes. The AAC&U's (2007) Liberal Education and America's Promise (LEAP) report was most influential in guiding decisions at institutions across the country about what students should know and be able to do as a result of college attendance. The report's essential learning outcomes have now been used as the basis for lists of similar outcomes tailored to the contexts of campuses throughout the United States.

The Essential Learning Outcomes

It is recommended a senior capstone or seminar at every institution be used to allow students to demonstrate learning across the following outcomes:

- *Knowledge of human cultures and the physical and natural world*. Beginning in school, and continuing at successively higher levels across their college studies, students should prepare for 21st-century challenges through study in the sciences and mathematics, social sciences, humanities, histories, languages, and the arts.

- *Intellectual and practical skills*. Focused by engagement with big questions, both contemporary and enduring, these skills include

  ○ inquiry and analysis,

  ○ critical and creative thinking,

  ○ written and oral communication,

  ○ quantitative literacy,

  ○ information literacy, and

  ○ teamwork and problem solving.

- *Personal and social responsibility*. Practiced extensively, across the curriculum, in the context of progressively more challenging problems, projects, and standards for performance, students should acquire

  - civic knowledge and engagement—local and global,
  - intercultural knowledge and competence,
  - ethical reasoning and action, and
  - foundations and skills for lifelong learning.

- *Integrative learning*. Anchored in active involvement with diverse communities and real-world challenges, students gain mastery by means of synthesis and advanced accomplishment across general and specialized studies and demonstrate integrative learning through the application of knowledge, skills, and responsibilities to new settings and complex problems.

Starting Course Design With Outcomes: The Problem

One ironic by-product of this push for outcomes-based education is the growing recognition that leading a course design process with identifying its learning outcomes frequently devolves into unhelpful generalities, philosophical knots, and sophistries (Knight, 2001). This concern is particularly acute at the senior course level where the outcomes of an entire undergraduate experience may be at issue. In a particularly harsh critique of outcomes-based education, Hussey and Smith (2002) suggested launching course designs with outcomes may, in actuality, do more harm than good.

> We are not denying the need for educators to indicate to, or discuss with, their pupils what is to be covered in a teaching session or what they are expected to learn, but we are claiming that the use of learning outcomes, as currently understood, can be damaging to education. Learning outcomes have value when properly conceived and used in ways that respect their limitations and exploit their virtues, but they are damaging to education if seen as precise prescriptions that must be spelled out in detail before teaching can begin … (p. 222)

Extended discussions about the *what* of teaching, these authors argue, may impede progress toward coming to agreement on the equally important *how* of teaching. Anyone with experience as a member of an institution-level curriculum committee or academic department curriculum team is likely to recognize the kind of scenario Hussey and Smith fear: After significant wrangling, including heated discussion around the purposes of higher education and/or a specific degree program, the group devises a list of learning outcomes that receives a majority vote and appropriate approvals outside the committee. The list is then used to structure an administrative accountability system where data on student-level or programwide achievement of those outcomes are to be collected. The outcomes may, at worst, merely make an appearance at the top of individual course syllabi. More earnest faculty members may attempt to describe where in the course students will be exposed to these outcomes. According to Knight (2001), the all-important answer to the How question in such a scenario is missing. The problem, he says, "comes when precise outcomes are linked with indeterminate processes" (p. 381).

Knight (2001) argues the outcomes-first approach to course design is especially problematic when demonstrations of complex learning are desired. Complex learning, as established in the mid-20th century by Bruner (1996), is distinguished by the level of autonomy expected of the learner in her or his ability to do something with the subject. If the activity, or what Knight refers to as the encounter, is paramount in complex learning, why would one not start with a description of that activity in course design? Knight suggests it is

> better to concentrate on the processes that might lead to the sorts of outcomes that are wanted, to provide ingredients from which a meal can be created, rather than to insist on cooking to a recipe. Applied to curriculum, this insight suggests that planning starts by imagining how to draw together the processes, encounters or engagements that make for good learning. (p. 375)

Fortunately, educators responsible for designing curricular learning experiences to promote complex learning have abundant examples for determining activities in course design first. According to Elliott (2000), educators in the Pacific Rim are increasingly turning toward answering the How question before, but importantly not to the exclusion of, answering the What question. Desired learning outcomes are used later in the design process to hold the activity up to scrutiny to determine if it is worthwhile. This process is similar to that advocated by Stenhouse (1975) who recommended curriculum be viewed as a set of worthwhile activities related to important material within the expectations of a subject community. Knight (2001) points out elementary and secondary teachers have long used this activities-first outcomes-later approach. Teachers at these levels organize content and match it to learning activities that have, in the past, achieved their instructional plan. Once the learning activities are imagined, the teachers consider learning outcomes as a check against the quality of their plan and to retool that plan as necessary to increase the likelihood students will achieve desired outcomes. In this process model of course design, outcomes are critical, but they are not considered first.

Adoption of this process may also begin to put to rest the debate over the appropriate place in the curriculum for senior seminars and capstone courses, alternately advocated for as a requirement of general education and as a requirement of the academic major. Evidence from the 2011 National Survey of Senior Capstone Experiences indicates 84.7% of colleges and universities incorporate a discipline-based capstone course into the curriculum (Padgett & Kilgo, 2012). And still, promoters of general education argue that offering the culminating course outside the academic major affords opportunities especially for synthesis, reflection, and assessment of the student's learning across the entire undergraduate experience (Fernandez, 2006). Under a process model of course design, the decision about the curricular location of the capstone or senior seminar is driven by knowing *where* students have the greatest opportunities for engaging in activities designed to promote complex learning. Whether those opportunities are in general education or in the academic major is a secondary consideration.

Senior-Level Course Design

The senior-level course design outlined below is an adaptation of Knight's (2001) process approach to curriculum development and an example of what Argyris and Schön (1974, 1996) label a *theory-in-use* (what people actually do) versus an *espoused theory* (what people say when they try to describe, explain, or predict their behavior). Outcomes-based education, used as a linear prescription, would have course designers plan activities after solidifying learning outcomes. This espoused theory contrasts to the methods actually more often employed and advocated for in a process approach to course design, as outlined below. A wide variety of senior seminars and capstone courses, across disciplines and types of institutions, have been produced by this theory-in-use and are offered below as exemplars of experiences that foster complex learning among seniors.

As noted at the beginning of this chapter, a process approach to course design assumes the senior year is not the first exposure students have to the kind and quality of learning expected in the senior seminar or capstone. Coherent, articulated supports to build the student's capacity for achieving learning at levels the institution considers acceptable for its graduates are assumed to have been present from the beginning. As noted earlier, this approach to design of senior seminars and capstones also assumes that a community of educators, either across campus or within an academic unit, has agreed to the methods to be used to help students learn, the kind of learning expected, and the level at which students will be considered ready to graduate. Again, the seven steps of a process I have labeled senior-level course design are

1. establishing values and products of course,

2. selecting methods for learning,

3. establishing the role of the instructor,

4. building in increasing complexity and student independence,

5. committing to depth of study,

6. committing to collaboration, and

7. determining individual and group learning assessment and feedback procedures.

Examples of courses developed through this process are offered below.

Step 1: Establishing Values and Products of the Course

More often than in other undergraduate courses, the senior seminar or capstone course asks students to demonstrate they have learned important concepts or skills by generating an original product, performance, or project relevant to those concepts and/or skills. A first step in process course design is determining the nature of that values-driven artifact.

At Philadelphia University, for example, the capstone course for general education asks students to complete a seminar project that establishes how well they have internalized the liberal-professional mission of the institution. Students produce original work that demonstrates their learning as it relates to this mission by analyzing how a global issue has impacted their intended profession. The Integrative Learning Project at Salve Regina University in Rhode Island, completed as part of the Core Curriculum capstone, asks students to demonstrate their level of understanding of the institution's four goals: (a) education with a Catholic identity; (b) liberal education, (c) responsible citizens of the world, and (d) lifelong learners. As is the case for students at many institutions, seniors at Salve Regina are allowed to choose from various mediums (e.g., writing, performance, art) to convey their understanding of these goals. In Ohio, Miami University's Urban Leadership Internship program immerses students in an experience that aligns with the institution's interest in developing students as scholars. The program requires that students create a tangible product at sophistication levels worthy of the label *scholarly output*. At these and other institutions, building courses that foster complex learning at the senior level begins with asking and answering two questions: (a) What is the overarching takeaway lesson for students who have completed an education here? and (b) What product will be the centerpiece of this course that will allow them to demonstrate they have learned this lesson?

Step 2: Selecting Methods for Learning

Once the centerpiece project is selected, developers of courses intended to foster complex learning at the senior level consider what methods students will employ to complete that project. Portland State University's capstone, Portland 2003: Oregon Community Visions, allowed students to work with the mayor's office, City of Portland staff, and other members of the community to begin implementation of the city's new vision. Methods for completing this project included conducting research, attending community meetings, drafting ideas and plans, and working with community organizations. Each aspect of the course related to completion of the end product. Students involved in the Mexica program at Southern Illinois University Edwardsville also focus the entirety of their learning experience in the capstone on completion of one project, a major exhibition of artworks inspired by their experience learning weaving and ceramic skills from indigenous artists in Tlaxiaco, a small town in Oaxaca State. Organizing and advertising the exhibition and the accompanying gala reception culminates the weeks-long trip to Mexico, an experience students report as being one of the most profound of their college careers (Sill, Harward, & Cooper, 2009). The Senior Year Experience at Otterbein College in Ohio offers seniors the opportunity to integrate learning from the academic major, the college's Integrative Studies program, and elective courses through one large final project. Saint Louis University's Senior Legacy Symposium showcases students' academic accomplishments through display of their original work. Monmouth College in Illinois asks students to build on their past studies to address important social issues through final individual and group projects. Across institutions, every learning opportunity at the end of the student's academic career is linked in meaningful ways to the final project.

Step 3: Establishing the Role of the Instructor

Instructors in courses designed to foster complex learning at the senior level typically assume a supportive advisory role as students complete the culminating project or prepare for a final performance. This may be particularly true in online academic environments where new technologies allow learner-directed, project-based learning to replace teacher-directed content delivery (Smith, 2002). These online environments support the notion that knowledge is constructed. In distributed learning environments, "teaching is akin to coaching, and learning is active or interactive" (Smith, 2002, p. 40).

Whether in the traditional or online classroom, such an approach may be seen as sympathetic coaching (Keagan, 1994). As a coach, the instructor understands and acknowledges the student's current level of expertise while encouraging higher levels of achievement. Educators typically see themselves in this facilitative role as graduate students complete original research or generate new knowledge and are increasingly being called on to assume this coaching role throughout graduate education (Bot, Gossiaux, Rauch, & Tabiou, 2005; Gunzenhauser & Gerstl-Pepin, 2006). Likewise, instructors of senior seminars and capstone courses designed to facilitate complex learning view themselves as coaches.

At Pennsylvania's Allegheny College, where a capstone experience has existed since 1821, a senior-project advisor works with each student to prepare him or her for review of the project, which is completed by a second faculty reader and project review board. The Capstone Seminar II in Environmental Science at California State University Monterey Bay (CSUMB) provides a typical example of the instructor's role in a culminating senior course. In the syllabus, students are introduced to their last academic task before graduating and how their instructor will help them complete it.

> The final requirement for your degree in ESTP is your capstone. In completing your capstone, you will further develop and demonstrate your ability to use an integrated ESTP approach to address current environmental issues. Capstone Seminar provides the structure and support you need to ensure that by the end of the semester you have

produced a capstone project that meets all of the required capstone outcomes. Capstone Seminar will guide you through the various stages of the capstone process starting from identifying what it means to develop an interdisciplinary ESTP capstone project and ending with the oral presentation of your capstone project. *My role as capstone coordinator is to facilitate this process* [emphasis added]. (CSUMB, 2012, para. 3)

Step 4: Building in Increasing Complexity and Student Independence

This aspect of senior-level course design is highly dependent on students' previous exposure to the methods and outcomes that will be used for learning experiences they will encounter in their final year. The assumption is that tasks they will be asked to replicate, at increased levels of sophistication, will be introduced in their first year and that feedback on their progress will support their efforts to improve over time. This scaffolding to foster complex learning presumes that early in college, students will engage in original research, field placements, study abroad, service-learning, and other opportunities to test out their capacity for complex learning (see discussion of HIPs in chapter 4). The learning outcomes related to this work in the first year will match those in their senior year with the difference being expected levels of achievement.

AAC&U's (n.d.) Valid Assessment of Learning in Undergraduate Education (VALUE) project is guiding the work of many campuses as they design series of courses (and cocurricular experiences) to foster increasingly sophisticated levels of student learning up to and including the senior year. Through this project, 15 *metarubrics*—statements of expected learning—have been developed and are being used to inform instructors and instructional teams about what assignments are effectively supporting learning at beginning (benchmark), intermediate (milestone), and mastery (capstone) levels. The rubrics are intended to be tailored for use in different contexts to serve as a set of expectations students and educators hold in common across courses and academic disciplines.

Developers of senior seminars and capstones are using these and other explicit statements of expected learning in designing opportunities for students to demonstrate what they have achieved in college. The VALUE rubrics have been introduced for capstone use at a number of institutions, including the University of Wisconsin-Oshkosh, the College of Wooster in Ohio, Baruch College-City University of New York, California's San Jose State University, the University of North Carolina at Chapel Hill, Indiana University-Purdue University Indianapolis, and the University of Delaware. As of January 2012, nearly 80 partner institutions were listed by AAC&U (n.d.) as using the VALUE project's metarubrics and providing the organization feedback. A wide variety of courses across disciplines, including senior seminars and capstone, are increasingly being designed to allow students to demonstrate their progress toward the capstone level of learning as measured by these metarubrics.

Step 5: Committing to Depth of Study

Senior seminars and capstone courses designed to foster complex learning do not suffer from the kind of content overload that cognitive psychologists have identified as preventing meaningful and useful understanding (Paige, 2010; Sweller, 1988; Sweller, van Merriënboer, & Paas, 1998). The single topic explored by students in these courses is typically personally relevant and selected to showcase the progress they have made over time in learning important content and skills.

Philadelphia University's required capstone asks students to select just one global issue they believe has altered the context of their chosen profession and explore that issue in depth through a term-long project. New York's LaGuardia Community College fine arts capstone studio project asks for similar depth of study. As they end their LaGuardia experience, students choose a single topic to link museum research, a mixed media project, a written research paper, and reflection to demonstrate their learning. Augustana College in Illinois offers a flexible menu of projects to allow students to choose how they will demonstrate learning. Students may decide to conduct laboratory research, create a portfolio of artwork, compose a work of music, or conduct classroom research on their student teaching experience. A public Celebration of Learning Student Research Symposium at Augustana, first held in 1997, provides these advanced students the opportunity to share the results of their work with the campus community and online (e.g., YouTube). In every case, these courses assume meaningful learning comes through in-depth study.

Step 6: Committing to Collaboration

Learning environments are comprised of discourses, practices, interactions, tasks, patterns of power, and resources (Knight, 2001) where students learn through the instructor's designed curriculum and with the help of others sharing the experience—their peers. An effective senior seminar or capstone course is one that allows students to practice their increasing understanding with the help of others through group work, peer evaluation, interpersonal contact, and opportunities to build networks with others in the class and beyond. Researchers involved in Project DEEP (Documenting Effective Educational Practice) discovered "Teaching, assisting, and evaluating peers places students at the center of their learning experiences. They learn to work as colleagues with faculty mentors and realize they are able to help others learn" (Kuh, Kinzie, Schuh, & Whitt, 2005, p. 195). Learning from, and with, their peers is well established as an important ingredient in the cognitive and social development of college students (Ender & Newton, 2000; Hunter, 2004).

The capstone experience at the Johnston Center for Integrative Studies, an alternative education program at the University of Redlands in California provides one intensive example. Typically as part of finalizing their contract for graduation, Johnston students are encouraged to teach, or coteach with their peers, a course that best exemplifies their accumulated learning. While a faculty adviser contributes to the syllabus, the students are in charge. Previous courses taught by Johnston Students include Books That Make You Want to Write, Feminism in Literature, Media Bias, Woodworking Haphazardly, Survivalism, Ecology and Interactions, Ecofeminism, Industriomasculinity, Nietzsche's Philosophy, and Sustainable Agriculture. More typical are capstones like that offered to literature majors at Appalachian State University in North Carolina. Prior to graduation, students complete the literature capstone project, reflective statement, and public presentation with reliance on support and guidance from faculty and their peers. The University of South Florida's Foundations of Knowledge and Learning Core Curriculum dictates skill development at all levels, including the capstone, with a reliance on peer-to-peer learning. The peer-based discussion seminar, IDST 4930 Liberal Studies Capstone, is completed by liberal studies students in the first term of their senior year at Georgia College. Working together, students apply advanced interdisciplinary material to contemporary social issues. Knight (2001) notes, whether the academic task demands it or not, collaboration is present in any environment intended to foster complex learning.

Step 7: Determining Individual and Group Learning Assessment and Feedback Procedures

If students know what sort of learning is intended, then their achievements tend to be better (Flavell, Miller, & Miller, 1993). While this statement seems axiomatic, in many undergraduate courses, the type and quality of learning expected is opaque to students. Huber (1992) even went so far as to suggest too many college professors hide expectations about learning as well as a cat guards cream. Expectations in senior seminars and capstone courses, on the other hand, are among the most transparent of any in the undergraduate curriculum. Those courses designed to facilitate complex learning follow the advice of Knight (2000) who suggests that they provide clear process standards for students and then help students make claims about their levels of achievement of these standards. Finally, these courses use assessment systems as venues for communication in the network impacted by the product or products of the student's work. Groups interested in and consumers of the product of an advanced college student's work are typically much broader than those for products of student work earlier in the curriculum. This farther-reaching interest requires greater collaboration in design of senior seminar or capstone course activities and assessments of those activities. While Ewell (2004) has argued this type of assessment—collective, coherent, and connected—is necessary throughout the undergraduate curriculum, designers of senior seminars and capstone courses intended to foster complex learning are most adept at enacting this vision.

The list of questions students may address in the reflective component of Augustana College's Senior Inquiry (SI) course are indicative of the broad impact expected of the student's work and of the intense level of reflection on the sources of their learning.

> Who outside of Augustana would care about my SI project? Who are my conversation partners in this discussion? What did I learn from this project? What do I know now that I didn't know before? Communities are constructed in part by ideas and values: What are the essential ideas that my project offers or advances? How does my project question or test received wisdom? How did my education at Augustana prepare me to do this properly? And what will my education and this project prepare me for? How will this work relate to future goals? What will the meaning of this work be to me in five years? In fifty? What questions did this project fail to answer? How did the experience change my view of the discipline? What are the implications of my work for those in my field? What community does my project contribute to? What did I do for my projects? Why did I do this project? What difference does it make? Why might this matter? How does this project fit into my story? Why do I care about it? Who was I when I came to Augustana, and who am I now? (Schermer, 2009, p. 25)

Use of information and communications technologies is now standard for widening the reach and impact of the work students produce in advanced undergraduate courses, including senior seminars and capstone courses. Over the years, a number of capstone courses in Portland State University's Senior Inquiry program have resulted in web-based products useful to the larger community. Past products have included information websites on nearby Johnson Creek, the Columbia Slough, living with colon cancer, motor vehicle fuels, and the middle ages. In a project piloted at Washington State University (Brown, DesRosier, Peterson, Chida, & Lagier, 2009), 87 students enrolled in a business marketing course were asked to use blogs to create an electronic poster for a portfolio presentation of their market forecasting project. They presented their poster for formative feedback at midterm and were asked to revise the electronic poster as a final project. Six industry professionals representing companies with global distribution networks participated in assessing the students' work as did seven faculty members in the program and the course instructor. Students also rated themselves and each other using the same critical thinking rubric as the working professionals and instructor group.

Electronic portfolios are also increasingly used to allow students in senior seminars and capstone courses to demonstrate and reflect on their learning and to disseminate the products of their learning. Assessments of these portfolios are increasingly being carried out by individuals representing a variety of stake-holder groups. In 2006, Clemson University in South Carolina implemented the ePortfolio program requiring all undergraduates to create and submit a digital portfolio as evidence of mastery of the University's common learning outcomes. The student's collected work connects to these outcomes and is drawn from both their curricular and cocurricular experiences. Portfolios in several categories are assessed by campus panels and the best are announced at a campuswide ePortfolio reception. A Best of Clemson ePortfolio award is presented to the student who demonstrates the highest level of creativity, originality, and reflection specific to the Clemson experience and whose work reflects the kind of collective, coherent, and connected curriculum and assessment design process advocated by Ewell (2004). In fact, a widely acknowledged need for similarly transparent expectations for learning across entire degree programs and within institutions has recently prompted the launch of AAC&U's Quality Collaboratives project. With support from the Lumina Foundation (2011), work is under way nationally to establish the Degree Qualifications Profile, a framework for illustrating what students should be expected to know and be able to do after earning their degree, regardless of major or specialization. Senior seminars and capstone courses, ultimate showcases for accumulated student learning, are certain to play a key role in this effort.

Conclusion

The outcomes-based education movement most recently spurred by advances in cognitive science and increasing pressure on colleges and universities to demonstrate their value has elevated the profile of senior seminars and capstone courses. When courses intend to allow students to develop and demonstrate complex learning, they are sent through a 7-step process referred to in this chapter as senior-level course design. While developers of these courses may use other descriptors for the process they employ, I have argued it fairly describes their theory-in-use.

The opportunities for success of senior seminars and capstone courses are greatest when their instructional methods and expectations for learning are introduced in courses students complete prior to the final undergraduate year. Senior seminars and capstone courses are also more likely to succeed if they are built on a commitment to these methods and expectations shared by a community of educators. Simplistic learning is differentiated from complex learning by the level of sophistication and autonomy expected of the student. The process described in this chapter, and modeled by senior seminar and capstone course designers at institutions across the country, is intended to help students demonstrate that college completion has, indeed, helped them to become both sophisticated and autonomous learners.

References

Argyris, C., & Schön, D. A. (1974). *Theory in practice: Increasing professional effectiveness.* San Francisco, CA: Jossey-Bass.

Argyris, C., & Schön, D. A. (1996). *Organizational learning II: Theory, method, and practice.* Reading, MA: Addison-Wesley.

Arum, R., & Roksa, J. (2011). *Academically adrift: Limited learning on college campuses.* Chicago, IL: University of Chicago Press.

Association of American Colleges & Universities (AAC&U). (n.d). *VALUE: Valid assessment of learning in undergraduate education.* Retrieved from http://www.aacu.org/value/

Association of American Colleges & Universities (AAC&U). (2002). *Greater expectations: A new vision for learning as a nation goes to college.* Washington, DC: Author.

Association of American Colleges & Universities (AAC&U). (2007). *College learning for the new global century: A report from the national leadership council for liberal education and America's promise.* Washington, DC: Author. Retrieved from http://www.aacu.org/advocacy/leap/documents/GlobalCentury_final.pdf

Bot, L., Gossiaux, P., Rauch, C., & Tabiou, S. (2005). Learning by doing: A teaching method for active learning in scientific graduate education. *European Journal of Engineering Education, 30*(1), 105-119

Brown, G., DesRosier, T., Peterson, N., Chida, M., & Lagier, R. (2009). Engaging employers in assessment. *About Campus, 14*(5), 5-13.

Bruner, J. (1996). *The process of education.* Cambridge, MA: Harvard University.

California State University Monterey Bay (CSUMB). (2012). *ENVS 403: Capstone seminar II, spring 2012.* Retrieved from http://sep.csumb.edu/class/ESTP_capstone/main/syllabus403.html

Deresiewicz, W. (2011, May). Faulty towers: The crisis in higher education. *The Nation.* Retrieved from http://www.thenation.com/article/160410/faulty-towers-crisis-higher-education

Elliott, J. (2000). Revising the national curriculum, *Journal of Education Policy, 15*(2), 247-255.

Ender, S. C., & Newton, F. B. (2000). *Students helping students: A guide for peer educators on college campuses.* San Francisco, CA: Jossey-Bass.

Ewell, P. (2004). *General education and the assessment reform agenda.* Washington, DC: Association of American Colleges and Universities.

Fernandez, N. P. (2006). Integration, reflection, interpretation: Realizing the goals of a general education capstone course. *About Campus, 11*(2), 23-26.

Fischer, K. (2011, May 15). Crisis of confidence threatens colleges. *Chronicle of Higher Education,* pp. A1-A4.

Flavell, J. H., Miller, P. H., & Miller, S. A. (1993). *Cognitive development* (3rd ed.). Englewood Cliffs, NJ: Prentice-Hall.

Gardner, J. N., Van der Veer, G., & Associates. (1998). *The senior year experience: Facilitating integration, reflection, closure, and transition.* San Francisco, CA: Jossey-Bass.

Gunzenhauser, M. G., & Gerstl-Pepin, C. I. (2006). Engaging graduate education: A pedagogy for epistemological and theoretical diversity. *Review of Higher Education, 29*(3), 319-346.

Huber, R. M. (1992). *How professors play the cat guarding the cream: Why we're paying more and getting less in higher education.* Fairfax, VA: George Mason.

Hunter, D. (2004). Peer to peer: Effective college learning. *Change, 36*(3), 40-44.

Hussey, T., & Smith, P. (2002). The trouble with learning outcomes. *Active Learning in Higher Education, 3*(3), 220-233.

Kegan, R. (1994). *In over our heads: The mental demands of modern life.* Cambridge, MA: Harvard University Press.

Kinzie, J., McCormick, A. C., & Nelson Laird, T. F. (2010). *Capped off: Assessing college capstone courses* [PowerPoint slides]. Retrieved from National Survey of Student Engagement website: http://cpr.iub.edu/uploads/Capped%20Off%20Assessment%20Institute%202010%20Kinzie,%20McCormick%20&%20Nelson%20Laird.pdf

Knight, P. T. (2000). The value of a programme-wide approach to assessment. *Assessment and Evaluation in Higher Education, 25*(3), 237-251.

Knight, P. T. (2001). Complexity and curriculum: A process approach to curriculum-making. *Teaching in Higher Education, 6*(3), 369-381.

Kuh, G. D., Kinzie, J., Schuh, J. H., & Whitt, E. J. (2005). *Student success in college: Creating conditions that matter.* San Francisco, CA: Jossey-Bass.

Lumina Foundation. (2011). *Degree qualifications profile.* Retrieved from degreeprofile.org

Padgett, R. D., & Kilgo, C. A. (2012). *2011 National Survey of Senior Capstone Experiences: Institutional-level data on the culminating experience* (Research Reports on College Transitions No. 3). Columbia, SC: University of South Carolina, National Resource Center for The First-Year Experience and Students in Transition.

Paige, R. (2010). Beyond student-centered instruction a model for teaching learning-to-learn strategies. *International Journal of Interdisciplinary Social Sciences, 5*(5), 299-307.

Schermer, T. (2009, October). *The senior capstone: Transformative experiences in the liberal arts.* Retrieved from Augustana College website: http://www.augustana.edu/Documents/facultynewsletter/Capstone_Experiences_Proposal.pdf

Sill, D., Harward, B. M., & Cooper, I. (2009, Summer). The disorienting dilemma: The senior capstone as a transformative experience. *Liberal Education, 95*(3), 50-55.

Smith, N. (2002). Teaching as coaching: Helping students learn in a technological world *Educause Review, 37*(3), 38-47.

Stenhouse, L. (1975). *An introduction to curriculum research and development.* London, UK: Heinemann.

Sweller, J. (1988). Cognitive load during problem solving: Effects on learning. *Cognitive Science, 12*(2), 257-285.

Sweller, J., van Merriënboer, J., & Paas, F. (1998). Cognitive architecture and instructional design. *Educational Psychology Review, 10*(3), 251-296.

van Merriënboer, J. G., Kirschner, P. A., & Kester, L. (2003). Taking the load off a learner's mind: Instructional design for complex learning. *Educational Psychologist, 38*(1), 5-13.

—

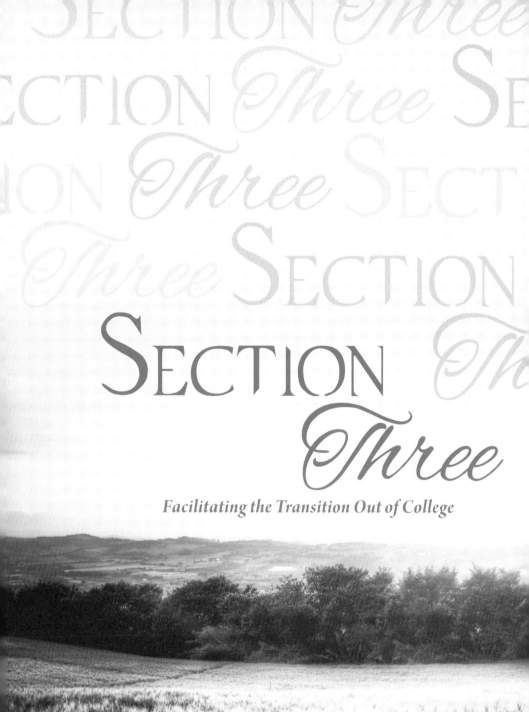

SECTION

Three

Facilitating the Transition Out of College

CHAPTER Six

Career Development in the Senior Year

Heather Maietta

Abby is a 20-year-old undergraduate senior studying history. Originally a communications major, Abby decided in her junior year that communications was not an area of study she wanted to pursue because it did not hold her interest. Without consulting her advisor, she switched her major to history—a subject in which she earned good grades in high school and found fascinating. Abby was sure history was an area of study where she would excel—and she was right. Since changing her major, she has made Dean's List. Now in her final semester, Abby's parents are pressuring her about what she is going to do after graduation. Abby never bothered to visit the career center or participate in any career-related programming. Truthfully, she has not given much thought to her postgraduate options and is at a loss about where to start.

Tia is a 22-year-old undergraduate senior studying human development, which she chose as a first-year student because it sounded interesting and was a new major on campus. When Tia first declared her major, she did not know what to do with a degree in human development; however, she formed a relationship with the career services office in her first year and, during her time as an undergraduate, researched career options related to her chosen field, as well as the type of skills and abilities required of individuals seeking careers in human development. Tia discovered a match in herself and enjoyed the process of self-discovery. She learned how her academic coursework influenced her career path by the informational interview research she conducted in her career planning course and was able to connect with professionals in the field through networking events hosted by her alumni association. Now as a second-semester senior, Tia feels confident with her career direction and is excited about the college-to-career transition.

These vignettes exemplify two very different career planning experiences: The first illustrates very last minute (maybe too late) career planning, and the second reflects a positive sequential, career-planning experience as the result of interventions during various stages of the undergraduate experience. Career development research reinforces the importance of logical career planning as a preface to successful job searches and long-term career management (Folsom & Reardon, 2003). Interventions designed to enhance career decision-making skills, self-efficacy, career information-gathering behavior, the ability to narrow one's options, awareness of interests and work values, and skills development can facilitate the transition from college-to-career (Gore, 2011). College is the time to seek out and take advantage of these career interventions; however, these services must first be available for students, and second, students must know they exist, have access to them, possess an interest in participating, and make meaningful connections between career interventions and academic course-work. Consequently, viewing career preparation not as a service to students but as an integral part of the core academic experience seems plausible and necessary to successfully prepare students for the demands of a modern-day workforce.

Astin (1993) describes the primary purpose of attending college as preparing for a career. Therefore, the ability to examine aspirations closely to ensure postgraduate goals are aligned with personal values, skills, and abilities, as well as achieve a balance between academics and marketable, transferrable skills could be argued as an essential outcome of undergraduate education. Providing students with a greater sense of self-awareness, goals clarification, job-seeking skills, and knowledge of personal attributes are necessary precursors to positive career decision making and workforce preparation.

Yet, today's college students and their parents have increasingly high expectations for the experiences and the outcomes of an undergraduate education. Entering now more as consumers, students are anticipating an increased return on their investment. Employers' expectations for college-educated prospects are also changing, and recent graduates frequently do not live up to them. For example, research conducted by Hart Research Associates (2010) on behalf of the Association of American Colleges and Universities indicated employers want employees to use a broader set of skills and exercise higher learning and knowledge levels at a more rapid pace than in the past to meet the increasingly complex demands of the changing workplace.

The intent of this chapter is to focus on career development in the senior year, but ideally, career development should begin at the point students enter the university. To that end, an examination of career development from matriculation to graduation is included. This chapter begins with a discussion of the current challenges of delivering career development in higher education and provides a brief overview of transition theory and the importance of comprehensive career advising, followed by a snapshot of the current state of career services and a discussion of the importance for including cocurricular career planning initiatives in the undergraduate experience. In addition, the chapter serves as a call to the academy for comprehensive career development at the undergraduate level. Our stakeholders—parents, students, and employers—are looking to higher education for holistic preparation, fusing academic ability and professional preparedness.

Career Development in Higher Education: The Challenges

Career centers and career-service support programs are prevalent in higher education, playing a vital role in student development and college-to-career transitions. Broadly, career centers are charged with the responsibility of assisting students in making informed decisions about major selections, helping them develop self-awareness and see its relation to career choice, providing employment information and opportunities, and helping students develop the skill set needed in a competitive job market. Despite these objectives, Luzzo (1993) suggests existing programs are deficient. Wood (2004) concurred, claiming that both college graduates and employers are dissatisfied with the job competencies of the graduates and charged that students must be better prepared for entering the work world. Peng (2001) reports "there are some students who fail to see meaningful relationships between what they are being asked to learn and what they will do when they leave college" (p. 39). In a study of 302 employers, Hart Research Associates (2010) reported only one in four believes two-year and four-year colleges are doing a good job in preparing students for the challenges facing our global economy.

For many graduates entering the job market, the lack of preparation appears to not only be related to the academic content of their college education but to the students themselves. In a series of graduate interviews conducted by Greene and Greene (2008), it was discovered many college students never accessed the career and counseling resources provided by their institutions, nor set foot in their career and graduate school planning office. Further, Fisher (2006) reported 85% of new college graduates are woefully unprepared to be interviewed, and Ritter (2008) contends the average graduate of the Millennial Generation lacks the proper etiquette training and has not been taught the value of hands-on experience of older, more experienced generations.

Senior-year interventions, such as capstone courses, résumé writing workshops, and on-campus interviewing, can be powerful opportunities to support students in building confidence and skills as they assume new roles and identities (Gardner & Van der Veer, 1998). Successful strategies, however, must be presented in a manner that both encourages and increases the participation of seniors and develops the skills they will need in the workplace.

Seniors in Transition

As chapter 2 illustrates, the senior year can be a time of significant developmental change in a relatively short period. Many seniors are forming a sense of purpose while trying to understand the world around them. According to Chickering & Reisser (1993), decision making with regard to balancing career goals, personal aspirations, and commitments to family and self are becoming more of a reality. Teetering on the fence between student and young professional, the desire to preserve self-respect and develop integrity—for their own beliefs, values, and purpose as well as those of others—is also on the forefront of seniors' minds (Lemme, 2006).

In addition to these developmental changes, seniors face significant career transitional change. It is a common myth that seniors are ready for graduation. Quite the opposite—most are very uncomfortable with the impending transition, regardless of their preparedness or coping skills. Student concerns relate to a lifetime of professional enterprise as well as juggling such things as the end of academic coursework, finding a job, changes in personal relationships, and managing finances (Gardner, 1999). Many college seniors return home, forcing adjustment to new roles within family dynamics. Others are torn between going after professional pursuits and meeting familial expectations. Some, particularly first-generation college students, may be perceived as no longer speaking the same language as their lifelong peers because of their college degree (Davis, 2010). Facing this self-concept transition carries new and unknown connotations and expectations.

Transitions have lifelong implications, and seniors are aware of the importance of their decisions and the consequences. A deeper understanding of both developmental and transition theory as it impacts career decision making can assist higher education professional in helping seniors develop successful strategies to support them through this complex, often confusing, and exciting phase.

Three Stages of Preparedness

In terms of postcollege career transition, seniors can be separated into three broad stages of preparedness: *decided*, *undecided*, and *indecisive* (Sampson, Peterson, Lentz, Reardon, & Saunders, 1998). Decided students know what they want prior to or during the senior year and remain focused on achieving their goals. These students face low stress in the decision-making and transition process. Career professionals working with decided seniors provide services, such as job search and interview coaching or postcollege transitional support (e.g., salary negotiations, first year on the job feedback). The career professional serves as a resource and mentor, guiding the senior through logical, progressive stages of the postcollege transition in a positive, reinforcing manner.

Undecided students enter the senior year moderately anxious about postcollege options and spend their senior year contemplating various possibilities. An undecided student is one who is typically unwilling, unable, or unready to make educational and/or vocational decisions (Gordon, 2007). Although somewhat overwhelmed by the process, they are ready to explore possibilities. An undecided senior may declare a different dream job at each counseling session or convey inconsistent messages with regard to after graduation plans (e.g., apply to graduate school and work for the family business and study abroad). Career professionals can work successfully with undecided students by providing self-discovery counseling (i.e., goals, interests, and skills) and vocational counseling, interventions that can help link the student's aspects of self with potential occupations (Buescher, Johnston, Lucas, & Hughey, 1989; Heppner & Hendricks, 1995).

An indecisive student is one having difficulty making any decision (Appel, Haak, & Witzke, 1970). Gordon (2007) described an indecisive student as having characteristics deriving from the "result of unsatisfactory habits of thinking that permeates the individual's total life" (p. 11). Indecisive seniors typically experience high levels of stress and anxiety obstructing their ability to make decisions and perceive "major life choices as permanent, thereby locking them into a secure employment pattern without addressing their desire to explore and experiment with career dreams" (Feitler-Karchin & Wallace-Schutzman, 1982, p. 59). Career professionals working with indecisive students should first focus on whether a student has a general inability to make any type of decision and also pay attention to other signs of social or psychological problems. If these problems are detected, the student may need to be referred to counseling services. Career assessment tools (i.e., interest inventory), personal values and priorities clarification, career education, and assertiveness training can be appropriate strategies; however, one-on-one personal attention is key to helping these students identify the nature and extent of the indecisiveness along with contributing factors.

Career professionals can assist at each level of the students' transitional experience, provided the student seeks out and/or is offered career interventions (e.g., individual or group counseling, workshops, computer career-guidance systems) delivered in a variety of environments, such as classrooms, counseling centers, or residence life (Gore & Carter, 2011). As Abby's vignette at the beginning of the chapter indicates, we are missing students, creating a potentially negative impact on future alumni relationships, including financial contributions; new student recruitment; and an institution's relationships with workforce partners and other constituents of the college. The remainder of the chapter describes traditional approaches to academic and career advising and presents integrated approaches as an alternative for positively impacting a broader range of students.

Traditional Approaches to Academic Advising and Career Development

Here, I offer some definitions and descriptions of the work of academic advising and career development. While these functions have been separated historically, there is increasing emphasis on their collaboration and integration to support student learning, development, and success (Gordon, 2006; Gore, Harney, & McCalla-Wriggins, 2007). The discussion in this section serves to highlight possible points for integration while the following section offers examples of more comprehensive, integrated approaches.

Academic Advising

O'Banion (1972) defined academic advising as a process that helps students explore life goals, vocational goals, program choice, and course choice. It also assists students with scheduling courses. More recently, Pardee (1994) characterized advising as using a developmental lens to help students identify aspirations, interests, and abilities for the purpose of integrating personal characteristics into academic, career, and life planning. Both definitions provide an overview of advising as a process spanning the undergraduate experience and developing as the student progresses through college. Effective advising is one major factor in increasing student retention since students who receive it tend to feel positive about the institution overall (Noel, 1978). By capitalizing on the benefits of quality advising, colleges can more effectively help students select programs of study and concurrent courses that will retain and focus them towards educational and career goal achievement (ACT, 2004).

Significant overlap exists between academic and career advising, and advisors must have a solid base of knowledge in both the academic core related to their institution and career paths associated with degree offerings. An advisor who sits with a student to discuss a major may also be helping the student learn information-seeking and problem-solving skills that can be valuable for successful experiential learning, cocurricular achievement, and future employment.

Career Counseling, Coaching, and Advising

According to the National Career Development Association (NCDA) there are 12 basic competencies in which career practitioners should be proficient when working with clients at any level in career decision-making process (Harris-Bowlsbey, Suddarth, & Reile, 2008). These include

1. **helping skills** or having proficiency in basic career facilitation process, including productive interpersonal relationships;

2. **labor market information and resources** or understanding labor market and occupational information and trends and being able to use and disseminate current resources;

3. **assessment** or comprehending and using (under supervision when appropriate) both formal and informal career and self assessments with attention to the population served;

4. **diverse populations** or recognizing unique needs of various groups and adapting services to meet their needs;

5. **ethical and legal issues** or following NCDA career development facilitator code of ethics and know current legislative regulations;

6. **career development models** or understanding various career development theories, models, and techniques as they apply to lifelong development, gender, age, and ethnic background;

7. **employability skills** or knowing job search strategies and placement techniques, especially in working with unique groups;

8. **training clients and peers** or preparing and developing materials for training programs and presentations;

9. **program management and implementation** or understanding various career development programs and implementation and work as a liaison in collaborative relationships;

10. **promotion and public relations** or marketing and promoting career development programs with staff and supervisors;

11. **technology** or comprehending and using a variety of career development computer applications and media technologies; and

12. **consultation** or accepting suggestions for performance improvement from consultants, supervisors, colleagues, or peers.

Career counseling is defined by Crites (1981) as an interpersonal process focused on helping individuals make appropriate career decisions. The purpose of career counseling is to identify a problem or concern and then come to a resolution. There are various methods or techniques by which a counselor assists students, but some of the more common are individual or group sessions, assessment testing, reflection exercises, and resources.

Career coaching combines a number of the original techniques of career counseling, such as helping clients identify skills; assisting with career choices and transition; and supporting individuals to become more productive, valuable workers (Chung & Gfoerer, 2003). However, in the coaching relationship there is the absence of a therapeutic problem-solving component (Gordon, 2006). Career coaches should use many of the above competencies in working with all students at the undergraduate level, particularly seniors who will be employing many of these resources for their individual job searches during the final year. Career coaches come from a variety of backgrounds; some are professional counselors while others transition from industry-specific fields, such as business and education, bringing their expertise and knowledge of the field to the career-planning relationship.

Career advising may be thought of as a less psychologically intensive approach to student support than career counseling (Gordon, 2006) with a focus on future goals, information, and exploring the connections between students' educational choices and career possibilities. Gordon states "career advising helps students understand how their personal interests, abilities, and values might predict success in the academic and career fields they are considering and how to form their academic and career goals accordingly" (p. 12). According to Brown and Ryan Krane (2000) effective career advising should incorporate five key ingredients: (a) written exercises, (b) individualized attention, (c) world-of-work information, (d) vicarious learning experiences, and (e) attention building support. Career advising is the most integrated approach of academic advising and career coaching, although not all advisors perform career advising—either because they lack proper training or because they do not view it as part of their responsibility.

Integrated Approaches

Given the information above, many of the responsibilities and aptitudes of academic advisors and career professionals overlap. Traditionally, academic departments perform the majority of academic advising, typically in the form of course registration. Most students do not get exposure or access to the career center during their early college years unless they seek out services individually. According to the National Association of Colleges and Employers (NACE, 2012), only 23% of college career centers provide some type of academic advising to students, and this service is predominantly located at smaller schools where there tends to be some overlap in functions. Between late junior and early senior year, students are directed to the career center for coaching and advising on things like internships, co-ops, résumés, interviews, graduate school options, and job searches. However, as Greene and Greene (2008) pointed out, many students never enter their institution's career center, and others may receive poor advising, may not be aware of campus services, or make use of resources late in their undergraduate experience. Gordon (2006) reports there is a critical need to integrate academic and career information to appropriately assist students with curricular and cocurricular decision making at all stages of the undergraduate experience. Yet, comprehensive advising systems can be challenging to implement in an era of shrinking budgets and limited resources. Several strategies for enacting comprehensive systems are discussed below.

One-Stop Advising Services

Providing a one-stop shop consisting of academic and career advising is a model that could offer a centralized flow of uninterrupted services ensuring students, such as Abby in the opening vignette, do not fall through the cracks and that better decision making happens throughout an undergraduate education. In a one-stop advising model, students are paired with a professional advisor at orientation who remains their advisor for the duration of their undergraduate experience, regardless of major declaration or change. Professional advisors work with academic advisors to provide an additional layer of support for students with regard to academic decision making as it relates to the world of work, coordinate referrals to other services as needed, and assist with the post-college transition. This integration allows the office to provide the best, most up-to-date information to all students at every juncture of their academic and career planning.

This model also offers an insurance policy for students because (a) counselors are housed in one location; (b) all staff are using one computerized management system for counseling observation notes; (c) students maintain the same counseling structure for the length of undergraduate experience, regardless of major change; (d) staff and systems regularly talk to one another; (e) academic and career-related programming come out of the same office; and (f) assessment and learning outcomes are centralized.

Integrated academic and career advising units are a uniquely student-centered approach, providing academic, curricular, and cocurricular help; career preparation and world-of-work transitional assistance; and, especially relevant to college seniors, social support. Murphy, Blustein, Bohlig, and Platt (2010) found that social support is one of the highest predictors of a successful post-college transition, noting students with high levels of social support seemed to perceive their transition in a much more positive light than their peers with lower support levels. Integrating the roles and duties of the academic advisor, career counselor, career coach, and career advisor and offering these services in a single center can effectively meet student transitional needs while providing a strong foundation for campuswide curricular and cocurricular programming.

Mandatory Career Advising

Another strategy for a more integrated approach to academic advising and career development is to assign a mandatory career advisor to all undergraduates in addition to their academic advisor. The career advisors would come from career services and work with students from inception to completion of the undergraduate experience. Career advisors are trained to work with students to help them understand themselves, and their academic and career choices (Gordon, 2006). Like the one-stop shop, this approach not only provides for continuous advising, adding an extra layer of support to the community that comprises the life of the college student. In this way, it may also serve as a retention tool. This model also addresses the need to improve career-related support programming for underserved populations, such as low-income and first-generation college students. Additionally, it provides a bridge between academics and student affairs since more than 59.4% of career centers report to student affairs (NACE, 2012). According to Grites (1979), "advising cannot be done in isolation. This process must be integrated among all constituents of the institution" (p. 6). Assigning mandatory career advisors primes students for career preparation early. They become accustomed to visiting the career centers as first- and second-year students, which can provide a seamless transition between exploration of self and major to exploration of the world-of-work and postgraduate options.

Comprehensive Career Services

Creating an environment that promotes career development and facilitates career decision making among students in transition, particularly seniors, depends largely on two factors: (a) the amount of time and effort students devote to career-related activites and (b) the ways in which institutions allocate resources and organize opportunities and services to maximize student participation and learning (Kuh, Kinzie, Schuh, Whitt, & Associates 2005). Strategies for creating optimal environments to support student learning and engagement with respect to current career development practice are the focus of this section.

Career-Related Programming

Career centers must work with, and within, their institutions to help students achieve important outcomes related to career planning, choice, and vocational identity. To realize these outcomes, career centers must extend their reach across campus in a variety of curricular and cocurricular ways. Opportunities for both on- and off-campus career-related programming are described below.

Partnering across campus. Building and sustaining cross-campus partnerships is probably one of the most fruitful and value-added ways to provide career-related programming to students. Since employment is an obvious outcome of an undergraduate education, these partnerships indirectly enhance visibility for career services. Partnering with the alumni office, student affairs units, health services, international programs, campus ministry, athletics, and academic departments can create countless opportunities to collaborate on campuswide events and share resources; marketing efforts; and, most importantly, students' time. Two examples of cross-campus collaborations are

- **University Leadership Academy (ULA)**—Framingham State University offers ULA as a cross-campus preparatory program engaging junior and seniors in leadership activities (e.g., clubs, organizations, athletics, admissions tour guides, orientation leaders, resident assistants) to develop individual passions and apply them to a career beyond the university experience. Now in its second year, the program is voluntary and runs on five consecutive Fridays in early spring semester—timed for seniors preparing for the postcollege transition. The five-week curriculum builds upon itself structurally with topics such as (a) Start Your Engines, (b) Résumé and Cover 411, (c) Using Others to Get What You Want, (d) Self Presentation, and (e) Put on Your Game Face. Students leave the program with a better understanding of self; polished professional documents; interviewing practice; networking skills; confidence; and most importantly, a connection to career services.

- **Reality MC**—At Muhlenberg College, seniors entering their final spring semester participate in a three-day weekend in January with a focus on developing personal, finance, and life management skills. Based loosely on reality TV, these fun, interactive sessions position seniors as the stars of their own reality. The program offers one-on-one time at fireside chats, group writing assignments, speed networking and other sessions, and small-group discussions. Anecdotes from faculty and staff confirm that thinking, planning, and rethinking continue long after Reality MC ends. Discussions around one's uniqueness and plans for the future facilitate the directed integration of academic and cocurricular activities. Finally, the concrete transition skills (e.g., money management, cooking, apartment hunting,) continue to be the most popular and highly valued programs for the college-to-career transition.

Technology. As Luzzo and MacGregor (2001) noted, the Internet and other technological advances have direct relevance to the practice of career counseling. Rather than lagging behind in the application of technology in the profession, career professionals have forged ahead with the examination and consideration of ways to harness the benefits of such technology in advancing the profession for the benefit of students. Tech tools that support distance engagement are abundant, inexpensive, and easy to use and offer career centers the ability to extend and supplement existing services. Virtual communication tools (e.g., Skype, Google Chat, Meebo) are becoming more widely accepted methods of connecting for students. In fact, 66.6% of career centers provide some form of online counseling (NACE, 2012). For example, some use Meebo to chat virtually with students about appointment scheduling and to answer basic questions about services. Other centers offer virtual career-related workshops to co-op and study-abroad students, ensuring this population receives the same services as campus-based students. Nearly 81% of career centers have a Facebook page and just under half report having an active Twitter presence (NACE, 2012).

Technology is also instrumental in a career center's job placement functions. For instance, students are now able to use software programs to practice their interviewing techniques, and many employers conduct virtual interviews or host virtual career fairs. The career services website and online job postings are the most commonly used technologies, and online job postings and interview scheduling systems were rated as being the most effective technology tools available (NACE, 2012).

Classroom-Based Interventions

As noted above, many students may never visit the career center, or, if they do, it may be very late in their careers. Because students increasingly balance work and family obligations with college attendance, the classroom may be the only time to reach some students. Strategies for providing career development support in the classroom are described below.

Career development courses. Some institutions are slowly realizing the benefits of educating students using a broad approach to career development, one that combines job-related knowledge and skills development with self-awareness counseling (Shivpuri & Kim, 2004). To proactively meet the needs of students and employers, comprehensive, structured, career and skills preparation programs at the undergraduate level are fundamental. One way to ensure this is happening is to embed career planning into the general academic core curriculum so students receive the benefits of comprehensive career development, such as job search preparation, skills-based training, and personal assessment.

Career development courses to assist students with career decision making and planning have been used in higher education for years, but the practice has been inconsistent and sporadic. NACE (2012) reports that fewer than 34% of colleges and universities offer career classes for credit; a figure that has been constant for several years. While research points to the need for, and expansion of, student support programs related to career decision and preparation (Collins, 1998), no studies have specifically explored outcomes related to continuous, mandatory, credit-bearing, career development programs for college students. Often, institutions will focus career-related attention on the first year as students prepare to select a major and, then again, in the senior year in anticipation of graduation. This delivery method has left a gap in career development, offering little or no services for second- or third-year students. Smith and Gast (1998) maintain "programs focusing on career needs of students should be evaluated to ensure a comprehensive approach during all years of the undergraduate experience" (p. 200). Additionally, Maietta (2009) found students who began career preparations in their junior or early senior years were often rewarded with a successful job search and transition into the workforce. These findings suggest students could benefit from a comprehensive career development program offered as part of, and throughout, their undergraduate education. Career courses help students realize how their developing values, interests, skills, and abilities contribute to positive career development and allow for more informed decision making, both during and after college.

The Professional Development Seminars (PDS) program at Nichols College is an example of a continuous, mandatory, credit-bearing, career development model. Since 1998, the College has been preparing a diverse student body for professional careers by offering a practical-oriented, business education that develops foundations skills readily transferable across a range of industries (Maietta, 2009; Maietta & Sherman, 2011). During the first year of PDS, students are provided with campus support services and helpful strategies for achieving academic success and a smooth campus transition, including faculty-student interaction and class attendance tips; time management, study, and research skills, diversity training, and self-discovery tools. Second year builds upon the first by providing a forum to address some of the uncertainty associated with the middle years of college. Students are encouraged to examine where they are and where they are headed in terms of career and professional growth in a structured, supportive environment through investigative course topics, such as major or minor exploration, employment options during college, creating and developing one's professional documentation (i.e., cover letters, résumé, mission statement, recommendations, and references), understanding how one's major translates to various industries, and examining how academic knowledge interconnects with employer expectations. Preparing for, and participating in, an extensive mock interview process is a primary focus of the third year as students begin to fully understand employer expectations and how their unique talents transfer to the world of work. The course allows students to thoroughly explore the job recruitment process, including involvement in professional organizations and social networking; the value of service-learning; and other options for contributing in and out of the classroom. Finally, as seniors, students are challenged to consider their role not only as students but as emerging leaders in our global society. Through the creation of individual recruiting plans, students delve heavily into the job search process and the various postgraduate options. Negotiating salary and benefits, managing expectations when taking that transitional leap out of college, first year on the job, ethical leadership, etiquette, and personal finance are some of the course topics discussed.

Many college students have concerns and uncertainty about how to establish goals and plans leading to a professional career (Collins, 1998); however, Super (1990) theorized traditional-aged college students are typically making the transition from tentative vocational preferences to more specific goals and plans. Comprehensive career planning programs are designed to grow with students, inviting them to consider what is most important academically, as well as reflect on their innate talents, interests, skills, and abilities as it relates to career planning. It is an approach for assisting undergraduates with career decision making and skills building, and a prescription for facilitating life-long career development.

According to Blustein, Prezioso, and Schultheiss (1995), career exploration is a process by which individuals seek information and make decisions about themselves, as well as education and career options related to their area of study. The process of gathering information, exploring options, self-discovery, and problem solving takes time. In addition, regular, structured, meeting times and frequent student-advisor interaction is needed for achieving important career outcomes and strengthening services offered to students. Mandatory career development courses embedded in the core curriculum can provide the time required to develop this process and an efficient structure for the delivery of services.

In-class activities. Most colleges do not offer credit-bearing, mandatory, career development courses; however, career center professionals can establish an in-class presence in the following ways:

- **Substitute instructor**—The career center could promote a campus-wide service to provide a substitute instructor in lieu of cancelling a class for faculty members faced with a conflict (e.g., conference, illness, personal matter). A career advisor would deliver a topical presentation appropriate for the student population in attendance (e.g., social networking for seniors, mock interviewing for juniors, résumé building for sophomores). This type of delivery can be more effective than traditional, optional career workshops in that it has the potential to reach more students while using fewer marketing resources.

- **Senior-year experience seminar**—At Kennesaw State University (KSU), this senior seminar provides students an opportunity to reflect on their collegiate educational experience, demonstrate proficiency, develop the skills necessary to successfully transition to and navigate postuniversity life, understand the civic and social responsibilities of being college-educated citizens, and connect with KSU in an on-going relationship. The three-credit, elective capstone course is taught in a hybrid format, blending traditional face-to-face instruction with online learning activities (e.g., discussions, assignments, assessments, creating a portfolio).

- **Career passport**—This concept has many design possibilities and can be linked to numerous departments across campus. At Merrimack College, for instance, students are given a passport of 10 career-related activities (e.g., virtual interviewing, creating a résumé, updating LinkedIn profiles, completing FOCUS assessment, career coach visits) and events (e.g., career fairs, alumni events, speed-networking nights, co-op or intern panels, recruiting programs). Students are required to complete five of the 10 events and activities and have their passports stamped as part of a business-writing course, which all first-year business students are required to take. The outcome of this cocurricular activity is threefold: (a) students gain exposure to career services of which they may not have been aware, (b) career services fosters positive relationships with academic departments, and (c) career programming is delivered to a greater number of students as part of a course requirement. Similar programs might be adopted for upper-level students, serving as a prerequisite for participation in on-campus recruiting programs.

In 1998, Gardner and Van der Veer proposed that colleges and universities must do more to enhance their students' readiness for transition by fostering collaborative initiatives among academic departments and career services units. Broadly, career centers provide a wide array of support to students in helping them develop the skills and contacts necessary for their postgraduate transition. These services are delivered in a variety of formats, such as on-campus interviews, career days, e-fairs, information sessions, job postings, résumé databases, open houses and special events, networking connections, coaching, mock-interviewing, advising, and more. Yet, studies suggest career interventions delivered one-on-one appear to be the most effective method in terms of student support followed by classroom and group-based interventions (Oliver & Spokane, 1988; Spokane & Oliver, 1983). Further, classroom-based interventions may be the most cost-effective (Gore, 2011). While a center may offer an abundance of support, it must also have strategies in place to ensure all students are made aware of, and take advantage of, the services, as well as enough staff for efficient delivery. Career services are only as effective as the number of students they serve.

Conclusion

Lyon and Kirby (2000) contend that few students prepare career plans on their own initiative; thus, Magner (1990) argues colleges and universities have a moral obligation to pay more attention to the preparation of their students for practical success beyond graduation. Yet, higher education must undergo a paradigm shift in the conceptualization and delivery of career-related services if it is to meet this obligation.

Students arrive on campus in their first year with high academic and career aspirations, and the senior year marks the culmination of these practical expectations at the undergraduate level. Unfortunately, many also enter college with unrealistic plans and information about what they will get out of their college experience and how these experiences relate to the world of work. Career centers are charged with the responsibility to ensure students leave the institution more informed not only about themselves, but also about their own decision-making abilities and the options available to them. To achieve this task, it is necessary to educate students from the moment they matriculate and work with them proactively throughout their undergraduate education, teaching them about self and weaving aspects of career advising and world-of-work exploration throughout their growth process as emerging adults. Because career development is a continuously evolving process (Luzzo, 1993), this integration must include not only career professionals but also academic advisors, academic departments, and student affairs professionals. Moreover, it needs to be seamlessly integrated into students' curricular and cocurricular experiences.

References

ACT. (2004). *Closing the gaps: Challenges and opportunities* (ACT Annual Report). Iowa City, IA: Author.

Appel, V., Haak, R., & Witzke, D. (1970). *Factors associated with indecision about collegiate major and career choice.* Washington, DC: American Psychological Association.

Astin, A. W. (1993). *What matters in college: Four critical years revisited.* San Francisco, CA: Jossey-Bass.

Blustein, D. L., Prezioso, M., & Schultheiss, D. E. (1995). Attachment theory and career development: Current status and future direction. *The Counseling Psychologist, 23,* 416-432.

Brown, S. D., & Ryan Krane, N. E. (2000). Four (or five) sessions and a cloud of dust: Old assumptions and new observations about career counseling. In S. D. Brown & R. W. Lent (Eds.), *Handbook of counseling psychology* (3rd ed., pp. 740-766). New York, NY: Wiley.

Buescher, K. L., Johnston, J. A., Lucas, E. B., & Hughey, K. F. (1989). Early intervention with undecided college students. *Journal of College Student Development, 30,* 375-380.

Chickering, A. W. & Reisser, L. (1993). *Education and identity* (2nd ed.). San Francisco, CA: Jossey-Bass.

Chung, Y. B., & Gfoerer, M. (2003). Career coaching: Practice, training, professional and ethical issues. *Career Development Quarterly, 52*(2), 141-154.

Collins, M. (1998, Winter). 1997 Career services survey: Snapshot of the profession. *Journal of Career Planning & Employment, 58*(2), 1-11.

Crites, J. O. (1981). *Career counseling: Models, methods, and materials.* New York, NY: McGraw-Hill.

Davis, J. (2010). *The first generation student experience: Implications for campus practice, and strategies for improving persistence and success.* Sterling, VA: Stylus Publishing.

Feitler-Karchin, B., & Wallace-Schutzman, F. (1982). Campus to career: Bridging the gap. *Journal of College Placement, 43,* 59-61.

Fisher, A. (2006, May 26). Learning what they don't teach in college: How to get a job. *Fortune.* Retrieved from http://money.cnn.com/magazines/fortune/fortune_archive/2006/05/29/8378027/

Folsom, B., & Reardon, R. (2003). College career courses: Design and accountability. *Journal of Career Assessment, 11*(4), 421-450.

Gardner, J. N. (1999, April). The senior year experience. *About Campus,* 5-11.

Gardner, J. N., & Van der Veer, G. (1998). The emerging movement to strengthen the senior experience. In J. N. Gardner, G. Van der Veer, & Associates (Eds.), *The senior year experience: Facilitating integration, reflection, closure, and transition* (pp. 3-20). San Francisco, CA: Jossey-Bass.

Gordon, V. N. (2006). *Career advising: An academic advisor's guide.* San Francisco, CA: Jossey-Bass.

Gordon, V. N. (2007). *The undecided college student: An academic and career advising challenge* (3rd ed.). Springfield, IL: Charles C. Thomas.

Gore, P. A., Jr. (2011). Career interventions: What works, why, and other important issues. In P. A. Gore, Jr., & L. P. Carter (Eds.), *Students in transition: Research and practice in career development* (Monograph No. 55, pp. 3-16). Columbia, SC: University of South Carolina, National Resource Center for The First Year Experience and Students in Transition.

Gore, P. A., Jr., & Carter, L. P. (2011, March). Using critical ingredients to design career interventions. *E-Source for College Transitions, 8*(2), 1-3.

Gore, P. A., Jr., Harney, J. Y., & McCalla-Wriggins, B. (2007, April 26). *Academic and career advising: Keys to student success* [Teleconference broadcast]. Columbia, SC: University of South Carolina, National Resource Center for The First-Year Experience & Students in Transition.

Greene, H., & Greene, M. (2008, October 1). A considered life: Helping students make deliberate career choice. *University Business.* Retrieved from http://www.thefreelibrary.com/A+considered+life%3a+helping+students+make+deliberate+career+choices.-a0187623911

Grites, T. (1979). Academic advising: Getting us through the eighties. In D. Crockett (Ed.), *Advising skills, techniques, and resources: A compilation of materials related to the organization and delivery of advising services* (pp. 5-7). Iowa City, IA: ACT.

Harris-Bowlsbey, J., Suddarth, B. H., & Reile, D. M. (2008). *Facilitating career development: Instructor manual* (2nd ed.). Broken Arrow, OK: National Career Development Association.

Hart Research Associates. (2010, January). *Raising the bar: Employers' views on college learning in the wake of the economic downturn: A survey of employers on behalf of The Association of American Colleges and Universities.* Washington, DC: Association of American Colleges and Universities.

Heppner, M. J., & Hendricks, F. (1995). A process and outcome study examining career indecision and indecisiveness. *Journal of Counseling and Development, 73*(4), 426-38.

Kuh, G. D., Kinzie, J., Schuh, J. H., Whitt, E. J., & Associates (2005). *Student success in college: Creating conditions that matter.* San Francisco, CA: Jossey-Bass.

Lemme, B. (2006). *Development in adulthood* (4th ed.). New York, NY: Pearson Education.

Luzzo, D. A. (1993). *Evaluating the relationship between college students' vocational congruence, academic success, and career maturity: Career counseling implications and future directions.* Chicago, IL: Mid-Western Educational Research Association. (ERIC Document Reproduction Service No. ED 369947)

Luzzo, D. A., & MacGregor, M. W. (2001). Practice and research in career counseling and development—2000. *The Career Development Quarterly, 50,* 98-140.

Lyon, D. W., & Kirby, E. G. (2000). The career planning essay. *Journal of Management Education, 24*(2), 276-287.

Maietta, H. N. (2009). *Guiding students from matriculation to graduation: Analysis of a four year professional development program for undergraduates* (Unpublished doctoral dissertation) Central Michigan University, Mount Pleasant, MI.

Maietta, H. N., & Sherman, D. C. (2011). A four-year professional developmental model prepares students for successful careers. *E-Source for College Transitions, 8*(2), 4-6.

Magner, D. K. (1990, March 21). Many colleges design courses and programs to prepare seniors to live in "real world." *The Chronicle of Higher Education,* pp. A33-35.

Murphy, K. A., Blustein, D. L., Bohlig, A. J., & Platt, M. G. (2010). The college-to-career transition: An exploration of emerging adulthood. *Journal of Counseling & Development, 88,* 174-181.

National Association of Colleges and Employers (NACE). (2012). *NACE 2011-12 Career services benchmark survey for four-year colleges and universities.* Bethlehem, PA: Author.

Noel, L. (Ed.). (1978). *Reducing the dropout rate.* San Francisco, CA: Jossey-Bass.

O'Banion, T. (1972). An academic advising model. *Junior College Journal, 42,* 62-69.

Oliver, L.W., & Spokane, A. R. (1988). Career-intervention outcome: What contributes to client gain? *Journal of Counseling Psychology, 35,* 447-462.

Pardee, C. F. (1994). We profess developmental advising, but do we practice it? *NACDA Journal, 14,* 59-61.

Peng, H. (2001). Comparing the effectiveness of two different career education courses on career decidedness for college freshmen: An exploratory study. *Journal of Career Development, 28,* 29-41.

Ritter, B. (2008, August 4). Rise of the millennials: Why they know so much … yet understand so little. *The Real Truth.* Retrieved from http://www.realtruth.org/articles/080804-002-society-print.html

Sampson, J. P., Jr., Peterson, G. W., Lenz, J. G., Reardon, R. C., & Saunders, D. E. (1998). The design and use of a measure of dysfunctional career thoughts among adults, college students, and high school students: The Career Thoughts Inventory. *Journal of Career Assessment, 6,* 115-134.

Shivpuri, S., & Kim, B. (2004). Do employers and colleges see eye-to-eye? College student development and assessment. *Journal of Career Planning & Employment, 65*(1), 37-44.

Smith, D. D., & Gast, L. K. (1998). Comprehensive career services for seniors. In J. N. Gardner, G. Van der Veer, & Associates (Eds.), *The senior year experience: Facilitating integration, reflection, closure, and transition* (pp. 187-209). San Francisco, CA: Jossey-Bass.

Spokane, A. R., & Oliver, L. W. (1983). Outcomes of vocational intervention. In S. H. Osipow & W. B. Walsh (Eds.), *Handbook of vocational psychology* (pp. 99-136). Hillsdale, NJ: Lawrence Erlbaum.

Super, D. E. (1990). A life-span, life-space approach to career development. In D. Brown, L. Brooks, & Associates (Eds.), *Career choice and development* (2nd ed., pp. 197-261). San Francisco, CA: Jossey-Bass.

Wood, F. B. (2004). Preventing postparchment depression: A model of career couseling for college seniors. *Journal of Employment Counseling, 41,* 71-79.

CHAPTER *Seven*

Transitioning Into the 21st Century Workplace: Will Seniors Be Ready?

Philip Gardner and April L. Perry

During a recent class where I was relating concerns employers had about young adults transitioning into the workplace (e.g., lack of maturity, work ethic), a young man asked me, "Dr. G, what was it like when you graduated?" Touché! I admitted that the Woodstock (i.e., Baby Boomer) Generation was looked at very unfavorably by corporate managers for the same reasons as today's youth. The difference, however, was the magnitude of the transition from college into the workplace. At the time of my graduation, jobs were relatively abundant, and with a lengthened stride, I could cross over to the world of work without much effort and without knowing a great deal about the workplace or my specific position since it was assumed I would spend the first five to seven years of my new career learning the ropes. Today, I told the young man, you are leaping, no longer striding, just hoping to reach the other side (i.e., land the job). The gap has widened and continues to widen; the landing site is constantly shifting; and the leap has to be upward (i.e., needing expertise already in place to hit the ground running) as well as across (i.e., obtaining employment)—almost a superhuman feat. You have to know your competencies and perform like a superstar from day one.

FAST! One simple word profoundly describes the 21st century economy and workplace. The pace of business transactions, development initiatives, and work assignments is fast and prone to constant change. Lea McLeod, a recent

Hewlett-Packard retiree who is now assisting young adults transition into the work force adds that "the complexity, ambiguity, and chaotic nature of the workplace" surprises new college hires (personal communication, January 5, 2011). Assignments seldom have a simple solution, or even one solution, and require collaboration across organizational, cultural, and political boundaries, increasing their complexity. Ambiguity stems from anxiety over one's role (e.g., conflicting job demands and multiple supervisors), flaws in organizational communication, and confusion over knowledge and information. The constant churn in the workplace drives the organization but, at times, with little sense of structure or stability. New hires must construct their own agendas (gone are the 15-page course syllabi to serve as guides). To meet the challenges of today's workplace, graduates must traverse a widening chasm between "town and gown."

The transition can be viewed through its two components: (a) professional competencies and skills and (b) attitudes toward work and work behaviors. This distinction can be murky as some of the behaviors are embedded within the professional competencies component. In this chapter, we embrace both dimensions with the intention of

- identifying the professional competencies employers expect new college hires to possess,

- examining employer concerns over the attitudes and behaviors young adults bring into the workplace, and

- offering several suggestions on how to address the professional preparation of students.

The chapter opens with a brief background on the dynamic forces that collided in the late 20th century to form the economic reality now shaping the transition from college to work. After discussing the gap in skills and competencies, we examine concerns over work attitude and behaviors, the role of professional practice (e.g., internship, practicum), and the emerging concept of a 21st century professional. To highlight the real experiences and perspectives of individuals in the midst of the postuniversity transition, quotations from a recently completed qualitative study involving graduates within their first year out of college (Perry, 2012) are included throughout the text.

The 21st Century Economy and Workplace

Sweeping forces converged in the past decade transforming the U.S. economy from a linearly organized production structure to a complex networked structure. Technology (Freidman, 2006), new financial services (Smick, 2008), demands and innovations in education (Kamenetz, 2010; Slaughter & Rhoades, 2009), and economic forces (*The Economist*, 2001) have rearranged how this country and the world produce goods and services, resulting in a realigned workforce where many jobs have simply been eliminated. Shapiro (2008) states that the economy, once the domain of individual nation states involved in trade, became truly global with the emergence of new world markets (e.g., China, India, South Korea, Brazil). He notes these countries supply low-cost, quality labor to a global economy, which has significantly altered the implicit, historical arrangements between employer and employee in developed economies. Cheaper labor and open access to markets has shifted manufacturing and other routine professional tasks to low-cost labor centers. The opportunities that are now emerging in developed economies require higher skill proficiencies and a higher level of readiness than previously expected of graduating seniors. Branden (1995) summarized this shift to higher complexity as follows:

> In the past two or three decades, extraordinary developments have occurred in the American and global economies … We have witnessed the transition from physical labor to mind work as the dominant employee activity. We now live in a global economy characterized by rapid change, accelerating scientific and technological breakthroughs, and an unprecedented level of competiveness. These developments create demand for higher levels of education and training than were required of previous generations … these developments also create new demands on our psychological resources. Specifically, these developments ask for a greater capacity for innovation, self-management, personal responsibility, and self-direction. This is not just asked at the top, it is asked at every level of a business enterprise, from senior management to first-line supervisors and even to entry-level personnel … Today, organizations need not only an unprecedentedly higher level of knowledge and skill among all those who participate but also a higher level of independence, self-reliance, self-trust, and the capacity to exercise initiative. (pp. 22-23)

The situation is further complicated by the demographic shifts that most western economies face with the pending retirement of a significant portion of their workforce born in the decades following World War II (Kotlikoff & Burns, 2005; Magnus, 2009). Even in the midst of a global economic recession, businesses are scrambling to find qualified young talent to succeed their older workers (DeLong, 2004). The surge of retirements over the next two decades may offer new college graduates some respite from economic oscillations, barring another global recession.

Other factors influencing the range of jobs available in the U.S. economy are *sourcing*—moving jobs from one location to another (e.g., Michigan to South Carolina; Ohio to China)—and *technological advances* (e.g., high-speed wireless Internet, cost-effective computerized processes, robotics). Both of these phenomena allow employers to take advantage of lower labor costs or rearrange their labor force. Businesses can either tap into a highly educated pool of talent dispersed across the globe or replace workers performing routine tasks with technical equipment (e.g., robotics). For example, the field of law is being transformed through advanced discovery software, reducing the need for new lawyers to conduct research on cases (Markoff, 2011). Accountants doing basic corporate accounting activities using standardized procedures and software are now being located across the globe, rather than at corporate headquarters (Pink, 2005). Advancement in laboratory equipment for clinical tests has transformed the job functions of medical laboratory technologists, and repetitive tests are now performed by technicians with two-year degrees (Gardner & Estry, 1990).

Retirements (i.e., workforce succession), technological advances and integration, and sourcing all have implications for college seniors by influencing the number of opportunities and the types of positions that will be available to them throughout their careers. Routine and repetitive job functions have been and are being replicated with technology, eliminating many openings that would have traditionally been targeted by college graduates. Young adults in other countries (e.g., Canada, South Korea, Hong Kong, Singapore, Finland) are now competing with American students for the same positions. These foreign students come to the labor market with excellent academic qualifications, performance-oriented work attitudes and behaviors, and demonstrated professional competencies gained through professional practice. U.S. employers are looking for the same qualities in American graduates.

Professional Competencies

Concerns about college graduates being prepared for the workplace have intensified during the first decade of the 21st century as witnessed by reports from eminent educational associations and foundations (Hart Research Associates, 2010; Lumina Foundation, 2011), employer-focused associations (The Conference Board et al., 2006), researchers (Autor, Levy, & Murnane, 2003; Dorn & Autor, 2011), and the popular literature (Barry, 2007; Coplin, 2012). The information presented in this section is drawn from work done over the last decade at the Collegiate Employment Research Institute (CERI) at Michigan State University.

During the 1999-2000 academic year, Michigan State University's Board of Trustees approved 12 core competencies deemed essential in the preparation of undergraduates to meet the new demands of the workplace. These 12 essentials serve as the foundation competencies for workforce readiness (Career Services Network, 2006):

1. developing professional competencies,
2. communicating effectively,
3. solving problems,
4. balancing work and life,
5. embracing change,
6. working effectively in a team,
7. working in a diverse environment,
8. managing time and priorities,
9. navigating across boundaries,
10. acquiring knowledge,
11. thinking critically, and
12. performing with integrity.

This list was further refined by Hanneman and Gardner's (2010) work with employers. Their research resulted in seven über-skills, which included variations of the 12 essentials (e.g., communication, critical thinking) as well as additional abilities:

- demonstrating initiative;
- building and sustaining professional relationships;
- analyzing, evaluating, and interpreting data and information;
- communicating effectively through justification and persuasion;
- creating new knowledge or services;
- engaging in continuous learning; and
- articulating global understanding.

The importance of the first two of these über-skills is illustrated by these comments from students in Perry's (2012) study:

> You have to personally get your name out there by connecting with personal friends, local business men and women, and local staffing firms to assist you in finding opportunities (paid/unpaid, full-time/part-time) to start your career in the world.

> I want to communicate the extreme importance of relationships and networking. One of my favorite phrases is "Life is all about one thing—relationships." Meeting, connecting, and networking with people are the top ways to connect and get interviews for jobs.

With this elevation in skill-level expectation for entry-level jobs, the learning curve for new hires has become almost perpendicular. Employers in advanced economies are seeking potential new employees who can handle assignments that are unique (versus repetitive or routine), assemble knowledge from multiple sources (cross-disciplinary training), manage one-of-a-kind events, and create new knowledge for the production or delivery of new products or services. As this study participant (Perry, 2012) notes,

> I should have gotten a "real" job my junior year and built up my work experience. I feel that if I would have done at least that, I would be working in a job that truly uses all of my talents. At the end of the day, an inexperienced worker is still a risk, and most companies are not willing to take that risk on their new hires.

Attitudes and Behaviors

Embedded in the competency sets addressed in the previous section are attitudes and behaviors (e.g., performing with integrity, engaging in continuous learning), which are more often emotional or mental responses to an environment or stimulus. Skills, competencies, attitudes, and behaviors can all be taught; however, attitudes and behaviors frequently are best learned through modeling and explicit expectations. For example, students can develop punctuality (a behavior) through clearly outlined assignment due dates in a syllabus or observing the promptness of an instructor arriving for class, as well as practicing being on time.

A recent report from the Center for Professional Excellence (2012) has identified several attitudes and behaviors associated with professionalism that trouble managers about young adults: specifically, work ethic, sense of entitlement, and appearance. These findings echo results from several of CERI's Recruiting Trends studies showing employers (i.e., managers and human resource professionals) believe that recent graduates feel more entitled (i.e., have unrealistic expectations), display less of a work ethic, are less mature, and present themselves less professionally than graduates of five years ago (CERI, 2011). None of these findings suggest today's young adults are in any sense vastly different from previous generations. For example, Jennings (1961) noted the same lament in the 1960s. Yet, because today's economy is moving at a much faster pace, the deficits in attitude and behaviors appear more pronounced as this Perry (2012) study participant's comment illustrates.

> I thought I would get out of college and would be making about $60,000 a year … and I do think the economy has a huge impact on that, but my expectations haven't been met.

Youth entitlement has borne the brunt of manager criticism about this generation. Twenge (2006) and Twenge, Campbell, and Freeman (2012) have confirmed in their studies that sense of entitlement continues to rise throughout the youth culture with possible, profound impacts on the workforce. The boomers also came with a sense of entitlement (and are still possessive of what they are entitled to) that was intrinsic in nature, meaning it was the individual who was entitled, and entitlement was gained through hard work (bases for a meritocracy). Young adults today express their entitlement more extrinsically, making it much more visible as it pertains to them as a collective group. When a member fails to receive what they believe he or she is entitled to, the entire group is affected (Neil Howe, personal communication, April 12, 2012). The economic disruptions of the first decade of the 21st century have undermined the expected entitlements of our youth. Unfortunately, they have failed to reset their expectations in light of the economy's new reality. Perry's (2012) research participants demonstrated this:

> I don't want to work as a clerk somewhere, because I have a degree … and a good degree, and I want something that's equal to my degree.

> I probably applied for about 20 to 30 jobs within the first few months after graduation, and only got responses from three of them. I thought my application was better than that, and that I'd hear back from more.

One attitude or behavior that has definitely changed with this generation concerns work identity—a construct measuring how important one's work is to shaping personal identity. Chao and Gardner (2007) found young adults today hold significantly lower levels of work identity than boomer youth at the same age. In other words, today's youth are more likely to define themselves by other aspects of their life (e.g., family, social group, avocation), in addition to work. Having a lower work identity does not mean that one is a slacker. In fact, most indications suggest that today's college graduates do work hard (albeit differently, in some cases). Perry's (2012) study participants provide insights on how today's young adults grapple with work identity.

> My personality hasn't changed, my desire to help others hasn't changed, the main thing that has changed in my life is that I work 40 hours a week instead of go[ing] to school 40 hours a week.

> Since I didn't have an environment defining me, I had to start answering questions… and that's been everything. My identity isn't student anymore … or student body president. I'm far from being done in this process, but I'm recognizing it and trying different things to do something about it.

Work identity should not be confused with work-life balance. Life balance may certainly be part of work identity, but it is not the sole reason for the shift. The college students in Chao and Gardner's (2007) study attributed the shift to observing their parents' obsession with work, resulting in constant stress and time pressures, and desired something else. Too often, employers associate this shift in work identity in young adults to a poor work ethic and lack of maturity, when in fact it is a different way to engage the workplace.

While the college environment offers numerous occasions for career-appropriate attitudes and behaviors to be taught (e.g., classes, workshops), modeled (e.g., mentors, instructors, peers), and made explicit (e.g., syllabi, style guides), faculty and staff must also strive to create ambiguous opportunities for students. Ambiguous, open-ended, or multiple-option assignments (e.g., flexible due dates, project- or case-based learning) can encourage individual thinking and creativity. A balance between explicitness and ambiguity is vital as this Perry (2012) study participant pointed out:

> Something needs to be done if we live in a society where the majority of parents/teachers plan out most kids' lives from kindergarten to their senior year of high school, and those same kids are supposed to magically figure everything out on their own when they become young adults. It just doesn't make sense.

Developing Transition Strategies

While the typical entry-level starting job of 10 years ago is disappearing from the workplace, it is re-emerging in the undergraduate experience as the internship or some form of professional practice appropriate for a student's major (e.g., clinical rotations, student teaching, practicum). Hanneman and Gardner (2010) found the skills required for obtaining an internship have followed a similar escalation as for full-time positions, and employer expectations for an internship closely match the job descriptions for entry-level, full-time jobs from five to seven years ago. In other words, the starting job is now the internship. Upcoming college and university students should expect that an internship be part of the undergraduate education experience for nearly all graduates. As one of Perry's (2012) study participants commented,

> I believe that the internships should be much more in-depth and more hands-on. It would be great to make it mandatory for students to job shadow a person in their career field. Also to help the student narrow it down to the exact career that they would like to explore.

Engagement through service-learning, study abroad, organizational leadership, and exploratory internships play a critical role in laying the foundation to launch a student's professionally focused internship. Prior to researching and selecting an internship, a student should have a good sense of self and know his or her interests and general career direction. Numerous tools (e.g., strengths assessments, learning style inventories, psychometric measures) are available to higher education professionals to help guide students on their self-discovery journey.

> My junior year, I participated in a strengths assessment, and that's when I learned what my top five strengths were. I think that I had always known those things about myself, but it wasn't until I took the assessment that I had language to describe it. And I think that's a very key factor when you're able to describe qualities about yourself. (Perry, 2012)

Furthermore, students should be encouraged to engage in a diverse array of cocurricular activities (balanced with their academic responsibilities) to broaden their scope and experience and make them eligible for more challenging internships as well as increase their selection chances. However, students may need assistance integrating these cocurricular experiences with their professional goals. For example, at Michigan State University, students who had participated in study abroad were having difficulty conveying the value of this experience to employers. A special unpacking workshop was created, based on results and feedback from several employer studies (Gardner, Gross, & Steglitz, 2008), that guides students through several exercises requiring deep reflection upon their experience. The most important step was to assist students in translating the value-added aspects of their international experience into language that had meaning to employers in a professional context. This process is now being used with other cocurricular activities at the University, and some faculty have begun holding sessions prior to students' engagement so that they have a better understanding of the learning outcomes to expect.

According to Gardner (2011), the high-stakes internship becomes the crucial bridge linking the university to the workplace. During this experience, students gain mastery in applying their learning to produce meaningful work as well as learn the fundamental professional competencies necessary for their career. Gardner stresses that successful internships must be difficult enough to challenge students in their actual career area of interest (i.e., more than front office reception). Moreover, faculty and workplace mentors should provide deep reflection on the experience before, during, and after. One of Perry's (2012) research participants had this to say:

I think there should be more requirements for interns. Believe it or not I didn't have to do much with mine, not to mention my supervisor and professor never communicated. Supervisors could care less … you're working for free! And the professors don't seem to really care as much either. Seriously, an internship to me is the most important class of your entire college career. It's preparing you for your future!

Discipline-based education remains a fundamental role of universities; however, students should also be offered opportunities to gain experience working (e.g., problem solving, project management, goal setting) with individuals from other disciplines. These cross-discipline opportunities can foster understanding among students and may even lead to a better use of their electives. Broadening students' knowledge base across disciplines will equip new graduates with the skills needed to interact with other professionals from a diverse range of fields. In addition to curricular, cocurricular, and extracurricular activities, students need to tap into the "human" resources available to them. Faculty, advisors, mentors, and parents can assist students in their journey through college to the workplace, as well as their lifelong journey, by being a/an

- **guide** for students in the discovery of their interests, showing how their career options are embedded within larger systems; providing relevant information about the transition experience into the workplace and assistance in dealing the uncertainty they will encounter; and strategizing ways to gain necessary skills and competencies;

- **promoter** who serves as an agent for students, making introductions to promising organizations, alumni, and community members to actualize the learning process;

- **coach** who engages students in reflective activities to find the common thread in their many and varied undergraduate experiences and challenging them to push their limits by exploring opportunities outside their comfort zone;

- **advocate** who can remove barriers that undermine students' growth and development (e.g., negotiating between two departments to enable a student to take a cluster of courses without declaring a major); and

- **teacher** who instills a thirst for lifelong learning.

Prehire Transition Challenges

The expectations of employers have been laid out in terms of the skills that they prefer seniors have, the work attitudes and behaviors they expect, and preprofessional experiences they require; however, the acquisition and demonstration of all this does not guarantee a successful transition. Even in the best of times, the workplace seldom greets new graduates on the graduates' terms. Too often, students are inspired and encouraged to pursue their dreams without a clear understanding of the terrain ahead. A realistic message of workplace conditions must be conveyed to students. Their concepts of starting salaries, initial assignments, and office perks, as well as the appropriate professional behaviors, can be skewed and may need reframing, as illustrated by this comment from a graduate in Perry's (2012) study:

> My expectations [of a degree] were not met … no, no, no, no! … My expectation was that it was going to be hard to get a job because I'm young, but I thought once people got to know me—who wouldn't hire me? And then I didn't have the job of my dreams right off, and I still don't have a job of my dreams [six months after graduation]. It's like—I went to college for four years to make $8.75 an hour, and not that it seems unfair, it just feels like—that was four years of my life, and I could have been doing this [working] the whole time … why did I have to do that [get a degree]?"

If students know and understand workplace norms from the outset, they will hold a healthier perspective of what to expect that first day on the job and avoid jeopardizing their early career success. Another participant in Perry's (2012) study offered this advice:

> I think that universities should start off being real with the students about the job market, what they can do with their major, what extra trainings they need, etc. I think our students feel lost when they leave because professors do not give applicable advice for graduates. If students knew going into graduation that they would more than likely still be looking for a job a year later, students might decide to continue their education or chose another career path that best suits them.

In addition to managing workforce expectations, students must be able to present their college experience as a "whole cloth" to future employers, rather than a series of isolated events. While in college, students are offered a wide variety of curricular, cocurricular, and extracurricular opportunities and may have difficulty finding the common thread weaving these experiences together into a comprehensive, intentional, and integrated whole. Higher education professionals are in a unique position to help students integrate their college experiences; manage their expectations; and understand the value of their degree, their abilities, and their worth to a prospective employer. A Perry (2012) study participant had this to say about a college faculty or staff interaction:

> One person that I worked for in college became a huge mentor and friend to me and taught me a lot about reflection. I think that's a lesson that I learned throughout college and something that I do now … to just focus on every moment as you're going through it and to reflect on what you're learning so that you can really grow in the midst of it.

For students, during their schooling the focus has been on them; but in the job search, the focus is on the employer. Employers do not want to hear about what a senior wants; rather, they want to know what that individual has to offer the hiring organization. Thus, the bottom line for new graduates is to be aware of (a) who they are (b) what they have to offer (i.e., skills and competencies), and (c) who is in their professional network. They do not need to be highly proficient in all the essential competencies listed above or identify their exact career path; however, they do need to be able to articulate their strengths (to the extent they have been developed) and stress their commitment to performing their assignments. Lastly, it is important for the graduating senior to keep in mind that his or her first job is only the beginning of a long journey in professional development, as this Perry (2012) study participant observed:

> It's almost been a year since I graduated, and yet I don't feel as far along in the process as I thought I would be. I still feel like I need be able to proverbially run faster, climb higher, swim longer, but yet I'm still this work in progress.

Posthire Transition Challenges

Even after all the hard work of preparing for and landing a job, the transition does not end there. Entwined with starting salaries, job assignments, new coworkers, and performance expectations, new graduates also have to manage their personal and emotional transition as their primary identity changes from student to professional. This shift may mean making decisions without assistance from family or friends, negotiating personal time, and relating to roommates or significant others in new ways. A recent graduate from Perry's (2012) study had this to say:

> The high school to college transition wasn't like this. Even though it was a different school and location, and probably living situation, you were surrounded by friends who were going through the same things and it's much more exciting. Whereas in this transition, you are often at a different place than your friends—even if it's happening at the same time for all of you. After college you stop being on track with other people. You are now moving at your own pace—whatever that may be.

Chao and Gardner (2008) and Perry (2012) noted that being aware of potential college-to-work transition challenges can mentally and emotionally prepare seniors and recent graduates for leaving one comfort zone (college) and finding a new one (the workplace).

> I don't much care for change, so it was uncomfortable changing life, but I feel like I am starting to get comfortable again. I think I have realized that just because it is the next step does not mean I'm full out grown up. I still go out and have fun and that's ok … I'm not married and that's ok for now too. I have more responsibility and more stress, but I am learning to understand this new stage of life. (Perry, 2012)

Becoming a professional and gaining respect does not happen on the first day on the job. Even with all the right preparation and establishing reasonable expectations, the initial years in the workplace can be challenging and humbling, as a new hire in Perry's (2012) study experienced:

> I'm getting really frustrated at work because I'm trying to get stuff done, but people still treat me like a student worker. There's been stuff that people will not do that I ask of them, then I'll e-mail my boss and he'll e-mail that person, and it's done in five minutes … so that's getting really frustrating.

However, recent graduates from Perry's (2012) study found that having a good support system and feeling part of a group were critical to ease this transition:

> I think that having a group of people that support me in this time of life makes things a lot easier to deal with. I like that I have people going through something similar to discuss things with, but I also have other people in my life to bounce ideas off of and to get advice from.

The postuniversity transition is multifaceted. To successfully move through it, new hires will need to have persistence, consistently demonstrate and improve their competencies, and use or develop a support system to manage these challenging times.

Becoming the Ultimate Professional

Many college seniors possess the raw material to transform themselves into the ultimate young professional. Brown (2005) popularized the concept of the *T*-shaped professional (Figure 7.1), who has a combination of skills that blend mastery in a chosen field with knowledge of other disciplines and an array of skills that allows him or her to easily cross various boundaries—organizational, social, and cultural. Estrin (2009) referred to these types of professionals as adaptive innovators and further articulated their dimensions. In addition, to mastery in a field of study and competency in boundary-crossing skills, adaptive innovators also possess a deep passion to engage in finding solutions to major issues or problems and an inquisitiveness and drive to find new ways to generate value to an organization or personal enterprise (commonly referred to as *tinkering*). Hanneman and Gardner's (2010) analysis of skill-set acquisition and performance strongly supports the contention that employers across all sectors are striving to find talent that embodies *T*-shaped skills.

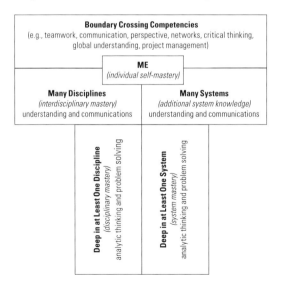

Figure 7.1. The *T*-shaped professional.

Adapted from *T-Shaped Professionals* by J. Spohrer, 2010, Collegiate Employment Research Institute website. Copyright 2010 by Michigan State University.

The elements that make up a *T*-shaped professional include

- **Boundary-crossing competencies**. These skills facilitate the traversing of disciplinary, organizational, cultural, and social boundaries that allow *T*-shaped professionals to act as adaptive innovators.

- **Me (individual self-mastery)**. This element encompasses the understanding of the self in terms of values that direct one's life, purpose for engaging in a career, and possible career directions.

- **Many disciplines (interdisciplinary mastery)**. Competence in this area involves the ability to communicate and understand how knowledge from another discipline(s) affects a problem.

- **Many systems (additional system knowledge)**. A system is an area of interest (e.g., food, water, energy, finance, information technology, transportation, health). As individuals mature in their careers, they can add more areas of interest to their knowledge base, focusing on the places the systems overlap or form niches where future economic activity and career opportunities can emerge.

- **Depth in at least one discipline (disciplinary mastery)**. This branch of the *T* requires command of the fundamental knowledge of one's discipline, including communication literacy, analytical literacy, technical literacy, and the ability to problem solve.

- **Depth in at least one system (system mastery)**. The final segment in the trunk of the *T* involves learning as much as possible about a system because of a passionate interest and/or the need to address a specific problem in that system.

Fully formed *T*s do not emerge from the initial four or five years of university. Instead, the trunk of the *T* can (and must) be developed and nurtured during the undergraduate experience as well as an inquisitiveness and desire to continually learn and grow. Becoming a lifelong learner will enable graduating seniors to develop the cells in the *T* crossbar (limbs) as they progress and thrive over their professional careers.

Concluding Thoughts

FAST! The transition from college into the workplace is challenging, and learning how an organization operates and how one fits in takes time. In the early 1990s, *Fast Company* magazine began publication with a mission to prepare its readers for dealing with and leading in a fast work environment. The suggestions offered over the years are pertinent to the future of today's seniors—a future for which colleges and universities must be prepared and equipped to provide the necessary tools and capacities for their students to succeed.

- *Initiative*. An individual is solely responsible for his or her career. Employers provide little guidance in nurturing and maintaining employee careers. Undergraduates need to be focused when they initiate their transition. They do not have to know exactly where they are going, but they do need to know where to seek the most appropriate opportunities that move them along in the right direction. This journey requires a foundation built upon curricular and cocurricular experiences that assist students in growing the skills and competencies they will need. Therefore, we have to be committed to developing comprehensive professional competencies among our undergraduates.

- *Innovation*. This is critical to the survival of every organization and its members. College students need to be aware of the cultural, social, technical, economic, and political changes emerging and how those changes can affect their career fields. The ability to restructure and create new services, products, and knowledge is essential to a new graduate's contribution to an organization. Therefore, we have to be committed to providing an environment where students from all disciplines can experiment with their ideas, work on solving emerging problems, and organize knowledge in new ways.

- *Learning*. It takes place 24/7. The four years of undergraduate study are merely a down payment. New graduates will be expected to initiate their own learning, constantly furthering their disciplinary mastery as well as broadening their reach into other fields that support their work. Therefore, we have to be committed to ensuring that students will be enthusiastic life-long learners.

- *Change*. This will be a constant part of students' lives. They need to embrace and adapt to it. Rather than a threat, change can be full of potential opportunities. Therefore, we have to be committed to helping students understand how to handle change and be accountable for their response to it.

- *Boundaries*. Students need to learn how to establish healthy boundaries between work and the rest of their lives. Modern technologies allow work to intrude into one's life every hour and every minute of the day.

Therefore, we have to be committed to teaching students healthy strategies to handle the stress that arises when work collides with other life commitments.

The success of recent graduates and new hires is a three-fold partnership with each party having a buy-in and return on their investment. The first partner is the individual whose successful transition includes gaining mastery in a chosen discipline and an understanding of related disciplines, securing a challenging professional experience as part of an undergraduate program, articulating one's skills and competencies, and acquiring self-knowledge regarding one's sense of purpose and direction. Universities, as the second partner, can assist students by offering opportunities for career exposure, professional work experience, and career skill-building and providing emotional support to guide students' expectations, foster reflection, and help understand the uncertainty that often accompanies this transition. Employers complete the partnership and can facilitate a workplace introduction through on-boarding programs that orient new hires to the organization's values, processes, and staff structure and help them understand and manage their expectations. A commitment and collaboration from all three partners can ensure our seniors will be ready.

References

Autor, D., Levy, F., & Murnane, R. J. (2003, November). The skill content of recent technological change: An empirical exploration. *The Quarterly Journal of Economics*, 1279-1333.

Barry, N. (2007). *When reality hits: What employers want recent graduates to know.* Dallas, TX: Brown Books Publishing.

Branden, N. (1995). *The six pillars of self-esteem.* New York, NY: Bantam.

Brown, T. (2005, June). Strategy by design. *Fast Company.* Retrieved from http://www.fastcompany.com/magazine/95/design-strategy.html

Career Services Network. (2006). *12 essentials for success.* East Lansing, MI: Michigan State University. Retrieved from http://careernetwork.msu.edu/pdf/Competencies.pdf

Center for Professional Excellence. (2012). *2012 professionalism in the workplace.* York, PA: York College, Center for Professional Excellence. Retrieved from http://www.ycp.edu/media/yorkwebsite/cpe/2012-Professionalism-in-the-Workplace-Study.pdf

Chao, G., & Gardner, P. D. (2007). *How central is work to young adults?* (White paper prepared for MonsterTrak). East Lansing, MI: Michigan State University, Collegiate Employment Research Institute. Retrieved from http://ceri.msu.edu/publications/pdf/work_young_adults.pdf

Chao, G., & Gardner, P. D. (2008). *Young adults at work: What they want, what they get and how to keep them.* East Lansing, MI: Michigan State University, Collegiate Employment Research Institute. Retrieved from http://www.ceri.msu.edu/young-professionals/

Collegiate Employment Research Institute (CERI). (2011). *Recruiting trends 2011-2012.* East Lansing, MI: Michigan State University, Retrieved from http://www.ceri.msu.edu/wp-content/uploads/2010/11/Recruiting-Trends-2011-2012.pdf

The Conference Board, Inc., The Partnership for 21st Century Skills, Corporate Voices for Working Families, & The Society for Human Resource Management. (2006). *Are they ready to work? Employers' perspectives on the basic knowledge and applied skills of new entrants to the 21st century U.S. workforce.* Retrieved from http://www.careers-marts.com/21/Are%20They%20Ready%20to%20Work.pdf

Coplin, B. (2012). *10 things employers want you to learn in college, revised: The know-how you need to succeed.* Berkeley, CA: Ten Speed Press.

DeLong, D. (2004). *Lost knowledge: Confronting the threat of an aging workforce.* New York, NY: Oxford University Press.

Dorn, D., & Autor, D. (2011). *The growth of low-skill jobs and polarization of the U.S. labor market* (MIT working paper). Retrieved from http://economics.mit.edu/files/1474

The Economist. (2001). *Globalisation: Making sense of an integrating world.* London, UK: Profile Books.

Estrin, J. (2009). *Closing the innovation gap.* New York, NY: McGraw Hill.

Friedman, T. L. (2006). *The world is flat.* New York, NY: Farrar, Straus, & Giroux.

Gardner, P. D. (2011). *Internships as high stakes events* (CERI Research Brief). East Lansing, MI: Michigan State University, Collegiate Employment Research Institute. Retrieved from http://www.ceri.msu.edu/wp-content/uploads/2010/01/High-Stakes-Internships.pdf

Gardner, P. D., Gross, L., & Steglitz, I. (2008). *Unpacking your study abroad experience: Critical reflection for workplace competencies* (CERI Research Brief 1-2008). East Lansing, MI: Michigan State University, Collegiate Employment Research Institute.

Gardner, P. D., & Estry, D. W. (1990). Changing job responsibilities in clinical laboratory sciences: A report on the 1989 AMST National Personnel Study. *Clinical Laboratory Science, 3*(6), 382-388.

Hanneman, L., & Gardner, P. D. (2010). *Under the economic turmoil a skill gap simmers* (CERI Research Brief 1-2010). East Lansing, MI: Michigan State University, Collegiate Employment Research Institute.

Hart Research Associates. (2010). *Raising the bar: Employer's views on college learning in the wake of the economic downturn.* Washington, DC: Association of American Colleges and Universities. Retrieved from www.aacu.org/leap/documents/2009_EmployerSurvey.pdf

Jennings, E. E. (1961). How to teach the young men to work. *Nation's Business, 49*(2), 40.

Kamenetz, A. (2010). *DIY U: Edupunks, edupreneurs, and the coming transformation of higher education.* White River Junction, VT: Chelsea Green Publishing.

Kotlikoff, L. J., & Burns, S. (2005). *The coming generational storm: What you need to know about America's economic future.* Cambridge, MA: MIT Press.

Lumina Foundation. (2011). *The degree qualification profile.* Retrieved from www.luminafoundation.org/publications/The_Degree_Qualifications_Profile.pdf

Magnus. G. (2009). *The age of aging: How demographics are changing the global economy and our world.* Singapore: John Wiley & Sons.

Markoff, J. (2011, March 5). Armies of expensive lawyers, replaced by cheaper software. *The New York Times,* Retrieved from http://www.nytimes.com/2011/03/05/science/05legal.html?_r=1&ref=johnmarkoff

Perry, A. (2012). *Treading through swampy water: Graduates' experience of the post-university transition.* (Unpublished doctoral thesis). University of Canterbury, Christchurch, New Zealand.

Pink, D. H. (2005). *A whole new mind: Moving from the information age to the conceptual age.* New York, NY: Riverhead Books.

Shapiro, R. J. (2008). *Futurecast: How superpowers, populations and globilization will change the way you live and work.* New York, NY: St. Martin's Press.

Slaughter, S., & Rhoades, G. (2009). *Academic capitalism and the new economy: Markets, states, and higher education.* Baltimore, MD: John Hopkins University Press.

Smick, D. M. (2008). *The world is curved: Hidden dangers to the global economy.* New York, NY: Penguin Books.

Spohrer, J. (2010). *T-shaped professionals.* East Lansing, MI: Michigan State University, Collegiate Employment Research Institute. Retrieved from the CERI website: http://www.ceri.msu.edu/t-shaped-professionals/

Twenge, J. M. (2006). *Generation me.* New York, NY: Free Press.

Twenge, J. M., Campell, W. K., & Freeman, E. C. (2012). Generational differences in young adults' life goals, concern for others, and civic orientation, 1966-2009. *Journal of Personality and Social Psychology, 102*(5), 1045-1062. doi: 10.1037/a0027408

CHAPTER *Eight*

Seniors, Symbolism, and Solidarity: Collegiate Transition Rituals

Peter M. Magolda and J. Michael Denton

In a sensible world, I would now congratulate the Class of 1995 and sit down without further comment. I am sure the Class of 1995 wishes I would do so; unfortunately, for the Class of 1995, we do not live in a sensible world.

We live in a world so far more slavish in its obedience to ancient custom than we like to admit. And ancient commencement day custom demands that somebody stand up here and harangue the poor graduates until they beg for mercy. The ancient role has been: Make them suffer. —Russell Baker, 1995 address to Connecticut College (Albanese & Trissler, 1998, p. 17)

Russell Baker, Pulitzer Prize author and humorist, began his commencement address with this amusing insight about university graduation ceremonies to counter the perception that keynote speakers are serious and humorless pontificators. Yet embedded in this amusing interlude is the serious message that the sacredness of enacted "ancient custom," as Baker suggests, has the potential to enslave organizers and participants in sustaining the status quo (e.g., suffering), even if the status quo is antithetical to an espoused value (e.g., a transformative and celebratory transition of seniors from college to the "real world") of the institution. We begin the chapter with this passage to remind readers that campus ceremonies involving seniors, such as commencement, convey important core institutional values, can transform students, and, therefore, are worthy of scholarly scrutiny.

Thus, the overarching goals of this chapter are to (a) introduce and carefully examine the myriad programs—aimed at easing transitions from college to life after college—that university staff typically sponsor for seniors and the events seniors plan for themselves; (b) examine the cultural norms (e.g., collegiate accomplishments merit commemoration) embedded in these ceremonies as well as participants' reactions to these expectations (e.g., acceptance, resistance); and (c) reveal how scholarship about ritual can enrich understanding about these familiar, although seldom scrutinized traditions, resulting in better support for college seniors. Unlike many commencement speakers, we refrain from offering prescriptive advice for success. Instead, readers are invited to use ritual as a theoretical lens through which to carefully examine these social scenes with the hope of "making the obvious obvious, making the obvious dubious, and making the hidden obvious" (Patton, 1990, p. 480).

Campus Traditions for Seniors

When I began to prepare for this [commencement] address, I spoke to a number of friends who (because of their distinguished work) had practice with this sort of thing. Their advice and collective wisdom was very helpful. One said to avoid clichés like the plague ... But one said, "By all means, don't tell them their future lies ahead of them. That's the worst."

I thought about this, and I think our future lies behind us ... In the last dozen years, I have learned many things, but that history is our greatest teacher is perhaps the most important lesson. —Ken Burns, 1987 address to Hampshire College (Albanese & Trissler, 1998, p. 131)

Ken Burns, famed documentary film director, during his commencement address invited graduates to study and reflect upon on the past before trying to influence the future. We heed this sage advice by introducing and briefly examining long-standing campus traditions for seniors. As Burns notes, examining the past—a potent teacher—allows us to think more complexly about the intentions, processes, and outcomes of and reactions to senior-year events—ensuring history does not repeat itself (pardon the cliché).

Gardner, Van der Veer, and Associates (1998) introduced and analyzed a multitude of campus programs sponsored exclusively for seniors—an indisputably unique collegiate subculture. Many of the century-old, senior-oriented, annual events mentioned in their work continue to thrive on most American campuses. Departmental curricular programs for seniors (e.g., capstone seminars, senior theses, internships) are commonplace and tightly woven into the fabric of campus life. The same is true for cocurricular offerings for seniors, such as career advising and professional development workshops, leadership achievement award ceremonies, financial planning seminars, and senior fund-raising competitions.

Some annual grand ceremonies, such as commencement, appeal to the masses, while other little traditions (e.g., joining the class of 2012 Facebook group) target niche audiences (e.g., nostalgic seniors). Some senior programs are formal and sanctioned by universities, like the administration of the Graduate Record Examination (GRE); others are informal, created, and sustained by seniors for seniors (e.g., student-run exam preparation sessions for students aspiring to take the GRE). Regardless of whether programs are in the curriculum or cocurriculum, formal or informal, grand or small, regularly scheduled or sporadic, or initiated by students or for students, these historically rooted and potent events share a common goal of supporting seniors as they celebrate college and prepare for the future. These programs also reveal much about universities' and seniors' deep-seated espoused and enacted values.

An examination of excerpts from five commencement addresses subtly reveals institutional norms, values, and intended outcomes for many senior-only events.

> But as you step into life I can give you three watchwords: first, you are Negroes, members of that dark, historic race that from the world's dawn has slept to hear the trumpet sermons sound through our ears. Cherish unwavering faith in the blood of your fathers, and make sure this last triumph of humanity. Remember next, you are gentlemen and ladies, trained in the liberal arts and subjects in that vast kingdom of culture that has lighted the world from its infancy and guided it through bigotry and falsehood and sin . . . And finally, remember you are the sons of Fisk University, that venerable mother who rose out of the blood and dust of battle to work the triumphs of the Prince of Peace. —W.E.B. Du Bois, 1898 address to Fisk College (Albanese & Trissler, 1998, p. 233)

To the graduates, I offer my heartfelt congratulations. This is the payoff for all the late nights in the library and the long hours of studying. —Madeleine Albright, 1997 address to Mount Holyoke (Albanese & Trissler, 1998, p. 138)

Being a Texan, for better and for worse, means you're going to be special for the rest of your lives ... You remember during World War II Winston Churchill used to flash the V for victory sign, like this. Who knows? If Churchill had flashed the hook 'em horns instead, he might have won the war in half the time. —Dan Rather, 1995 address to The University of Texas (Albanese & Trissler, 1998, p. 33)

So what exactly do I want to pass on to you?...Continue searching harder, deeper, faster, stronger, and louder and know that one day you'll be called upon to use all that you've amassed in the process. —Jodie Foster, 1993 address to Yale University (Albanese & Trissler, 1998, p. 15)

It's special because I get to look out over some of the most talented young people in America getting ready to march off and tackle the toughest problems this world can throw at them. —Colin Powell, 1992 address to Fisk University (Albanese & Trissler, 1998, p. 72)

Du Bois invoked a sense of *solidarity* amongst Fisk University graduates— alluding to the importance of unity, cultural awareness, and social networks. He argued these qualities that benefitted Fisk collegians while undergraduates are equally important after college. Albright acknowledged and celebrated the astonishing *achievements* of Mount Holyoke seniors as she reminded these serious and hard-working women about their preparedness for life. Rather declared University of Texas seniors received a one-of-a-kind education and sustaining their *loyalty* to their alma mater was essential. Foster invited Yale seniors to *reflect* on the knowledge they gained during college to ensure their actions make the world a better place to live. And finally, Powell acknowledged the monumental tasks that awaited college graduates as they *transitioned* from college seniors to world citizens.

The wisdom conveyed in these commencement addresses exemplify five important and discrete outcomes for many senior-year programs posited by Kuh (1998): "(1) recognizing achievement, (2) encouraging students to reflect on the meaning of their college experience, (3) cultivating loyal graduates, (4) unifying the senior class, and (5) easing the transition to life after college" (p. 155). These discrete, purposeful, and intuitively appealing elements centering on integration, reflection, closure, and transition account for the proliferation and endurance of these events.

Recognizing and working to purposefully achieve these outcomes makes sense, because as Gardner (1999) noted, "as college seniors leave their undergraduate careers behind, these new alumni will face the complex demands of a new economy, ever-changing technology, an increasingly diverse America, and a demanding, fluctuating, and highly competitive job market" (p. 6). Many senior-oriented traditions and programs assist students and universities in attaining Kuh's five vital outcomes (e.g., cultivating loyal graduates, easing the transition to life after college). Yet, these ceremonies are more than a means to numerous ends; they are complex and multilayered sociocultural scenes, filled with meaning and often with competing and contested ideologies (Bailey & Gayle, 2003). These scenes reveal differing views of what counts as good. A cursory examination of Gardner's position reveals what he believes is good: preparing seniors to navigate the perils of new economies, become tech-savvy, appreciate diversity, and secure meaningful employment—American values, while prevalent, not universally endorsed in academia.

Magolda (2000) noted campus traditions "(1) are seldom scrutinized, (2) are important sources for revealing social and cultural conditions, (3) reveal much about … organizers and participants, and (4) are political acts that communicate expectations and norms for behavior and performance (that is, transmit culture)" (pp. 32-33). Carefully examining senior traditions and programs reveals competing visions among and between seniors, staff, faculty, administrators, and other stakeholders (e.g., parents, governing boards) of what counts as good. For example, one senior might interpret her senior capstone seminar as a perfunctory requirement for graduation—an empty rite of passage of sorts, with minimal symbolic meaning. Her acquiescence or this-too-will-pass philosophy (i.e., what she deems as good) challenges the espoused purpose of a capstone experience (i.e., critically reflecting on and synthesizing years of learning), while sustaining the status quo (i.e., an academic prerequisite for graduation). A second senior might interpret the same capstone seminar as highly symbolic and transformative—representing a rite of passage from knowledge recipient to knowledge creator (e.g., honing intellectually curiosities, designing and conducting original research, integrating knowledge, defending intellectual ideas). A third senior might also value the capstone seminar but more highly prize the esprit de corps amongst seniors than the particular seminar content.

Examining the past—using ritual as an analytic guide—allows us to think more complexly about the intentions, processes, and outcomes of and reactions to these events, such as subculture norms and competing ideologies. Exploring the many different ways university communities, including seniors, have historically ascertained what is good can lead to the sponsorship of more meaningful events and programs for seniors based on negotiations involving individuals who subscribe to different viewpoints.

Ritual and Rites of Passage: An Overview

Graduation is one of the few genuine rites of passage left in our society. You are, individually and collectively, passing symbolically from one place to another, from an old to a new status. And like all such rites, it is both retrospective and prospective. You are graduating (or being graduated) from college, which is the end of something. But the ceremony we are participating in is called commencement ... If your liberal arts education has meant anything, it has given you some notions of a critical opposition to the way things are ... This attitude of opposition is not justified as strategy, as a means to an end: a way of changing the world. It is, rather, the best way of being in the world. —Susan Sontag 1983 address to Wellesley College (Albanese & Trissler, 1998, pp. 157, 159)

Sontag—literary theorist, feminist, and political activist—in her commencement address purposefully uses the term rite to describe the elaborate, dramatic, and planned cultural change that commencement ceremonies hope to induce. Although she intentionally uses the term rite of passage (a type of ritual) to convey this significant life transition (van Gennep, 1960), many faculty, administrators, students, and alumni are more cavalier when they interject anthropological terms, such as rites of passage or ritual into campus conversations.

For example, when colleagues discuss ritual, their definitions widely vary. The Greek life community uses the term ritual to communicate to outsiders that their organizations follow a proscribed set of secret practices that define the essence of their organizations. In this context, rituals separate insiders from outsiders. Student affairs staff members may use the term ritual to describe annual or transitional events that may have significance for both staff and students, such as residence halls move-in/move-out days and orientation. Athletic administrators and alumni talk about tailgating rituals that precede football games (i.e., events where fans engage in fanatical behaviors, such as arriving six hours before kickoff to pledge their allegiances to college athletics and their universities); in these instances, solidarity and loyalty reign. Seniors talk about the ritual of taking the Medical College Admission Test (MCAT) or Law School Admissions Test (LSAT)—rites of passage, of sorts, into respected professional fields. In contrast, custodians often refer to their daily rituals when describing mundane work routines.

Some faculty and staff interchange the terms *ritual* and *commencement* since commencement is formal, large-scale, and distinct from ordinary life, which are widely accepted characteristics of ritual. Yet others would argue the little acts, or interaction rituals (Goffman, 1967), such as graduates tossing their caps into the air as soon as the university president confers degrees, is synonymous with ritual. Despite these smaller, unspectacular, and informal social scenes, some posit these micro-interactions symbolically affirm or challenge the location and status of individuals in the larger social network. McLaren (1986) concludes, "A great deal of conceptual confusion still surrounds the meaning of the word ritual" (p. 55).

Unfortunately, when campus community members interject the word ritual into conversations, either an anything-goes mentality (i.e., ritual can mean whatever you want it to be) or rigid competing definitions (e.g., Greek life lavaliering ceremonies are rituals while custodians' routines are not rituals) prevail. Regrettably, in both of these instances opportunities to fully understand and appreciate the potency of ritual and its influence on the university and its constituents is severely hindered.

Deconstructing Rituals

In the spirit of Sontag, it is imperative to critically oppose efforts to ignore careless references to ritual without seeking clarification. Likewise, simply cataloguing complex, multivoiced, and multifaceted social scenes (i.e., this is a ritual and this is not a ritual), and then debating which definition is "correct" leads to contentious, futile, and exhausting discussions; essentialized definitions; and, at best, moderate insights. Instead, it is proposed the belief that ritual is a *type of action* (Quantz & Magolda, 1997) be abandoned and, instead, conceptualized as an *aspect of action*, which better reveals its utility for scholar-practitioners.

Consequently, we should first enquire about how individuals use ritual discourse and for what purposes, rather than ask what ritual is. Quantz (1999, 2001) offers a conceptualization of ritual (without claiming this is what ritual actually is) helpful in shifting conversation from types of ritual action to aspects of ritual embedded in all social scenes. He describes ritual as a *formalized, symbolic performance* (1999). First, it is a performative rather than a linguistic act. As such, performers physically act out something for an audience to observe, conveying messages not easily communicated in everyday language. For example, when a senior woman dances into the living room of her apartment and announces to her housemates that she has accepted a job offer, her intention is for her friends to view and participate in this celebratory scene. During this performance, distinct roles emerge. The recently employed senior's role may be that of the euphoric, relieved, and proud soon-to-be college graduate. The woman's housemates, who too follow an implicit and often unconscious script, may act as supportive friends. Quantz (1999) states,

> The point of performance is that the action is not simply instrumental to achieving an overt end, but is acted in a manner to be seen or heard and "read" by others; therefore, it is also a text, a dramatic text. (p. 507)

Recognizing and then studying the scripts and actions of these performances can lead to invaluable reflective opportunities and profound insights.

Second, ritual involves *symbols*, which are mechanisms that convey meaning indirectly and over and beyond the specific situational meanings. In this example, announcing the job news is not simply an instrumental task (i.e., to communicate news of the day). For this senior, sharing her career attainment news symbolizes an educational milestone, and her peers' euphoric reaction may affirm the group's solidarity. The mode of communicating the news (i.e., dancing) is also symbolic. Depending on context, dancing may convey feelings of elation and/or superiority; it can be inviting and build unity or be used to exclude and emphasize difference, as high school prom attendees can attest. Rituals are "never neutral" (McLaren, 1985, p. 85); they create and transmit values, expectations, and cultural norms (Magolda, 2000). During these cognitive, emotional, spiritual, and experiential performances, participants manipulate symbols to convey and reaffirm shared values.

Lastly, symbolic performances have a recognizable and expected form, meaning that individuals familiar with a ritual expect it to occur in certain predetermined ways and these individuals are likely to recognize whether or not the ritual is performed correctly. In order for people to believe the ritual and its meaning, the ritual must follow form and be convincing. The participants must enact (i.e., perform) the ritual as expected (i.e., preserve its form). When someone performs a ritual act, but violates some important aspect of the form, doubt about the legitimacy is a likely outcome. Embedded in symbolic performances are explicit and implicit rules that convey to participants whether the ritual was done correctly. If the peers' responses to the news about the job offer were indifference, disappointment, or sarcasm, the legitimacy of the ritual (in this context) would be called into question. Yet, forms of support may vary wildly among different social groups. For some, an expected or appropriate performance of support could be real or feigned envy, while others might expect friends to show support differently. Over time, rituals acquire "a sense of rightness" (Young, 1999, p. 11). Carefully examining senior events, by paying particular attention to the performances, symbolism, and form, can lead to keen and in-depth insights about event organizers and participants.

Shifting attention away from what is and is not a ritual and instead toward a conceptualization of ritual that examines social scenes in order to reveal sociocultural norms uncovers the power of ritual. For example, on some college campuses, the acquisition of a school ring is a significant experience reserved only for seniors. The social scene of a senior student acquiring and donning his or her ring in front of friends and/or family personifies ritual as an aspect of action. The senior here has an opportunity to perform, the experience has an expected form, and the scene has symbolic meaning (e.g., the student's rite of passage to being a senior and future alumni). Conversely, if the student merely purchases a ring as ornamentation and does not imbue it with any special significance, even in front of significant others, it is clearly not intended as a performance, but rather instrumental (i.e., buying jewelry), and not symbolic. The scene then becomes the antithesis of ritual as an aspect of action. The significant other (perhaps a parent), understanding the symbolic significance of the student's purchase, can be a gateway to conversations about what it means to be beginning the transition into "the real world." The rite of passage, reflected in this minor social exchange, is a powerful reminder of change and has implications for the student and possibly the significant other. A dialogue may even begin with a staff or faculty member who notices the new ring. The conversation about the transition has the potential to help the student critically reflect on his or her values, goals, hopes, and fears. In addition, the person interacting with the senior has the opportunity to provide mentorship and possible guidance while deepening the relationship with the student.

Manning (2000) states, "higher education is replete with ritualistic activities … rituals are rich depositories of accumulated meaning within a college culture. By examining the forms of rituals and ceremonies, the meanings of college culture can be understood" (p. 3). McLaren (1985) adds rituals are "carriers of culturally … coded messages … [that] channel meaning contextually" (p. 85). Deconstructing rituals and analyzing them provides insights about higher education and its seniors. For instance, when seniors write about their final days on campus on Facebook or Twitter, enroll for classes for the final time, apply for jobs, or purchase caps and gowns for graduation, are these events simply treated as instrumental tasks by staff and faculty? Are they merely things most seniors tend to do—or are they "rich depositories of accumulated meaning within a college culture?" These and the following set of questions provide a starting point in the deconstructing process to examine rituals: What are the coded messages? In what ways do ritual participants interpret these messages? What roles do the performers adopt? What do the performances convey? Are the performances convincing? Do the performances evoke cognitive, emotional, or spiritual reactions? If the performance appears askew, do we reflect on what is wrong? Since rituals are never neutral, what values and cultural norms do these actions transmit?

There are multiple reasons the academy avoids asking and answering questions such as these. Some senior-oriented events are small, informal, unspectacular, and occur irregularly; others possess a sacred-like quality or are so steeped in tradition that scrutinizing their worth seems sacrilegious and ill advised. Some senior ceremonies are admired to such a degree that busy organizers simply replicate rather than tweak them—adhering to the adage, "if it ain't broke, don't fix it." Yet, to truly support seniors, architects of senior programs need to answer these questions so they can recognize, understand, and respond to the core values that guide actions. For example, if the multitude of ways seniors envision and enact the values of unity, achievement, loyalty, reflection, and smooth transitions are understood (Kuh, 1998)—by examining the formalized, symbolic performances—then rituals can be created that are meaningful to seniors and engage them in conversation about the messages their informal rituals convey.

Rational and Nonrational Analysis

When studying ritual, a rational (e.g., symbolic) analysis can yield useful insights as discussed above; however, it is also important to include a nonrational (i.e., not to be confused with the irrational) examination, which works side-by-side with rational analysis to enrich understanding about ritual and its knowledge potential. Nonrational social mechanisms (e.g., inspirational speeches, collective singing at sporting events, induction ceremonies) remain mostly ignored, despite the influence of the nonrational on social interactions.

For example, during the final home game of the season for most collegiate sports teams, coaches and fans pay tribute to senior team members. The multitude of formalized, symbolic performances embedded in this celebratory event (based on a rational analysis) could yield volumes of data, interpretations, and findings (e.g., analyzing the meaning of symbols, such as the recognition of parents, the cheering crowds, the coach's comments about the unique contributions of each graduating senior). But focusing exclusively on spoken words or actions (i.e., rationality) would be to miss an equally important aspect—the nonrational influences resulting from the university community gathering together to collectively celebrate the contributions of these seniors. The act of coming together—team members, their families, fans, peers, administrators, alumni, and community members—creates a sense of solidarity. This solidarity is "produced by people acting together, not by people thinking together" (Kertzer, 1988, p. 76). The feelings of community that arise result less from the sharing of some common idea and more from the sharing of a common experience. Quantz and Magolda (1997) elaborate on other outcomes as well as the importance of the nonrational in ritual analysis:

> But while these performances help construct solidarity, they not only lead to the construction of a single, egalitarian "community," they may also work to reconfirm social hierarchies (Warner, 1941; 1959) or to increase social conflict (Gilmore, 1975) even to assist in revolution (Kertzer, 1988). Ritual is important to study because it is one of the major social mechanisms that utilizes nonrationality to construct schools as places of community (Hays, 1994) or as places of domination (Bernstein, 1977) or of places of resistance (Hall & Jefferson, 1976; McLaren, 1993) or as places of struggle.

The last game of the season celebration, in other words, serves purposes, intentionally or not, other than building solidarity. Nonrational outcomes of such a recognition ceremony may include reinforcing a privileged status for college athletes and/or the athletic team. Conversely, such a ceremony could counter-intuitively convey to college athletes that a failure to balance the intense schedule of training along with a heavy course load is their fault and not that of the program since, clearly, other athletes are graduating. Because such reactions are rooted in the nonrational, we can only speculate as to how individuals or a community construct them. Dialogue with participants in rituals may expose invisible, unexpected, and potentially unintended messages being conveyed in rituals. Human actions are not always logical and rational; they are often inconsistent, incoherent, and sometimes performed against our better interests and strongly held values. We may nonrationally construct unintended meanings and messages. This nonrational aspect of our existence can be found in our rituals.

Thinking of ritual as being an aspect of many, perhaps even most, actions will help organizers of senior transition programs to shift their attention from the larger, higher profile, and less important rituals, such as commencement, to the more mundane and more important ritualistic performances of ordinary collegiate life (Bjork, 2002). For instance, inquiring as to how student athletes celebrate graduating or attaining senior status among themselves, away from official university functions, may provide useful insights into how student athletes think and feel about their experiences. How do various student organizations choose to recognize or celebrate their graduating members, if they do at all? The mostly unseen, largely unknown, and usually unexamined rituals seniors engage in reveal through action the complexities, tensions, and contradictions they may feel about their university, their transition into professional careers or advanced academic work, their peers, and themselves in ways they would not or possibly could not otherwise articulate. Examination of these (and other) micro social scenes is central to understanding our universities and students, especially seniors.

Rituals, Rites of Passage, and Senior Transition

Humans have always had rites of passage for critical, transitional moments in our life histories. This is a tradition going back not just hundreds of thousands of years, but millions. —Carl Sagan, 1993 address to Wheaton College (Albanese & Trissler, p. 55).

As Carl Sagan, famed astronomer acknowledges in his commencement address, senior rituals are a time-honored rite of passage. The senior year is replete with critical, transitional, and transformative moments. For instance, each year at Miami University in Ohio, the two days in early May between final examinations and commencement are inundated by hundreds of senior events—large and small, informal, and student-sponsored celebratory evenings—some involving the excessive consumption of alcohol and resulting in extensive property damage on and off campus. These senior rituals exemplify the rites of passage Sagan references—that have been going on for about 200 years at the institution. Seniors who partake in these events describe it as "our last fling … before entering the 'real world.'" From the vantage point of University administrators and town leaders, the senior celebratory events that involve the excessive consumption of alcohol and property damage are dangerous, antithetical to institutional values, and a public relations nightmare. Despite administrators' and town leaders' concerns about these dangerous occurrences;

each year, a vocal majority of seniors who participate in the outings resist efforts to alter the status quo. Juxtaposing these informal, spontaneous, small, and student-initiated pregraduation celebrations with the more formal university commencement ceremony, the multitude of transition events for seniors comes in sharper focus. These two contrasting events are used to summarize key points raised in this chapter and offer concluding insights about ways to better support seniors and higher education.

Senior Programs Are Worthy of Scholarly Scrutiny

I was quite impressed to learn that the doctorate that I am receiving today is one of Humane Letters. I'm not really sure what Humane Letters are, but I've heard of it before. So thank you for inducting me into that esteemed academic community. —Ben Cohen, 1995 address to Southampton College (Albanese & Trissler, p. 45)

Like Ben Cohen, of Ben and Jerry's fame, who during his commencement speech acknowledged he did not know what was meant by Humane Letters, many university faculty, staff (in particular individuals responsible for events for seniors), and students are unaware of scholarship written about ritual, and that ritual is worthy of examination. McLaren (1986) points to this lack of scrutiny and invites questioning of underlying ideologies in school rituals: "a great deal has been written about education as the transmission of cultural knowledge, but almost no exploration of the way culture, as a ritual action, constitutes and fosters ideology and behavior in school settings" (pp. 56-57).

Long-standing senior traditions, such as pregraduation celebrations (PGC) and commencement, remind us there are literally thousands of different kinds of programs marketed to seniors, worthy of critical examination. Many of these programs—especially those that are formally linked to the curriculum and cocurriculum, regularly occurring, university-sponsored, and larger scale—immediately come to mind when brainstorming senior ceremonies or programs. Yet, smaller, informal, senior-sponsored, sporadically occurring events, such as the PGC described above, are ignored. These events, especially the latter, escape scrutiny despite their importance and capacity to reveal social, cultural, and political conditions; organizers' and participants' expectations and norms for behavior and performance; social strata; privileged subcultures, power differentials, or hierarchies; and what is good.

Thinking broadly about what counts as senior transition programs, events, or celebrations and then inventorying them are useful first steps. Whitt's (1993) cultural audit provides a formal, although, flexible discovery framework for identifying senior transition events and surfacing their important historical roots. If senior programs are worthy of sponsorship, they are worthy of scholarly scrutiny.

Senior Programs Are Political Acts

Most important, our stories include our own justifications for our actions and our motives—in light of our own values. —Stephen Breyer, 1997 address to Stanford University (Albanese & Trissler, p. 87)

Supreme Court Justice Breyer, in his commencement address, underscored the influences of values, ideologies, and politics on everyday life. McLaren (1986) echoed this sentiment when he stated, "A political program which does not recognize the unconscious elements of ideology and its embodiment in social routines and rituals at all levels of social existence ... is doomed to failure" (p. 60). Programs supporting and honoring seniors are political acts (i.e., actions intended to have an effect on the established social order). As much as institutions might want to disguise this fact, senior programs—both PGC and commencement programs—are political acts, predicated on particular ideologies. An ideological intention of PGC organizers, who sponsor all-night-anything-goes parties, is to challenge the established social order of "appropriate" behaviors for seniors mandated by university standards. Likewise, commencement organizers challenge the established social order of an "ordinary" day on campus by organizing a grand, one-of-a-kind hypercelebratory event replete with processions, academic regalia, dignitaries, decorum, and pageantry. Commencement organizers' political agenda includes bringing closure to seniors' collegiate careers, celebrating academic achievements, and cultivating devoted alumni, among others. In both contexts, the performers convey what is perceived as normal. In the PGC context, seniors who party are normal and represent the privileged few. In the commencement context, academically successful students, for example, are normal and represented as the upper strata in this collegian hierarchy. Failing to recognize the dominant values and participants' reactions to these values will lead to squandered learning opportunities. Recognizing the politics and values embedded in senior events can reveal answers to the important question: Whose interests are being served? Answering this political question can lead to meaningful campuswide dialogue about the common good, resulting in more purposeful and powerful programs for seniors. For as Gardner (1999) notes, "We have a moral obligation to define and improvethe senior year experience" (p. 5). Meaningful change of senior-year experiences is more likely to occur if change agents understand their own and others' values and political agendas.

Analyzing Senior Ritual Discourse Can Enhance Practice

We must look with the greatest skepticism toward those who promise easy and quick solutions. —Bill Clinton, 1996 address to Princeton University (Albanese & Trissler, p. 123)

As President Clinton suggests, we do not propose that understanding how ritual impacts institutional culture will lead to sudden or even necessarily easy change. Shifts in rituals and culture more often than not occur incrementally and gradually. Magolda (2000) notes, "Carefully analyzing rituals can reveal an institution's core values, a small but important step in closing the gap between what institutions say and what they do"(p. 43). All social entities (e.g., institutions, subcultures), large and small, have core values that guide actions. While individuals enact and react (e.g., agree or disagree) to these values each day, often they remain implicit and part of individuals' subconscious. Even when clarity is gained about these core values, an inevitable gap between what is espoused and enacted persists. Carefully analyzing seniors' ritual discourse can make these values explicit, lessening this espoused-enacted gap. Engaging in these processes is one example of the potency of rituals.

For example, if an espoused goal of the PGC is to challenge the status quo of campus life in a small, sleepy, college town, examining the many social scenes embedded in these events—paying particular attention to the formal, symbolic performances—can assist in assessing how well the organizers enacted this goal, which could lead organizers to alter the program in the future. PGC opponents could also examine these social scenes—again paying attention to formal, symbolic performances—which could possibly lead to interventions aimed at altering these events (e.g., minimizing the amount of alcohol consumed). Rituals can reveal moral or political imperatives, which is a prerequisite to understanding what is good.

Likewise, in the commencement context, an espoused goal could be recognition for all seniors, but a symbolic analysis of the event may reveal numerous subcultures of students who the ceremony marginalizes (e.g., seniors who worked full time and earned average grades, rendering them virtually invisible in an event that celebrates the accomplishments of the best and the brightest). By examining the many social scenes embedded in this grand event, positive changes can result, such as affirming a wider body of students. Since nongraduating students often attend these ceremonies in solidarity with graduating friends, these students also stand to benefit from feeling more central to the university community. Further, commencement ceremonies offer an opportunity to convey or reinforce to faculty and staff important core institutional values and the importance of their role in transforming students. Who and what counts (i.e., is good) in a university is often reflected in commencement ceremonies, sometimes in conflict and tension with espoused values.

Examining ritual discourses suggests what purposes the ceremony serves, for example, sustaining the status quo or seeking transformation. The process can also unfold how rituals support logical arguments about senior experiences and education and nonrational components of the ritual (e.g., emotions, inspirational appeals, higher callings). In addition, an analysis of ritual discourses can reveal what the institution considers normal. Pockets of resistance construct their own discourse for those who disagree with these normalizing expectations (e.g., the rubber duck taped to a graduation cap as a form of resisting dialogue). Asking the following questions can lead event organizers, faculty, and staff deeper into this examination process: What does a specific resisting discourse (e.g., rubber duck on the cap) suggest about that student's relationship to the ritual and other ritual participants? To what extent does a capstone course truly embody and enact (i.e., perform) the values and principles of transformative education and to what extent does it exist to serve as a symbol of those values but fail to enact them? What values and principles do programs geared towards senior-year issues represent? To what degree might they reinforce or undermine the principles of a liberal education through their various emphases?

Ritual discourse reveals what counts as meaningful transitions for seniors; what seniors learned; how seniors integrated their collegiate experiences into a whole; how seniors forge and maintain communities; and the interpersonal, civic, political, spiritual, and vocational actions and aspirations of seniors. For campus community members who want to understand shared social interactions, change the culture, and respond to pockets of resistance, paying attention to ritual discourses is a viable means to achieve these aims—provided we heed Bill Clinton's reminder there are no "easy and quick solutions," especially as it relates to improving senior-year experiences.

Closing Thoughts

So, I will ignore tradition and try to say something you might remember for more than twenty-four hours. —John Grisham, 1992 address to Mississippi State University (Albanese & Trissler, p. 62)

We, like John Grisham during his commencement address, aspire to offer some insights that might pass the test of time. Gardner (1999) observed:

> While there appears to be a general acceptance of the need for specific interventions to help students successfully make the transition into college, the problems and needs associated with the transition out of college have received little attention from college and university personnel, let alone researchers. (p. 6)

Rituals play an important part in the transition into and beyond the senior year of college. When university administrators, staff, and faculty understand how their and students' actions constitute aspects of ritual and how those actions convey certain values and meanings, they can augment their ability to effectively address the transition needs of seniors. Examining formal and informal rituals on a large and small scale can illuminate the values institutions and students hold and how those values align, intersect, compete, or conflict. Finally, while rational and logical analysis of the symbolic meanings conveyed in various rituals will certainly offer up copious information and insights, attending to nonrational aspects of rituals may better explain actions taken by students and institutions through this period of transition.

References

Albanese, A, & Trissler, B. (Eds.). (1998). *Graduation day: The best of America's commencement speeches.* New York, NY: William Morrow.

Bailey, G., & Gayle, N. A. (2003). *Ideology: Structuring identities in contemporary life.* Peterborough, Ontario: Broadview Press.

Bjork, C. (2002). Reconstructing rituals: Expressions of autonomy and resistance in a Sino-Indonesian school. *Anthropology and Education Quarterly, 33*(4), 465-491.

Gardner, J. N. (1999, March-April). The senior year experience. *About Campus,* 5-11.

Gardner, J. N., Van der Veer, G., & Associates. (1998). *The senior year experience: Facilitating integration, reflection, closure, and transition.* San Francisco, CA: Jossey-Bass.

Goffman, E. (1967). *Interaction ritual: essays on face-to-face behavior.* Garden City, NY: Anchor Books.

Kertzer, D. I. (1988). *Ritual, politics, and power.* New Haven, CN: Yale University.

Kuh, G. D. (1998). Strengthening the ties that bind: Cultural events, rituals, and traditions. In J. N. Gardner, G. Van der Veer, & Associates, *The senior year experience: Facilitating integration, reflection, closure, and transition* (pp. 152-170). San Francisco, CA: Jossey-Bass.

Magolda, P. M. (2000). The campus tour ritual: Exploring community discourses in higher education. *Anthropology and Education Quarterly, 31*(1), 24-36.

Manning, K. (2000). *Rituals, ceremonies, and cultural meaning in higher education.* Westport, CT: Greenwood Publishing Group, Inc.

McLaren, P. L. (1985). The ritual dimensions of resistance: Clowning and symbolic inversion. *Journal of Education, 167*(2), 84-97.

McLaren, P. L. (1986). Making Catholics: The ritual production of conformity in a Catholic junior high school. *Journal of Education, 168*(2), 55-77.

Patton, M. Q. (1990). *Qualitative evaluation and research methods.* Newbury Park, CA: Sage.

Quantz, R. A. (1999). School ritual as performance: A reconstruction of Durkheim's and Turner's use of ritual. *Educational Theory, 49*(4), 493-513.

Quantz, R. A. (2001). On seminar, ritual, and cowboys. *Teachers College Record, 103*(5), 896-922.

Quantz, R. A., & Magolda, P. M. (1997). Nonrational classroom performance: Ritual as an aspect of action. *Urban Review, 29*(4), 221-238.

van Gennep, A. (1960). *The rites of passage.* Chicago, IL: The University of Chicago Press.

Whitt, E. J. (1993). Making the familiar strange: Discovering culture. In G. D. Kuh (Ed.), *Cultural perspectives in student affairs work* (pp. 81-94). Lanham, MD: University Press of America.

Young, R. B. (1999, September-October). Reexamining our rituals. *About Campus,* 10-16.

CHAPTER Nine

Cultivating Traditions of Engagement and Giving Among New Alumni

Meredith L. Fakas and Mary Ruffin W. Childs

Twenty-five-year-old Ryan received his bachelor's and master's degrees in architecture from a public university. His undergraduate studies were paid for with academic scholar-ships, but Ryan accrued significant student loans while earning his master's degree. Aside from attending an occasional football game, he was not involved in any student activity outside the requirements of his major. He graduated at the top of his class each time, walked in both commencements, and proudly wears his class ring, but he has yet to make a financial contribution to his alma mater. Employed at an architecture firm, he has paid off his car loan and accelerated the retirement of his student-loan debt.

Cameron, also 25 years old, received her undergraduate degree in education from a small, private liberal arts college. She was involved in first-year student orientation, Greek life, faith-based organizations, and student government. Her education was subsidized by student loans that grew to the size of a modest first-home mortgage. She walked in commencement, proudly wears her class ring, made her first gift to the college when she was a senior, and has made one every year since graduation. Currently unemployed, she was a school teacher for two years.

Ryan believes donating to his university is important, but it is something he intends to continue putting off until he feels financially healthier: "I really should start donating money to my alma mater now that I have an income," he explains, "but the only money

I have donated is the two-dollar bill they gave me at graduation to give back to them immediately so they could obtain my after-college contact information. I will soon begin donating more—right after I finish paying off my student loans" (Personal communication, September 9, 2011).

As her giving history suggests, Cameron has a different take. "My alma mater gave me my education, friends, and an all-around great experience," she says. "My annual donation is a very small way I can give back to the school that means so much to me" (Personal communication, September 9, 2011).

Determining the motivations for giving by alumni and using that information to encourage gifts from those who have previously not donated have been priorities of alumni offices for as long as fundraising has been necessary to advance colleges and universities. Monks (2003) surveyed 10,511 graduates from the class of 1989 at 28 private, highly selective colleges and universities and found the graduate's financial profile, major field of study, advanced degree attainment, financial aid support, marital status, and satisfaction with undergraduate experiences were all correlated with alumni giving, as were involvement in extracurricular activities and certain academic opportunities (e.g., internships). Among all of these factors, Monks states "the most significant determinant of alumni giving levels is the individual's satisfaction with his or her undergraduate experience" (p. 124). He found that survey respondents who indicated they were *very satisfied* or *generally satisfied* with their college experience gave 2.6 and 1.8 times more, respectively, to their alma mater than those who were *ambivalent, generally dissatisfied*, or *very dissatisfied*.

Yet, research on the motivations of young alumni (i.e., under 35 years old or up to 10 years postgraduation) has been more limited. Recent studies have provided valuable data to identify giving trends and common characteristics of younger alumni. Akers and McDearmon (2010) noted, "Several studies have found that younger donors typically donate less to their alma maters when compared to older generations" (p. 4). Clotfelter (2001) offered two reasons for this phenomenon, suggesting that disparities in income and generational characteristics may play the biggest roles in determining why older alumni are more likely to give. He argued age itself is relevant: "As documented by many econometric studies of charitable giving, contributions tend to rise with age, independent of income" (p. 7).

Another indicator of future giving is former gifts, as Akers and McDearmon (2010) pointed out:

> Even if the gifts of this generation are less frequent, cultivating young alumni is still a priority of college and university development offices especially since it has been found that past giving is the strongest single factor in predicting future giving. (p. 4)

Monks (2003) concurred, positing, "Identifying young alumni who are more likely to give and encouraging them to do so, even in modest dollar amounts, may have significant lifetime giving effects" (p. 124).

While gaining ongoing financial support is a chief objective of those working with alumni, this chapter will also examine strategies for creating lasting ties between the institution and its undergraduates. We begin with a discussion of the differences, as well as collaborative efforts, between alumni associations and offices of alumni relations before turning our attention to alumni engagement. This chapter also provides an in-depth discussion of the motivations driving young alumni to donate and offers examples of emerging trends in new alumni giving campaigns.

Alumni Associations and Offices of Alumni Relations

The alumni engagement efforts of college and universities are generally managed by two entities whose needs and goals are distinctly different, but which nevertheless can be easily confused by recent graduates. It is the joint responsibility of an institution's alumni association (or alumni relations office) and its office of annual giving to both *fundraise* and *friend raise* (i.e., offer engagement activities to keep former students connected to and informed about their alma mater).

Some schools have alumni associations, which are often separate nonprofit organizations; others have alumni relations offices that are departments existing and funded within the institutional structure. Many larger universities also have alumni relations representatives directly employed by a school, college, or department. These individuals often manage programs and events specific to their school's alumni and either drive fundraising efforts for the college or work alongside an institutional development officer dedicated to their department.

Development is generally considered the fundraising arm of an institution, and, therefore, the office of annual giving is often located within this area on an organizational chart. In addition to fundraising initiatives, this office manages the annual fund (i.e., the vehicle for alumni, parents, and friends of the institution to provide a yearly gift in support of various programs and critical operating funds). In many instances, the office of annual giving and the alumni association (or office of alumni relations) also act as strategic components for institutional advancement—the efforts to increase understanding and support of the institutional mission to attract high-caliber students and faculty, improve program quality and academic reputation, and expand scholarly productivity.

Measurements of success for offices of annual giving are quantifiable, whether it is the number of constituents who donate, amount of money pledged or collected, or percentage difference in a giving metric from one year to the next. Though most offices of annual giving are separate from alumni associations, institutions benefit when both offices work in conjunction to win the trust and generosity of former students and other constituent groups, such as donors and parents of current students. In addition, collaboration allows these two entities to share and benefit from critical data, such as accurate contact information for students, alumni, and donors.

Friend Raising—or Creating the Ties That Bind

As noted above, alumni associations and offices of alumni relations have two complementary objectives: (a) to create ongoing ties between an institution and its alumni and (b) to incent alumni to provide financial support for their alma mater. The second of these objectives will not be achieved if institutions are unsuccessful in meeting the first. As such, we examine strategies for alumni engagement before turning our attention to alumni giving.

New Graduate Engagement

Many alumni associations are nonprofit organizations independent, at least in part, from their institutions. Measurements of success, such as number of memberships sold, other sources of revenue earned, and scholarship money distributed, are relevant to fulfilling their missions and keeping their doors open. A less quantifiable but highly sought after goal is engagement (i.e., friend raising). Universally, alumni associations consider it a top priority to find ways of strengthening the bonds between alumni and their institutions, yet it is one that can be challenging to track.

Associations work to cultivate meaningful relationships with alumni on an individual basis and make every effort to challenge the common complaint that alumni do not hear from their alma maters until they are asked for money. Whereas offices of annual giving ask for contributions via direct mail, e-mail, or phone calls and dues-based alumni associations solicit for memberships and sponsorships, alumni associations also devote resources to creating engagement opportunities for alumni.

Potential results of these efforts are greater closeness to one's alma mater and an increased likelihood of future gift giving. As Andrew Christopherson, director of development for campus life and athletics at Emory University, notes:

> One trend I see is that some schools are giving graduating students the option of making a financial gift—or they can pledge their time. For example, they could pledge five volunteer hours with their alumni chapter instead of making a $50 gift. Then, after getting involved through the chapter, the idea is that they will be more likely to make the gift, as well. (Personal communication, September 12, 2011)

Alumni associations are actively working to change the belief that they only plan and manage fundraising campaigns and affairs for older members, such as class-year reunions and big-ticket events for high-level donors. Associations nationwide have recognized that young alumni need special consideration, and grouping them into memberwide mass appeals, events, or other initiatives may not be effective. A scan of websites of major university alumni associations around the country reveals young alumni programming has become a critical component. This intent is illustrated by comments from the Michigan State University Alumni Association (MSUAA): "Although the common perception of alumni association members is of older, wealthier donors to the university, MSUAA officials say involving young alumni has become one of the office's biggest focuses" (McKown, 2010).

Some of the most commonly organized methods of bringing together young alumni include volunteer opportunities and sports game-viewing parties. Scott Dahl, president of the Council for Alumni Membership and Marketing Professionals and director of membership and marketing at the Iowa State University Alumni Association, suggests strategies for engaging recent graduates, such as forming a young-alumni council, creating special programming for this age group, and sending them targeted communications (Personal communication, September 8, 2011). At Florida International University,

Duane Wiles, associate executive director of the university's alumni association, credits affinity grouping (i.e., an emphasis on reuniting alumni based on campus involvement, not just class years) as a catalyst for greater involvement. For instance, Florida International will host homecoming reunions for former students who were involved in Greek life, served as student government presidents, acted as student ambassadors, and provided leadership as residential assistants (Personal communication, September 9, 2011).

The University of South Carolina's award-winning and highly successful Face of Y'all campaign prioritizes education and communication over direct donation requests and personalizes the young alumni experience by creating a competition for new graduates to become spokespeople in collateral materials and other publicity vehicles for the year. "They get to talk about themselves, and who doesn't like to talk about themselves?" states Steven J. Farwick II, assistant director of annual giving at the University of South Carolina, referencing this age group's eagerness to share personal information. In its first three years, more than 5,000 young alumni have taken part in the initiative. In 2010, the University saw a 4% increase from the previous year in young alumni responses to a calling campaign, and Farwick credits this to the Face of Y'all program involvement. "I really think it's because we're in front of them more," he suggests. "We're trying to message them the way they want to be spoken to" (Personal communication, September 7, 2011).

Recruiting Current Students as Alumni

To begin the process of cultivating future donors, colleges and universities need to build relationships with students before they leave campus and instill in them the importance of giving. At the University of Virginia, first-year students sign pledges to start paying on a life membership upon graduation, which entitles them to free member benefits while they are undergraduates. The program began in the 1970s, and nearly 75% of the alumni association's current members joined as students. Patti Daves, director of membership, marketing, and affinity programs for Virginia's alumni association, states,

> Engaging students while they are in school is so important. They are our future alumni. Alumni associations should play a role in the [student] experience. If a student understands the value of an alumni association and sees the association as a part of college life, they will in turn lend their support. (Personal communication, September 9, 2011)

Iowa State's Scott Dahl agrees, believing there is a return on investment in programming for students early in their college tenure:

> This process must begin as soon as a student sets foot on campus. If your school has a traditions program, make sure the alumni association is a visible part of it. If you have an alumni center, make sure students have a real reason to be in the building at least once a year. Provide student members with the tools they will need to succeed after college, such as career networking programs in conjunction with college placement programs, mentoring programs and alumni "real world" panels. They may not use these tools early on, but as they become seniors and turn into new graduates, they will appreciate these opportunities. (Personal communication, September 8, 2011)

Laura Taylor, director of member services at the Southern Illinois University (SIU) Alumni Association, concurs, noting SIU's students tend to change their focus from their first year to their last, shifting from an emphasis on the discounts and free events offered by student membership to alumni networking and potential relationships. She had this to say about beginning the relationship-building process between alumni associations and alumni early on:

> To grow so much in maturity in four years means that our association has to keep up each year along the way; otherwise, we've left our future alumni without a strong connection to their alma mater upon graduation day. It is our responsibility to foster relationships and provide top-notch service to our students. As the saying goes, "students today, alumni tomorrow." (Personal communication, September 12, 2011)

Taylor also offered a marketing perspective on the relationship:

> There is no other time in a [student's] life that they are as readily available to us as when they are . . . on campus. That means it is to our advantage to introduce them to the association and all it has to offer while they are here. It's the basic idea of target markets at its finest . . . (Personal communication, September 12, 2011)

Though alumni associations do not necessarily vie for dollars with other schools when it comes to their single degree-holding graduates, they do compete with a multitude of other nonprofits as well as the debt and transition expenses many new alumni face. Establishing a bond and sense of loyalty to the university or college while young alumni are still students needs to be a top priority.

Helping Recent Graduates Weather Economic and Employment Challenges

As Monks (2003) noted, a graduate's financial profile is correlated with alumni giving. Yet, seniors often face a conflicting financial picture upon graduation: "The pot at the end of the rainbow, higher salaries and independence, sits next to 'loan payment due' notices and ever changing 'help wanted' lists'" (Barefoot, 2008, p. 79). Further, since the 2008 economic downturn, many new alumni "have graduated … into a no-jobs job market, and they are still, in large numbers, underemployed, dependent on their parents and saddled with big college debt" (Stern, 2010, para. 1). College debt now includes both student loans and credit card balances and reflects a 27% increase from 2004 to 2008 in the number of students graduating with student loan debt (The Project on Student Debt, 2010). Moreover, 30% of undergraduate students indicated using credit cards to pay tuition at an average debt of $2,000 per student (Sallie Mae, 2009).

This increased debt can also impact new alumni's satisfaction with their institution and, consequently, their engagement with the institution postgraduation. Dan Rhodes, vice president of marketing for the Purdue Alumni Association states,

> When students are paying debt for 15 to 20 years after graduation, they don't have the same level of respect for the opportunity afforded them as prior generations who come back and talk about how inexpensive their tuition was … As the value of a degree drops, the value of joining an association connected to that degree drops, as well. (Personal communication, September 13, 2011)

In response to this grim financial outlook, alumni associations have made recent efforts to support members in career searches with the intent of improving members' financial profiles, strengthening the link to the alma mater, and increasing the likelihood of donations. For example, Jodi Kaplan, director of marketing for the University of Connecticut Alumni Association, reported her association created a robust career services website, Alumni Career Resource. Free to alumni members, the site offers easy access to resources and tools that lend assistance with career planning, job searching, and career transitioning. Career fairs, networking opportunities, and webinars are just a few of the benefits of the career resource. The creation of the program is a result of a survey conducted among young alumni who responded overwhelmingly that they expected career services support from their alumni association (Personal communication, September 8, 2011). Michigan State University (MSU) has made networking among students and alumni a priority in order to "stay relevant and connected to people's lives after they graduate …" (McKown, 2010, para. 8). "One of the most important ways MSUAA is working to accomplish this goal is by aiding in career searches, providing interview tips and facilitating networking between young alumni and older graduates" (para. 9).

Keeping in Contact with New Graduates

Finding graduates once they have left campus is a challenge due to the uncertainty of postgraduate employment and increased mobility. When institutions do not collect accurate and updated contact information for their new graduates, they are often left with only the last-known permanent home addresses of graduates' parents. E-mail addresses may be more useful than physical addresses, since direct mail does not generally resonate with this generation and, because they are highly portable, e-mail addresses are less likely to change than mail addresses. Yet, as many institutions are discovering, e-mail may not be as successful a mode of communication as social networking accounts (e.g., Facebook, Twitter). For these reasons, alumni associations invest in creative strategies (e.g., applications for mobile devices) to assist them in obtaining all current contact information and locating lost alumni.

For example, the University of Arkansas has had success with an incentive-based initiative, Senior Walk, to collect seniors' postgraduate contact information, namely e-mail addresses not affiliated with campus accounts. Senior Walk is a university tradition in which all graduates' names are engraved in campus sidewalks. For students to receive their free Senior Walk t-shirt, they must access an online form, which captures contact data. At Oklahoma State University, University of California at Berkeley, and Iowa State University, new graduates are offered the convenience of a lifetime e-mail forwarding address, allowing them to continue receiving messages at their university e-mail address, which normally expires upon graduation. Though the actual account is deleted, the alias remains, making the university e-mail address essentially a placeholder sending the messages to another inbox the graduate has created elsewhere. For development professionals, this strategy provides a constant point of contact to the new graduate, and for the student, it offers something stable when everything else in his or her life is changing, as well as a long-lasting connection to their alma mater. As evidenced by the more than 14,000 lifetime e-mail users at Iowa State University alone, these programs are proving both popular and successful.

Giving Habits of New Graduates

In describing millennial graduates, Strauss and Howe (2003) predicted this group may very well become an "active, loyal, and giving generation of alumni … They will keep in touch with their fellows later in their career lives, return for reunions, and (most important) open their wallets for their alma maters" (p. 139). Data seem to support this prediction with results from a recent national survey showing alumni ages 34 and younger reported they donated 20% of their charitable giving to their university alma maters in 2009, compared to 8% of those between the ages of 35 and 49, 7% of those aged 50-64, and 12% of those 65 and older (Engagement Strategies Group, 2010).

Johnson, Grossnickle, and Associates (2011) completed a broader study of the giving preferences and history of approximately 3,000 20-35 year-olds and suggested "we need to embrace both their progressive ideas and deeply rooted values" (p. 3). In 2010, approximately 8 out of every 10 participants volunteered their time during the year. While 93% gave to nonprofits, more than half said their largest gift was less than $150 (Johnson et al., 2011). Factors that influence giving include the mission of the organization, understanding how money will be used, and a personal connection to the organization (Figure 9.1). For example, 59% of the survey participants gave in response to a personal ask (Johnson et al., 2011).

Young alumni, more than any other age group of former university attendees, have a desire to select which areas of their alma mater to support according to Masterson (2010b), possibly presenting "a challenge for colleges that prefer the financial flexibility of unrestricted gifts" (para. 13). Johnson et al. (2011) found recent graduates also want to know their gifts are making an immediate impact. In their survey, 82% of the respondents replied they would be *very likely* or *somewhat likely* to donate to organizations that specifically described how their donations would be used, and more than 70% were likely to give if they could increase their impact with a donor match. They summarized their findings as follows:

> Clearly, organizations must work to make their messages as compelling as possible and be specific as to how donations will be used. Millennials may not always have a lot to give, so they want to make sure they use it wisely. (p. 11)

Factors that motivate trust:
1. Endorsement of friends or family – 77%
2. Reports how financial support makes a difference – 60%
3. Meet the organization's leadership – 63%

Factors that motivate giving:
1. Compelling mission or cause – 85%
2. Personal connection with organization's leaders – 56%
3. Endorsement of a friend or peer – 52%

Factors that would make you Somewhat Likely or Very Likely (combined %) stop donating:
1. Lack of trust in the organization – 90%
2. Didn't know how the donation was making an impact – 78%
3. The organization asked for support too frequently – 73%
4. Didn't feel a personal connection to the organization – 72%

Figure 9.1. Highlights from millennial donor profile.

Adapted from *The Millennial Donors Report 2011,* by Johnson, Grossnickle, and Associates, 2011, pp. 10-11. Copyright 2011 by Achieve and Johnson, Grossnickle, and Associates.

Steven Farwick II at the University of South Carolina is on board with this trend, believing it does not threaten the future of unrestricted funds: "We absolutely encourage donors to support their passion." He continued,

> What we want our young donors to know is that their $25 makes a difference. They want to specifically know what cause will be impacted and how it relates back to them. [We tell them] The better the university becomes, the more valuable your diploma becomes, and the better chance you will have in the workforce. (Personal communication, September 7, 2011)

Young graduates also have clear preferences on how they would like to contribute. Johnson et al. (2011) reported that 49% of their respondents preferred to give online. A 2011 survey of alumni at the University of South Carolina confirmed this trend, revealing

> a strong desire for young alumni to be able to make gifts automatically via electronic debit or recurring credit card payments … They might not be able to give $120 at one time, but they could do $10 a month … Young alumni are more likely to give on a credit or debit card than other alumni because it's something they've grown up doing. (S. Farwick II, personal communication, September 7, 2011)

Farwick credited the go-green trend of using less paper to protect the environment as well as the ability to make an immediate impact as two additional factors that drive credit- and debit-card use by this age group.

Strategies to Promote Giving Among Young Alumni

The picture evolving from this research suggests (a) graduates want to be contacted by their universities for reasons other than simply being asked for money, (b) they wish to designate their gifts to specific departments or projects, and (c) they insist on knowing how their gifts will make a difference. Concurrent with the emergence of this young donor profile information are new fundraising strategies. One recent trend is face-to-face donation requests to young alumni— reflecting this group's desire to build trust and connect with an organization's leadership. Masterson (2010a) describes the efforts of the president of the College of the Holy Cross in Massachusetts who plans development trips to combine meetings with high-level donor prospects and visits with young alumni. The president not only reaches out directly to newer graduates but he also asks each of them to, in turn, ask 10 of their classmates to make contributions, resulting in more of a community-inspired effort to raise funds. The industry can expect to see more new and creative fundraising campaigns as development professionals seek to modify their donation requests to match the giving habits of young alumni. This section discusses key components to include in those efforts.

Philanthropy Education

The work of Akers and McDearmon (2010) and Monks (2003), as well as the giving history of Cameron (described in the student profile opening this chapter), supports the idea that recent graduates who give early are more likely to continue to do so. Masterson (2010b) made the case for encouraging early giving when she said:

> Though alumni tend to give less when they're younger, one day colleges will depend on them for the larger gifts. Also, colleges want to get younger alumni in the habit of giving, so they will be inclined to support the institution throughout their lives. (para. 5)

Educating prospective donors is key to this process. It is critical that young alumni understand and are made to feel their gift, no matter how large or small, matters. Also, pointing out that contributions can be designated to a specific residence hall, academic department, or student club or organization can effectively link their giving mindset to a tangible, recent positive experience. Steven J. Farwick II, at the University of South Carolina, commented new alumni

> always see the big-check presentation … and the first thing they think is, I can't make that kind of gift. So they think they can't give. They know that million-dollar gift is going to make an impact, but they don't think their $25 is going to make an impact, so we need to show them that, regardless of size, their gift matters. We have to show them how … If you can get them to give two years in a row, then the likelihood of their giving for the rest of their lives is a lot greater. (Personal communication, September 7, 2011).

Findings from the Engagement Strategies Group's (2010) research suggest that today's young alumni are generally open to giving of their time and financial resources but perceive they have already supported their alma maters financially through their previously paid tuition. Higher education institutions must continually strive to dispel this notion that tuition alone completely covers the cost of an education (Masterson, 2010b).

When Steven Farwick II hears this concern from new alumni at the University of South Carolina, he clarifies the role tuition plays in supporting the University (i.e., at Carolina, tuition comprises less than half of the University's total annual revenue). He also invites recent graduates to remember their student experiences and points out how much alumni were funding those experiences, especially in ways other than scholarships. Then he asks them: "Was there something you didn't like when you were here? Well, you can make a gift to help enhance that area." Farwick's office concentrates on educating young alumni rather than soliciting them directly, sending short, simple, and engaging postcards that challenge commonly held myths or assumptions about giving. He adds, "We educate students; why not educate alumni?" (Personal communication, September 7, 2011). Scott Dahl from Iowa State University echoes this sentiment, advising:

> Don't make everything about asking for money or becoming a member. You're still cultivating the relationship at this point. Spend more time talking about where contributions go or how your organization works to benefit the university or current students." (Personal communication, September 8, 2011)

Microphilanthropy: A New Giving Trend

Microphilanthropy is a relatively new form of giving that allows donors to choose small projects and can sometimes involve more direct interaction between the donor and project. Chuck (2010) describes a 28-year old microphilanthropist, Carlo Garcia, in Chicago who forsook his daily cup of Starbucks coffee to donate to a different worthy cause each day for an entire year. He then used social media (e.g., blogs, Twitter, Facebook) to attract approximately 5,000 online followers who added to and exceeded Garcia's donations, as well as shared ideas for new charities. As Chuck notes, "even though [Garcia] can only give a little, some experts believe that he and his fellow mini-donors have the potential to change the altruistic landscape" (para. 7).

With its focus on small, social, and passionate causes; emphasis on peer referrals; and use of technology, microphilanthropy has the potential to resonate strongly with young donors. Middlebury College in Vermont has adopted this model in the development of MiddStart, a program that helps current students attract contributors for campaigns that need a relatively small amount of financing. "By eliminating some of the barriers between students and their supporters, and integrating the site with online social media, the college hopes to tap into previously unengaged alumni, particularly recent graduates (Wiseman, 2011, para. 4). The program is attractive to young alumni who can easily donate online through microlending sites, such as Kiva, Kickstarter, and DonorsChoose. They also find the financial transparency when presenting the need for and proposed use of funds appealing. MiddStart not only helps young donors establish a habit of giving in a new fashion, but it serves the dual purpose of connecting alumni with current students and institutional initiatives in a meaningful way.

Alumni associations and other fundraising arms of universities should take notice of this new trend and find ways to use microphilanthropy to drive ongoing personal and financial investments in the institution among new alumni.

Conclusion

When relationships between alumni and their alma maters are mutually beneficial, former students are recipients of support and benefits as well as benefactors to future generations. It is the job of alumni associations and offices of annual giving to educate, remain relevant, and build relationships so that young alumni that do not concentrate solely on fundraising but embrace a culture of philanthropic giving and engagement. To be successful, universities and colleges must recognize and embrace the differences between newer graduates and other age groups and focus on providing networking opportunities that foster career growth.

The ways in which today's young alumni prefer to donate dictate that institutions make online giving available, strive to clearly articulate the need for and proposed use of donated funds, accept contributions via credit and debit card transactions, and allow gifts to be designated to particular areas. Colleges and universities need to make it known that modest donations are crucial, and they can make an immediate impact. To build trust, alumni associations and offices must exhibit financial transparency and should consider face-to-face meetings with young donors. Further, campaigns based on microphilanthropy should be part of an overall fundraising and friend raising vision.

Perhaps most important is to remember though this group of graduates is young, they are savvy, as Strauss and Howe (2003) remind us:

> Millennials are already the most achievement-oriented collegians in our nation's history, and by the time they leave the campus gates, they may be the most learned and capable graduates ever … Wherever they choose to go, and no matter how difficult the times, colleges and universities may enjoy a new golden age, as they serve this very special generation in what could be uniquely challenging times. (pp. 144, 146)

With the aforementioned new technologies so easily accessible to today's college seniors and a resurgence in volunteerism among this younger cohort, it seems alumni offices will indeed be breaking new ground as graduates of this decade and the next make their mark. They will expect to be listened to, and if alumni associations, offices of annual giving, and other alumni relations professionals take note of their desires, the results could very well be transformational, positively impacting higher education institutions for years to come.

References

Akers, K. S., & McDearmon, J. T. (2010, October). *Measuring the external factors related to young alumni giving to higher education.* Paper presented at MWERA Annual Meeting, Columbus, Ohio.

Barefoot, B. O. (2008). Collegiate transitions: The other side of the story. In B. O. Barefoot (Ed.), *The first year and beyond: Rethinking the challenge of collegiate transition* (New Directions for Higher Education No. 144, pp. 89-92). San Francisco, CA: Jossey-Bass.

Chuck, E. (2010). *For microphilanthropist, donations are a part of daily life.* Retrieved September 5, 2011 from MSNBC.com website: http://www.msnbc.msn.com/id/40607088/ns/us_news-giving/t/microphilanthropist-donations-are-part-daily-life/

Clotfelter, C. T. (2001). Who are the alumni donors? Giving by two generations of alumni from selective colleges. *Nonprofit Management & Leadership, 12*(2), 119-138.

Engagement Straegies Group. (2010, July). *Mood of alumni 2010.* Retrieved from http://im.dev.virginia.edu/wp/engagementcommunity/files/2011/11/Mood-of-Alumni-2010.pdf

Johnson, Grossnickle, & Associates. (2011) *Millennial donors report 2011.* Retrieved from http://millennialdonors.com/wp-content/uploads/2011/05/MD11_Report1411.pdf

Masterson, K. (2010a, February 21). Five colleges that inspire alumni giving, and how they do it. *The Chronicle of Higher Education.* Retrieved from http://chronicle.com/article/5-Colleges-That-Inspire-Alumni/64307/

Masterson, K. (2010b, July 18). Appeals to college loyalty are not enough to engage younger alumni. *The Chronicle of Higher Education.* Retrieved from http://chronicle.com/article/Appeals-to-College-Loyalty-Are/66319/?key=SDghL1BiMXgZYiNgcysTfyJVbHwpIxp/YCZAMC4aYlFT

McKown, L. (2010, September 7). Alumni association targets young grads, *The State News.* Retrieved from http://www.statenews.com/index.php/article/2010/09/alumni_association_targets_young_grads

Monks, J. (2003). Patterns of giving to one's alma mater among young graduates from selective institutions. *Economics of Education Review, 22,* 121-130.

The Project on Student Debt. (2010). *Quick facts about student debt.* Retrieved from http://projecton-studentdebt.org/files/File/Debt_Facts_and_Sources.pdf

Sallie Mae. (2009). *How undergraduate students use credit cards: Sallie Mae's national study of usage rates and trends, 2009.* Retrieved from http://static.mgnetwork.com/rtd/pdfs/20090830_iris.pdf

Stern, L. (2010, May 19). Generation Y: Educated, underemployed and in debt. *Reuters.* Retrieved September 5, 2011, from http://www.reuters.com/article/2010/05/19/us-column-personalfinance-idUSTRE64I4M220100519

Strauss, W., & Howe, N. (2003). *Millennials go to college.* Great Falls, VA: American Association of Collegiate Registrars and Admissions Officers.

Wiseman, R. (2011, July 3). Middlebury College draws young donors with microphilanthropy. *The Chronicle of Higher Education.* Retrieved from http://chronicle.com/article/Middlebury-College-Draws-Young/128427/

Chapter Ten

Implementing Effective Educational Change

John N. Gardner and Mary Stuart Hunter

This chapter is intended to help readers make decisions about moving from reading about the senior-year experience to the acting upon it. An overall theme of this volume is that for the concluding experiences of undergraduates to improve—today and in the future, change needs to occur, and that change needs to be skillfully managed. Often change is resisted because it is perceived as inevitably leading to winners and losers, the cost will be too high, and/or it will be at the expense of existing protocol or programs. With careful attention, this resistance can be overcome.

Taking a positive approach and focusing on those most likely to benefit from change will bring faculty and administrators from many corners of an institution into conversation around positive intended outcomes. Through intentional and well-designed interactions with seniors, many individuals and institutional units are likely to gain from increased attention to the senior year by achieving educational and student development goals. These winners include the academic units housing seniors' majors that benefit from helping students synthesize and make meaning of their major area of study as they begin the transition to the world of work or to graduate school and the alumni and development offices aspiring to cultivate more engaged alumni and increase the likelihood of long-term alumni giving. Other student service offices have opportunities to interact with students in meaningful ways while they achieve their missions through delivering direct services to seniors (e.g., career services, registrar and dean's offices); offices that manage and deliver end-of-college rituals, especially commencement; and individual faculty who direct undergraduate student-faculty research and senior capstone courses. Finally, and definitely most importantly, the seniors themselves are likely to experience a far superior culminating undergraduate experience than those who came before them. Who would be the losers from increased attention paid to seniors? It would be difficult to identify any.

Admittedly, in today's economic environment, change is more likely to be accepted if it is revenue neutral or positive. Further, any effort to institute change directed centrally is very likely to be resisted as it will be perceived to cost institutional units something; if there is not new money, then new initiatives can only be accomplished by internal reallocation throughout the institution. Most higher education institutions have highly decentralized cultures. This suggests change on behalf of seniors is more likely to be possible and supported if what is proposed is perceived as not costing existing units something. Many of the best practices espoused in this book are of minimal incremental cost, if any, and as noted above, may actually add value to an institutional unit.

Lastly, change is more likely to be embraced if it enhances institutional reputation (e.g., national recognition for commendable practices adopted for seniors) and desired educational outcomes. Change is also more likely to be possible when it is driven primarily by local unit impetus; helps attain high-priority institutional strategic objectives (e.g., increased levels of student engagement, enhanced graduation rates); and responds positively to increased external demands for accountability, from such varied constituencies as regional and specialized accrediting bodies, higher education professional associations, employers, government entities, and families. And finally, from the student perspective, change is likely to be embraced when it is supportive of activities that enhance student satisfaction, is voluntary, and is not externally imposed. So fundamentally, the goal of increasing the attention paid to the senior year is a change exercise. Change will occur and be sustained when there are multiple gainers and winners, and benefits can be shown to outweigh costs.

Change to Improve Reflection, Closure, Integration, and Transition

While this volume attempts to update and move beyond the Gardner, Van der Veer, and Associates 1998 work, *The Senior Year Experience*, there is value in returning to the central thesis of that work to encourage readers to consider possible action steps that would lead to enhancement of the senior-year experience. The primary intellectual argument of that work was that increased attention to the final period of undergraduate education was needed to encourage seniors' reflection, closure, integration, and transition. It is within this context that the following series of critical questions are offered to help frame the thinking on next possible steps.

Regarding reflection: Based on what the chapter authors in this book have offered, what additional steps might be taken to provide departing students structured, intentional opportunities for reflection on the value of their college experience? How could these reflections be made more intentional; be incorporated into academic coursework; be shared with other students, faculty, and staff; and become the basis for important decision making and action steps by senior students?

Regarding closure: What kinds of curricular and cocurricular requirements and assignments would give seniors a greater sense of closure on the most important learning experiences of their undergraduate experience? How can or should students be guided to demonstrate the mastery of knowledge and skills, both cognitive and noncognitive? What kinds of capstone experiences would be most valuable for our students? How could seniors achieve a more empowering sense of closure that would motivate them to more appropriate and purposeful courses of action postcollege? What kinds of rituals would enhance this important sense of closure? How can the most important rituals, such as commencement, be made more meaningful toward these ends?

Regarding integration: Given all the curricular requirements coupled with voluntary cocurricular experiences, how can these be integrated into a coherent whole before graduation? How can general education be integrated with the major? What strategies would help students understand the power of the liberal arts and think intentionally in terms of multidisciplinary perspectives? How can the powerful, multiple strands of the educational experience be intentionally integrated and not left to serendipity or chance?

Regarding transitions: How can institutions provide greater assistance to seniors to help them in ways they will long appreciate to make better choices in many areas of pending transition (e.g., living situations, personal and professional relationships, continued formal education or a first job, debt management, civic engagement)? In what ways can institutions help students understand and anticipate the process and stages of healthy and natural transition experiences so they can cope emotionally with separation, transition, and integration into new environments?

Change to Ensure Seniors Receive the Best Possible Treatment

It seems ironic that as seniors approach graduation, and after spending four or more years and significant financial resources to earn their degrees, many institutional policies and processes make the graduation experience one of increased financial burden and challenge (e.g., diploma fees, rental fees or purchase of caps and gowns, fees for transcripts for each prospective employer or graduate school). Often, students living in campus residence halls must vacate their rooms on the very day they are celebrating the culmination of their undergraduate education. Many students are also solicited by the alumni association to join, for an additional fee, sometimes before they even graduate, but most certainly before the glow of commencement fades.

Surely colleges and universities must and can do better. This volume has presented myriad reasons why seniors deserve and require special treatment. Another way then to ask what kinds of change might be necessary to improve the experience of seniors would be to consider whether or not seniors receive the level of attention befitting the institution's most loyal and long-attending students:

- Are there any perks to being a senior?

- Are resource allocations congruent with the high status of seniors?

- What kinds of attention and experiences are offered only to seniors?

- Are seniors recognized as the students with the longest period of involvement and most experience with the institution?

- Are seniors being rewarded appropriately for their institutional loyalty and perseverance?

The ability to answer such questions brings into focus the need to better understand the senior student experience. Significant, sustained, and broad-based attention must be paid to the senior year if institutions are to create and institutionalize a positive culminating experience for students. That is what this volume has attempted to address.

Recommendations for Improving the Senior-Year Experience

We offer the following insights and recommendations, drawn from the preceding chapters and the authors' experiences and ideas, to help higher education professionals and institutions develop successful senior-year experience programming initiatives.

Determine what constitutes an excellent senior year. This process begins by asking these fundamental guiding questions: What would be an excellent culminating college experience? What is excellence in the senior-year experience? and What are the outcomes desired related to the senior year? In exploring the answers to these questions and clearly identifying desired outcomes, programs and initiatives can be developed to achieve those outcomes. Further, developing an institutional vision for excellence in the senior year can provide a benchmark for self-study, evaluation, initiative development, and strategic planning.

Tie the goals of the senior-year experience to institutional mission. The basic underlying belief is that all institutions can have excellent transition experiences regardless of the extent of institutional wealth and resources. A vision of educational excellence for any component of the undergraduate experience should be connected to institutional mission. To operationalize their espoused missions, institutions vary in many ways—curriculum and degrees offered, control and funding, and the kinds of students served. Because the focus on the senior year in this book is on the student experience as created in an individual institutional context, the goals of the senior year experience should be tied to the realities of the students actually served and not designed for the students that were once served by the institution or those the institution would prefer to serve.

Analyze the current status of the senior year at the institution. Based on their unique visions of excellence, institutions need to determine how they are currently performing. They must identify and affirm what is working well and can remain in place and, conversely, what is not working so well and might need to be changed or eliminated. Higher education professionals will need to consider the evidence, suggestions, and support that is required to marshal the case for such changes.

Involve campus stakeholders in this important work. An institution-wide task force should be comprised of representatives from all the stakeholders for the senior year: academic and student affairs offices; the registrar (because of transcript requests and checks); career center; alumni and development offices; residence hall staff; and the faculty who are responsible for senior courses and academic, credit-bearing capstone experiences. Current or recent seniors must be included in the work of this group as their perspectives can be especially enlightening. Others may also be appropriate to involve based on the institution's mission (e.g., graduate and professional school admission officers, employers).

Become familiar with the demographic and other salient characteristics of seniors. Knowing who the seniors are at the institution and how they are defined is fundamental. Data from national surveys can provide a high-level perspective on seniors that is helpful, but an institution-specific understanding is critical. Examining the lived experience of the graduates by studying (a) degree completion pathways; (b) the opportunities seniors have available to them both in and beyond the classroom throughout their undergraduate years; (c) the workplace competencies students developed through general education and coursework in the majors; and (d) the level of engagement of all students—not just the outstanding or marginal students at the institution—can provide a solid base for improving the senior year.

Understand developmental theories of emerging adulthood. Knowing where seniors are developmentally allows for a more effective analysis of the efficacy of existing institutional programs, curriculum, and initiatives. Understanding the epistemological, intrapersonal, and interpersonal development of students will provide fertile ground for rich conversations concerning the experiences and needs of seniors. Such an understanding can then guide implementation of new strategies to better serve senior students and guide their progress along the developmental spectrum.

Acknowledge and harness the omnipresence of technology in the lives of seniors. Traditional-aged seniors today have lived their entire lives with computers. Technology influences how students learn, communicate, and develop; therefore, technological tools must be a part of any strategy to enhance the senior-year experience. Students' online identities, civil discourse, social capital, and casual communication modes all influence their senior year and their future. Educators must understand both the benefits and consequences of technology's impact on the lives and experiences of seniors and embrace available technologies (e.g., electronic portfolios) to help students engage in the senior year in more significant ways. The mobile nature of the student experience, where there is no boundary of time or place, needs to be considered as institutions strive to enhance the senior-year experience.

Lay the groundwork for the senior year by providing powerful learning opportunities throughout the undergraduate experience. Learning is a cumulative process, and attention to the senior year will produce significant results only if the experience students have had leading up to it is meaningful. High-impact practices (HIP) that are well done, widespread, and accessible to all students can have transformative effects on student learning and development. Both curricular and cocurricular HIPs can produce a range of desirable outcomes and serve as the foundation for seniors as they make meaning of their undergraduate experience. Institutional leaders need to be intentional as they create or enhance existing structures and appropriate sequencing for HIPs to meet their potential.

Recognize that the career development needs of students will become most pressing in the senior year. That some students do not take advantage of institutional career centers until they begin a job search and focus on life after graduation is lamentable. Although the ultimate purpose of career centers on many campuses may be to facilitate the placement process, work with students must begin much earlier if success is to occur. Career development includes a wide variety of learning activities that can be found in both the curriculum and cocurriculum. To meet the demands of the global workplace today, stakeholders (e.g., parents, students, institutions, employers) all recognize that career development initiatives must be comprehensive, intentional, integrated, and span the entire undergraduate experience.

Understand the expectations and demands of the 21st century workplace are a new frontier. Globalization has changed the character of the entry-level positions of the past. It is no longer sufficient for new graduates to have content knowledge alone to secure a position in their academic field. Students must develop new workplace competencies, have exposure to workplace norms and expectations, and gain experience through internships and work placements to find success in early career positions. Institutions must develop intentional workplace transition opportunities for students to remain competitive today's workforce.

Prepare students to be engaged alumni. Involving students in philanthropic giving education and engagement while they are still undergraduates has become a goal of many alumni associations, alumni relations offices, and development offices in recent years. As seniors prepare to transition out of college, an appropriate time exists to establish a bond and sense of loyalty to the institution. Such efforts pay dividends for both the institution (e.g., increased annual giving) and the student, in terms of increased networks for career development and connection to their alma mater.

Provide opportunities for students to synthesize and demonstrate their learning. The senior-year experience is strengthened by providing mechanisms in which students recognize the complex cognitive and social skills they (hopefully) have developed during the undergraduate experience. Senior seminars, integrative courses, and capstone courses provide a curricular structure for such reflection and synthesis.

Create faculty development initiatives to support and enhance curriculum development of senior-level courses. As faculty are encouraged and challenged to develop courses that allow students to synthesize and demonstrate their learning, faculty development initiatives will be critical. Helping faculty create courses that include the how of learning as well as the what of content mastery may be necessary. Incorporating such pedagogy and process elements that enhance student learning, engagement strategies, and integrative approaches may be new to some and will provide opportunities for faculty renewal and development.

Engage in an examination of the rituals that exist at the institution surrounding the senior year. Rituals and ceremonies play an important role in seniors' transition throughout the final year of college and beyond and have the potential to transform students. Having an understanding of how both sanctioned and unsanctioned events contribute to the senior transition can help institutions better understand their students and the institutional values that are transmitted to them. Meaningful dialogues among institutional leaders and seniors about the common good can assist colleges and universities in making these ending ceremonies the kinds of events that can drive attempts to make the senior year more positively meaningful to students and more reflective of institutional values and mission.

Consider linking needed changes to externally mandated self-study processes or engage in a similar voluntary process. It is axiomatic that some changes and improvements can be handled at the unit level. But if they are really substantive changes and improvements and would potentially involve a critical mass of seniors, then what is needed is a process of institution-wide assessment, planning, and action improvement strategy development. This is exactly the kind of high-priority and high-impact activity that some of the country's regional accreditors are now rewarding as they build in continuous improvement initiatives into the reaffirmation process (e.g., Southern Association of Colleges and Schools' Quality Enhancement Plan [QEP] process, Higher Learning Commission's Open Pathways and Academic Quality Improvement Program [AQIP] processes, Middle States' special topics process). Another option is to consider undertaking voluntary self-study that specifically uses the senior year as a unit of analysis for assessment and improvement purposes, resulting in the development of a comprehensive plan. This plan would provide the rationale for the implementation of programs and initiatives targeting a greater number of students throughout their undergraduate experience with a directed, long-range focus on the senior-year transition. Models for this approach have been used to improve the success of first-year and transfer students (e.g., the Gardner Institute Foundations of Excellence assessment and improvement processes) and could easily be adapted to focus on the senior transition. The argument for a self-study, either as part of an accreditation process or in a voluntary manner, assumes there is probably much that is not known or understood about the lived experience of our students and that institutions (and students) would greatly benefit from this knowledge.

Final Thoughts

Fundamentally, the case for improving the final period of the undergraduate experience all comes down to a mutual dependency. The stakes have never been higher for individual institutions and their students. Both need each other to be successful and to keep giving back. This inherent reciprocity ensures that all parties gain in this transaction of investing more attention and resources in the concluding college experiences, and the dividends will be both immediate and much longer term. We would argue that strengthening the senior year is, therefore, in the nation's interest, and we invite your individual and collective institutional applications of the ideas presented in this work. We are hopeful this book will inspire readers as much as it has us as to ask what could and should be happening for our most loyal and deserving students.

INDEX

NOTE: Page numbers with italicized *f* or *t* indicate figures or tables respectively.

Y

About the
CONTRIBUTORS

Mary Ruffin Weaver Childs is the assistant executive director of membership, marketing, and communications for My Carolina Alumni Association at the University of South Carolina. In her role, she oversees the entire alumni membership experience, including acquiring, retaining, and ensuring the satisfaction of the organization's 30,000-plus members. In addition, Childs manages all affinity partnerships and is responsible for generating all of the organization's revenue. Childs served as a contributing chapter author to "Marketing Opportunities for Financial Gain and Alumni Benefit" in *Alumni Relations—A Newcomer's Guide to Success* (2nd edition). She cofounded the Council of Alumni Association Membership & Marketing Professionals, a national organization, and My Carolina programs under her purview have won numerous awards from the Council for Advancement and Support of Education. Most recently, Childs was awarded the prestigious Forman Fellowship from the Council of Alumni Association Executives.

J. Michael Denton is a doctoral student at Miami University of Ohio in the Student Affairs in Higher Education program. Denton's academic interests include cultural studies, queer theory, HIV/AIDS, college student identity, and critical and transformative pedagogy. Prior to starting work on a PhD, he worked as a residence life professional at various colleges and universities in the southeastern United States, with a focus on first-year student learning and retention, academic and student affairs initiatives, and learning communities. Denton has presented at many conferences as a practitioner, and recently contributed a chapter on cultural theory to *Contested Issues in Student Affairs* (2011).

Meredith L. Fakas is the director of integrated marketing communications for My Carolina Alumni Association at the University of South Carolina. She earned a bachelor's and master's degree in communications from the University of South Carolina and has served as an instructor for its University 101 program. Fakas has played a vital role in maintaining and continuing to build upon the award-winning My Carolina brand for the University's alumni association, managing the organization's survey research and web-based initiatives, as well as driving the creative strategy for membership fulfillment and promotions.

John N. Gardner has led an international movement to enhance the first and senior years on campuses across the country and around the world. He is founder and senior fellow of the National Resource Center for The First-Year Experience and Students in Transition and distinguished professor emeritus of Library and Information Science at the University of South Carolina (USC). From 1974 to 1999, Gardner served as executive director of the National Resource Center and of the nationally acclaimed University 101 program at USC. He is currently president of the John N. Gardner Institute for Excellence in Undergraduate Education. In his capacity at the Institute, Gardner has been instrumental in the development of the Foundational Dimensions® of Excellence, a set of aspirational standards in the first-year and transfer-student experience. He is the recipient of numerous local and national professional awards, 11 honorary doctoral degrees, and several lifetime achievement recognitions. A frequent presenter and speaker at national and international conferences, Gardner has also authored and co-authored many articles and books, including *The Freshman Year Experience* (1989), *Ready for the Real World* (1994), *The Senior Year Experience* (1998), *Challenging and Supporting the First-Year Student* (2005), *Achieving and Sustaining Institutional Excellence for the First Year of College* (2005), and *Helping Sophomores Succeed: Understanding and Improving the Second-Year Experience* (2010).

Philip Gardner is the director of the Collegiate Employment Research Institute at Michigan State University (MSU). For three decades, he has studied the transition from university to work, national labor markets for young professionals, workforce readiness, early socialization in the workplace, and the impact of work-based learning on career outcomes. MSU's nationally recognized annual college labor market study is done under his direction each fall. Gardner holds a doctoral degree from MSU in economic development, resource economics, and organizational behavior. His undergraduate degree was earned at Whitman College where he majored in chemistry. In the spring of 2009, he served as a Fulbright specialist to New Zealand on work-integrated learning. Gardner has authored numerous reports, articles, and book chapters and was the senior editor of the *Journal of Cooperative Education and Internships* from 2002 to 2009.

Jean M. Henscheid is an associate professor of educational leadership and policy and senior scholar in student affairs at the Center for Academic Excellence at Portland State University. She also serves as executive editor of the Jossey-Bass/ACPA publication *About Campus*. She served as editor of the *Journal of The First-Year Experience & Students in Transition* from 2007 to 2011. She has authored and edited books and articles on topics related to the college student experience and conducts workshops across the United States and internationally on learning communities, general education, curriculum design, and learning assessment. Henscheid has also held administrative and teaching positions at the University of Idaho and Washington State University.

Mary Stuart Hunter is the associate vice president and executive director for University 101 Programs and the National Resource Center for The First-Year Experience and Students in Transition at the University of South Carolina (USC). Hunter's work centers on providing educators with resources to develop personal and professional skills while creating and refining innovative programs to increase undergraduate student learning and success. She was honored in 2010 with an honorary doctor of Humane Letters by her alma mater, Queens University of Charlotte, and with the Outstanding Leadership in the Field Award from the Division of Student Affairs and Academic Support at USC; in 2006 as the Outstanding Campus Partner by South Carolina's University Housing division; and in 2001 as the Outstanding Alumnae by South Carolina's Department of Higher Education and Student Affairs. She recently authored the nomination packet that earned USC's University 101 Program Faculty Development Program the 2011 NASPA Excellence Awards Category Gold Award and overall Silver Award. Her recent publications include *The First-Year Seminar: Designing, Implementing, and Assessing Courses to Support Student Learning and Success: Volume II: Instructor Training and Development* (2012); *Helping Sophomores Succeed: Understanding and Improving the Second-Year Experience*

(2010); *Academic Advising: New Insights for Teaching and Learning in the First Year* (2007); "The First-Year Experience: An Analysis of Issues and Resources" in *Peer Review* (2006); and "The Second-Year Experience: Turning Attention to the Academy's Middle Children" in *About Campus* (2006).

Reynol Junco is a faculty associate at the Berkman Center for Internet and Society at Harvard University where he is part of the Youth and Media project. As a social media scholar, Junco investigates the impact of social technologies on college students. His research interests focus on using quantitative methods to analyze the effects of social media on student psychosocial development, engagement, and learning as well as informing best practices in using social technologies to enhance learning outcomes. For instance, his research has shown that technology, specifically social media like Facebook and Twitter, can be used in ways that improve engagement and academic performance. A frequent contributor to the field, Junco co-authored, with Jeanna Mastrodicasa, *Connecting to the Net.Generation: What Higher Education Professionals Need to Know About Today's Students* (2007) and edited the New Directions for Student Services volume, *Using Emerging Technologies to Enhance Student Engagement* (2008). His latest research focuses on using online tracking data to create predictive models of student success, how digital identity is related to creativity, and how youth understand and implement privacy in online social spaces.

Jennifer R. Keup is the director of the National Resource Center for The First-Year Experience and Students in Transition at the University of South Carolina, where she is responsible for operational and strategic aspects of the Center. Before joining the staff of the National Resource Center, Keup had professional roles in the national dialogue on the first-year experience as well as higher education research and assessment as a project director for the Cooperative Institutional Research Program at the Higher Education Research Institute and was heavily involved in institutional assessment efforts as the director of the Student Affairs Information and Research Office at the University of California-Los Angeles. Her research interests focus on students' personal and academic development during the transition from high school to college; the influence of campus programming on adjustment to college; and issues of institutional impact, responsiveness, and transformation in higher education. Keup has been a frequent contributor in higher education, both as a presenter and author. Her most recent co-authored publications include *Crafting and Conducting Research on Student Transitions* (2011); *The First-Year Seminar: Designing, Implementing, and Assessing Courses to*

Support Student Learning and Success: Volume I: Designing and Administering the Course (2011); and *2009 National Survey of First-Year Seminars: Ongoing Efforts to Support Students in Transition* (2011).

Jillian Kinzie is the associate director for the Center for Postsecondary Research and the National Survey of Student Engagement Institute at Indiana University in Bloomington. Kinzie earned her PhD from Indiana University in higher education with a minor in women's studies. Prior to this, she served on the faculty of Indiana University and continued on to coordinate the University's master's program in higher education. She also worked as a researcher and administrator in academic and student affairs at several institutions, including Miami University and Case Western Reserve University. Her scholarly interests include the assessment of student engagement and the impact of programs and practices designed to support student success, as well as college choice, first-year student development, teaching and learning in college, access and equity, and women in underrepresented fields. She has co-authored numerous publications, including *Continuity and Change in College Choice: National Policy, Institutional Practices and Student Decision Making*, a monograph endorsed by the Lumina Foundation; *Student Success in College: Creating Conditions That Matter*; and *One Size Does Not Fit All: Traditional and Innovative Models of Student Affairs Practice*. Her service to the profession includes her work with the Documenting Effective Education Practices (DEEP) project and Building Engagement and Attainment of Minority Students (BEAMS).

Peter M. Magolda is a professor at Miami University, in Ohio, in the Student Affairs in Higher Education program. Prior to joining the Miami University faculty in 1994, he worked in the Division of Student Affairs at Miami University, The Ohio State University, and the University of Vermont. Magolda received his bachelor's degree from LaSalle College, a master's degree from The Ohio State University, and a doctorate in Higher Education Administration from Indiana University. He teaches educational anthropology and research seminars, and his scholarship focuses on ethnographic studies of college students and critical issues in qualitative research. Magolda's recent ethnographic research resulted in a 2009 publication entitled *It's All About Jesus: Faith as an Oppositional Collegiate Subculture*. In 2011, he co-edited, with Marcia Baxter Magolda, *Contested Issues in Student Affairs*. He also serves on the editorial boards of *Research in Higher Education* and the *Journal of Educational Research*. In 2012, Magolda received the American College Personnel Association's Contribution to Knowledge Award.

Heather Maietta is director of the O'Brien Center for Student Success at Merrimack College. Formally, she was the director of Career Services, assistant director of the Professional Development Seminars Program, and adjunct faculty at Nichols College. Prior to this, she earned her doctorate of higher education from Central Michigan University, where she also served as a faculty member. Maietta frequently speaks and publishes on topics related to career development in college and postcollege transitions for young alumni. She has authored and co-authored numerous publications, including "Virtual Job Club: A Social Support Network for Recent Graduates" (2012), "Job Club Helps Seniors Transition to the World-of-Work," (2010), "A Four-Year Professional Development Model Prepares Students for Successful Careers" (2011), and "Junior Business Card Project" (2010). Her scholarly interests include career development in college, first-generation college students, the senior-year experience and students in transition, and the impact of programs and practices designed to enhance and support student success. In 2011, Maietta received the National Association of Colleges and Employers and Spelman & Johnson Group Rising Star Award for her achievements in the field of career development

Jeanna Mastrodicasa is the assistant vice president for student affairs at the University of Florida (UF). Before joining the Vice President's office, she had been in several different roles at UF, including the associate director of the Honors program, assistant dean of students, and an academic advisor. Mastrodicasa is the co-author, with Reynol Junco, of *Connecting to the Net. Generation: What Higher Education Professionals Need to Know About Today's Students* (2007) She has also published a book chapter, "Technology Use in Campus Crisis," in the New Directions for Student Services Special Issue, *Using Emerging Technologies to Enhance Student Engagement* (2008) and an article about town-gown relations. Mastrodicasa is a frequent presenter about the trends of millennial college students, social media and technology, and generations in the workplace at conferences and on college campuses across the country. In addition to her higher education role, Mastrodicasa served in local government as an elected official from 2006-2012.

April L. Perry recently completed her PhD at the University of Canterbury (UC) in Christchurch, New Zealand. As a UC International Doctoral Research Fellow, originally from Oklahoma, she pursued a degree in Higher Education under the supervision of Dr. Judi Miller and Dr. Marion Bowl. For her research on the postuniversity transition, Perry conducted a qualitative exploration of the experiences, perspectives, and needs of recent graduates. Her findings have been instrumental in setting the scene for senior-year experience research, as her work has been presented in practitioner-focused publications (*Improving the Student Experience: A Practical Guide for Universities and Colleges,* 2011) and research-based publications (*International Handbook for Cooperative and Work-Integrated Education: International Perspectives of Theory, Research and Practice,* 2011). Perry holds a bachelor's degree in broadcasting and a master's degree in adult education. Before moving to New Zealand in 2008, she worked at the University of Central Oklahoma in student activities and leadership programs. Perry is passionate about student development in the college years and lives by the motto that the only thing better than watching someone grow is helping them grow.

Tracy L. Skipper is assistant director for publications for the National Resource Center for The First-Year Experience and Students in Transition at the University of South Carolina (USC). Prior to her work at the Center, she served as director of residence life and judicial affairs at Shorter College in Rome, Georgia, where her duties included teaching in the college's first-year seminar program and serving as an academic advisor for first-year students. She also served as director of student activities and residence life at Wesleyan College. She edited (with Roxanne Argo) *Involvement in Campus Activities and the Retention of First-Year College Students* (2003) and wrote *Student Development in the First College Year: A Primer for College Educators* (2005). She holds a bachelor's degree in psychology from USC, a master's degree in higher education from Florida State University, and a master's in American literature and doctorate in rhetoric and composition from USC. She has presented on the application of student development theory to curricular and cocurricular contexts and on the design and evaluation of writing assignments. Her research interests include the application of cognitive-structural development to composition pedagogy and the use of writing in first-year seminars. She teaches writing as an adjunct instructor in USC's English department.